Making Disciples in a World Parish

Princeton Theological Monograph Series

K. C. Hanson, Charles M. Collier, D. Christopher Spinks,
and Robin Parry, Series Editors

Recent volumes in the series:

Sherri Brown
Gift Upon Gift:
Covenant through Word in the Gospel of John

Christopher W. Skinner
John and Thomas—Gospels in Conflict?:
Johannine Characterization and the Thomas Question

Christopher L. Fisher
Human Significance in Theology and the Natural Sciences:
An Ecumenical Perspective with Reference to Pannenberg, Rahner,
and Zizioulas

Linda D. Peacore
The Role of Women's Experience
in Feminist Theologies of Atonement

Julie Woods
Jeremiah 48 as Christian Scripture

Randall W. Reed
A Clash of Ideologies:
Marxism, Liberation Theology, and Apocalypticism
in New Testament Studies

David Rhoads
Luke-Acts and Empire: Essays in Honor of Robert L. Brawley

David L. Balch
Finding A Woman's Place: Essays in Honor of Carolyn Osiek

Making Disciples in a World Parish

Global Perspectives on Mission & Evangelism

Edited by
PAUL W. CHILCOTE

Foreword by Gregory V. Palmer

☙PICKWICK Publications • Eugene, Oregon

MAKING DISCIPLES IN A WORLD PARISH
Global Perspectives on Mission & Evangelism

Princeton Theological Monograph Series 162

Copyright © 2011 Wipf and Stock Publishers. All rights reserved. Except for brief quotations in critical publications or reviews, no part of this book may be reproduced in any manner without prior written permission from the publisher. Write: Permissions, Wipf and Stock Publishers, 199 W. 8th Ave., Suite 3, Eugene, OR 97401.

Good New Bible: Today's English Version. New York: American Bible Society, copyright © 1992. Used by permission. All rights reserved.

Pickwick Publications
An Imprint of Wipf and Stock Publishers
199 W. 8th Ave., Suite 3
Eugene, OR 97401

www.wipfandstock.com

ISBN 13: 978-1-60899-880-7

Cataloging-in-Publication data:

    Making disciples in a world parish : global perspectives on mission & evangelism / edited by Paul W. Chilcote ; foreword by Gregory V. Palmer.

    Princeton Theological Monograph Series 162

    xxiv + 328 p. ; 23 cm. Includes bibliographical references.

    ISBN 13: 978-1-60899-880-7

    1. 2. I. Palmer, Gregory V. Title. II. Series.

CALL NUMBER 2011

Manufactured in the U.S.A.

*For Elisha Kabungaidze,
Zimbabwean United Methodist pastor,
a model disciple-making evangelist
in the Wesleyan tradition*

Contents

Contributors / xi

Foreword by Bishop Gregory V. Palmer / xix

Preface / xxi

Introduction: "Love, that never, never fails"
—*Paul W. Chilcote* / 1

Further Reading on Wesleyan Disciple-making / 13

PART ONE: Africa: Riding the Flood Tide

Introduction to Part One / 17

1. Being a Disciple of Christ in the African Great Lakes Region—*Lubunga W'Ehusha* / 19

2. Making Disciples in Kenya—*Nahashon Gitonga* / 28

3. Evangelism, Mission, and Discipleship in Southern Africa: How Hope is Overcoming Tragedy!—*Dion A. Forster* / 39

4. Local Church—An Arena for Making Disciples: A Case Study of Sherukuru United Methodist Church in Zimbabwe—*John Wesley Zvomunondiita Kurewa* / 48

5. Disciple-Making in a Zimbabwean Church—*Christinah Kwaramba* / 58

Further Reading on African Contexts / 68

PART TWO: Asia & Oceania: Navigating Cross-Currents

Introduction to Part Two / 73

6. Making Disciples in China: "When Christ calls a man, he bids him come and die."—*Lo Lung-kwong* / 77

7. Multi-Lingual Disciples—*Lenita Tiong* / 84

viii   Contents

8   Making Disciples in a Philippine Context
—*Daniel C. Arichea Jr.* / 93

9   Making Disciples in Singapore: Challenges and Opportunities—*Robert M. Solomon* / 103

10   The Spread of Missionary Congregations in Korea
—*Jong Chun Park* / 112

11   Making Disciples in the Tongan Diaspora
—*Tevita M. Siuhengalu* / 123

Further Reading on Asian and Oceanic Contexts / 131

PART THREE: Europe—Persevering through Ebb Tide

Introduction to Part Three / 135

12   Making Disciples in Estonia—*Kaja Rüütel* / 137

13   Making Disciples in a Eurasian Parish—*Lena Kim* / 147

14   Enabling People to Believe and Live: Mission and Evangelism in the German-speaking Context
—*Achim Härtner, trans. Paul W. Chilcote* / 155

15   Making Disciples in Britain—*Graham Horsley* / 165

16   Making Disciples in Eastern Europe
—*Pavel Procházka* / 175

Further Reading on European Contexts / 185

PART FOUR: Latin America & Caribbean—Tacking into the Wind

Introduction to Part Four / 189

17   Caribbean Perspectives on Mission/Evangelism
—*George Mulrain* / 191

18   The Mission of God and the Mission of the Church in Latin America—*Nidia V. Fonseca R.,
trans. Philip Wingeier-Rayo* / 200

19   Disciple-Making Systems and Models for Mexico
—*Raúl García de Ochoa* / 209

Further Reading on Latin American Contexts / 217

PART FIVE: North America—Exploring a New Ocean

Introduction to Part Five / 221

20 Making Disciples in a Canadian Context
    —*Dan Sheffield* / 223

21 Making Disciples in a Post-Christendom USA
    —*Elaine A. Heath* / 233

22 Graceful Articulation—*Kimberly D. Reisman* / 242

23 Discipleship and Empire—*Bryan Stone* / 251

    Further Reading on North American Contexts / 260

PART SIX: Cross-Continental Witness—Valuing the Confluence of Streams

Introduction to Part Six / 265

24 Holistic Mission and Evangelism—*Sarah F. Davis* / 267

25 A Permeable Church of New Disciples
    —*R. F. Leão Neto* / 276

26 Baptism of Water and Spirit: A Women's Discipleship
    —*Tumani Nyajeka* / 285

27 Becoming, Being, and Making Disciples in Cross-Cultural Appointments—*Helmut Renders* / 293

28 Christian Vitality in Cuba: An Apparent Contradiction in a Land of Paradoxes—*Philip Wingeier-Rayo* / 301

    Further Reading on Global Witness / 310

    Conclusion: Lessons from the World Parish
    —Some Concluding Observations / 312

Bibliography / 319

Contributors

DR. DANIEL C. ARICHEA JR. served for twenty-six years with the United Bible Societies in the Asia Pacific Region before his election (in absentia) to the United Methodist episcopacy in the Philippines in 1994. After retirement in 2000, he served for eight years as Bishop in Residence at Duke Divinity School. Currently, he is Translation Consultant for the Philippine Bible Society and Head of the Graduate Department of Religion and Philosophy, Philippine Christian University.

DR. PAUL W. CHILCOTE is Professor of Historical Theology & Wesleyan Studies, Ashland Theological Seminary, Ohio, USA. Born in the United States, Dr. Chilcote has taught on three continents in the areas of church history, mission/evangelism, and applied Wesleyan studies. He was a charter faculty member who helped to launch both Africa University in Zimbabwe and Asbury Theological Seminary in Orlando. His most recent publication in the area of evangelism is *The Study of Evangelism: Exploring a Missional Practice of the Church* (Eerdmans).

BISHOP SARAH FRANCES TAYLOR DAVIS is the 126th elected and consecrated bishop of the African Methodist Episcopal Church. Born in Beaumont, Texas, she lived and served in Lesotho (Southern Africa) as Bishop of the 18th Episcopal District AMEC (Lesotho, Botswana, Mozambique, and Swaziland), 2004–2008, and currently lives with her husband Claytie Davis Jr., in Kingston, Jamaica, serving as Presiding Prelate of the 16th Episcopal District (Caribbean Islands, Europe, France, Haiti, Dominican Republic, Guyana/Suriname, Virgin Islands).

REV. NIDIA V. FONSECA R. is a native of Costa Rica and a pastor in the Wesleyan Methodist Church. She has been associated with the Latin American Biblical University in San José (UBL) since 1998 and presently serves both as Professor of Contextual Studies and Vice-Rector at the UBL, responsibilities she assumed in 2006. Educated at the

University of Costa Rica, and holding advanced degrees from UBL, her primary teaching area is pastoral theology with specialization in pastoral psychology.

Dr. Dion A. Forster is a Methodist theologian and author who lives in Cape Town, South Africa. Having served previously as a seminary dean, he currently holds posts in New Testament at the University of Pretoria and in Systematic Theology at Stellenbosch University. Deeply involved in the Lausanne Movement and planning for the 2010 Cape Town Congress on World Evangelization, his most recent publication in mission, evangelism, and social justice is "Methodism in Southern Africa: A Celebration of Wesleyan Mission."

Rev. Raúl García de Ochoa was born in General Teran, state of Nuevo Leon, Mexico. He received his education at Universidad Valle del Bravo in Reynosa, John Wesley Seminary in Monterrey, and Asbury Theological Seminary, from which he received both MDiv and DMin degrees. He has served as a local church pastor, a District Superintendent, and is currently the bishop in the Conferencia Oriental of the Methodist Church of Mexico. Garcia is married to Martha Delia and has two children.

Rev. Dr. Nahashon Gitonga is Senior Lecturer in Theology and Chairman of the Department of Theology and Religious Studies, Kenya Methodist University, Meru, the first Methodist institution of higher education in this East African nation. Having served in both pastoral and academic settings, his most recent publication in the area of evangelism is *Evangelization and Inculturation in an African Context* (Today in Africa).

Professor Achim Härtner has served as E. Stanley Jones Professor of Evangelism at Reutlingen School of Theology in Germany since 1995. His homiletic and evangelistic textbook, *Predigen lernen* (2008), co-authored with Holger Eschmann and now in its second edition, was the product of both cross-cultural experiences and engagement in German churches. This resource is also published in Bulgarian and Russian, and the English edition is entitled *Learning to Preach Today*.

DR. ELAINE A. HEATH is McCreless Associate Professor of Evangelism and Director of the Center for Missional Wisdom, Perkins School of Theology, Southern Methodist University in Dallas, Texas. She is an ordained elder in the East Ohio Conference of The United Methodist Church. Her recent books on evangelism include *The Mystic Way of Evangelism: A Contemplative Vision for Christian Outreach* (Baker) and *Longing for Spring: A New Vision for Wesleyan Community* (Cascade).

REV. GRAHAM HORSLEY is the Coordinator of Evangelism, Spirituality and Discipleship for the Methodist Church in Great Britain. He has extensive experience as an evangelist, a pastor, and a church planter. He currently works equipping the church and Christian leaders in the area of evangelism and church planting. His most recent publication is *How to do evangelism without being religious* (Headway).

REV. LENA KIM is Director of Education & Church Development for The United Methodist Church in Eurasia. Born in Uzbekistan (at that time a part of the USSR) and of Korean origin, she represents the fourth generation of her family to live in Russia. During the period 2003–2008, as a part of her responsibilities in the church, she travelled extensively throughout Russia, Ukraine, Belorussia, Kazakhstan, Uzbekistan, Kirgizstan, Georgia, and Azerbaijan, promoting the work of mission and evangelism.

PROFESSOR JOHN WESLEY ZVOMUNONDIITA KUREWA is E. Stanley Jones Professor of Evangelism in the Kurewa Chair of the Faculty of Theology, Africa University, Mutare, Zimbabwe. He has served as a pastor, theological lecturer, Secretary for Evangelism with the World Council of Churches, Secretary to the Parliament of Zimbabwe, and was founding Vice Chancellor of Africa University. His latest book is *Drumbeats of Salvation in Africa: A Study of Biblical, Historical and Theological Foundations for the Ministry of Evangelism*.

REV. CHRISTINAH KWARAMBA (née Borerwe) is serving as Chaplain of Methodist Dallas Medical Center as she pursues doctoral studies at Southern Methodist University. Born in Zimbabwe, she served as a school teacher for eighteen years and pastored four United Methodist congregations in both rural and urban circuits. Having received theological degrees from Africa University in Zimbabwe and Perkins School of Theology, the topic of her doctoral dissertation is *A Personal Evangelism Model in an African Context*.

REV. PROFESSOR LUNG-KWONG LO is Director and Professor of New Testament and Pastoral Studies of the Divinity School of Chung Chi College, The Chinese University of Hong Kong, China. He is President of the Methodist Church, Hong Kong. Previously he served for more than ten years as the Chairperson of the Mission and Social Concern Committee of the Hong Kong Christian Council. His most recent publications in Chinese are *Church Management Makes Sense* (2009) and *Search for the Identity of Christianity in Acts and Letters* (2006).

REV. DR. GEORGE M. MULRAIN is Connexional President of the Conference of the Methodist Church in the Caribbean and the Americas (MCCA), with headquarters in Antigua. Born in the Caribbean twin-island Republic of Trinidad & Tobago, Dr. Mulrain pastored churches in the Republic of Haiti and then taught Theology, Missiology, and Biblical Studies at academic institutions in Birmingham (UK) and Jamaica. He has recently been involved in producing a hymnal for his Church that is more relevant to its context.

REV. DR. R. F. LEÃO-NETO is Brazilian by birth. He has been a Minister at Hinde Street Methodist Church in the West End of London and a Chaplain to the Social Work Ministry of the West London Mission since 2001. Dr. Leão-Neto is a Co-Chair of Grassroots Ecumenical Programme in Luton, a missional project which specializes in community and interfaith ministries. He has particular interest in cross-cultural ministry.

DR. TUMANI NYAJEKA, a native of Zimbabwe, has served in the Dorothye and Cornelius Henderson Chair of Evangelism as an E. Stanley Jones Professor of Evangelism at Gammon Theological Seminary in Atlanta since 2004. After completing her doctoral studies at Garrett-Evangelical Theological Seminary, she taught at Spellman College. Dr. Nyajeka's particular areas of expertise include congregational evangelism, missions, women's, and African studies.

DR. JONG CHUN PARK is Professor of Systematic Theology, Methodist Theological University, Seoul, Korea. Chair of the Theological Education Committee of the World Methodist Council and Co-President of the Oxford Institute of Methodist Theological Studies, he was a keynote speaker for the 19th World Methodist Conference held in Seoul in 2006. He has been a visiting professor at various seminaries in Russia, China, Indonesia, and the United States of America.

DR. PAVEL PROCHÁZKA is Professor of Applied Theology, Matej Bel University, School of Pedagogy, Department of Evangelical Theology and Mission, Banska Bystrica, Slovak Republic. Born in the Czech Republic, Dr. Procházka had served for many years as United Methodist District Superintendent in Slovakia. Since 1993 he has been university pedagogue. His most recent research project examines preaching in the Slovak evangelical churches as related to quality of life.

REV. KIMBERLY D. REISMAN is Executive Director of Next Step Evangelism Ministries (www.nextstepevangelism.org). Rev. Reisman received a B.A. from Emory University, an MDiv from Yale Divinity School, and is currently a Harry Denman Doctoral Fellow studying the Theology of Evangelism at Durham University in the United Kingdom. Her most recent publication is the co-edited volume, *44 Sermons to Serve the Present Age* (Epworth).

DR. HELMUT RENDERS is Professor of Theology and History and Secretary of the Wesleyan Study Center at the Theological Faculty of the Methodist University in São Paulo, Brazil. Ordained as an elder of The United Methodist Church in Germany in 1990, he has served in Brazil since 1998. Following pastoral appointments in Germany, he taught at the Methodist Institute of the Amazon (1998–2003) before his move to the Faculty of Theology. He was a contributor to *Prática Teológica na tradição metodista*, a volume celebrating the tercentenary of John Wesley.

MRS. KAJA RÜÜTEL completed her Master of Evangelism studies at Cliff College, England, in 2004, and worked there as the European Mission Enabler. After returning to her native Estonia, she has been working at the Baltic Methodist Theological Seminary, Tallinn, as a simultaneous translator and teacher in the area of the history of missions. She is a member of the Estonian Evangelical Alliance Missions Work Group and has been leading teams on mission to small ethnic groups in Russia. Currently she is raising two small children.

REV. DAN SHEFFIELD serves as Director of Global and Intercultural Ministries for The Free Methodist Church in Canada. A graduate of McMaster University, he pastored in Canada and served as a missionary educator and church plant and community development facilitator in Egypt and South Africa. He teaches as an adjunct lecturer at Tyndale Seminary in Toronto. His most recent book is co-authored with Dr. Joyce Bellous, *Conversations that Change Us: Learning the Arts of Theological Reflection*.

REV. TEVITA SIUHENGALU, a native of the South Pacific Kingdom of Tonga, is Parish Minister with his wife, Meleane, at St. David's Uniting Church in Albury, New South Wales, Australia. They have been actively involved in cross-cultural mission and ministry in their community. Rev. Siuhengalu also serves as a co-chairperson for the 2013 Oxford Institute of Methodist Theological Studies.

BISHOP ROBERT M. SOLOMON is Bishop of The Methodist Church in Singapore. Born in Singapore, Bishop Solomon served as a medical doctor, pastor, and taught at Trinity Theological College. His Episcopal responsibilities cover six other mission areas, from Nepal to Vietnam. Having preached and taught on four continents, his latest book is *The Prayer of Jesus: The Lord's Prayer in Daily Life*.

DR. BRYAN P. STONE is Associate Dean for Academic Affairs and E. Stanley Jones Professor of Evangelism, Boston University School of Theology. Dr. Stone's background is in urban ministry, and his current research interests are in the areas of evangelism and congregational development, urban ministry, Wesleyan theology, and theology and film/popular culture. He is the author of *Evangelism after Christendom: The Theology and Practice of Christian Witness* (Brazos).

REV. LENITA TIONG is an ordanied Elder with the Methodist Church in Malaysia. She is currently the pastor in charge of Wesley Methodist

Church in Sibu Sarawak. She served as the Academic Dean of the Cambodian Methodist Bible School in Phnom Penh before returning to Sarawak to take up pastoral duties. She is also the Chairperson of the Board of Missions of the Sarawak Chinese Annual Conference.

DR. LUBUNGA W'EHUSHA is a research assistant in the School of Religion and Theology at the University of Kwazulu Natal and also lecturer of Old Testament at the Evangelical Seminary of Southern Africa in South Africa. Dr. Lubunga works as Assistant Legal Representative of the Free Methodist Church in the Democratic Republic of Congo and gives part-time lectures in Bukavu Eastern Congo and at Hope Africa University in Bujumbura, Burundi. His area of research includes church leadership and peace-building.

DR. PHILIP WINGEIER-RAYO is Associate Professor of Religion at Pfeiffer University in Misenheimer, North Carolina. He and his wife were United Methodist missionaries assigned to Cuba by the General Board of Global Ministries, 1991–1997, and served a total of fifteen years as missionaries in assignments in Nicaragua, Texas, and Mexico. Philip is the author of *Cuban Methodism: The Untold Story of Survival and Revival* (2006) and *Where are the Poor? A Comparison of Pentecostalism and Base Christian Communities in Mexico* (2010).

Foreword

If a tour de force is an exceptional achievement, then this volume is one. The Christian Church in the broadest sense owes a debt to Paul Chilcote and this magnificent cast of scholars, authors, and practitioners of mission evangelism. In my judgment this is especially true for the churches shaped in the Wesleyan way of being and doing church.

I read most of the manuscript on my laptop computer while travelling from the United States to Liberia, West Africa. On the one hand, I could chalk up this timing to the simple coincidence of when I received the manuscript and when I would have an available large block of time to read it. Having read it when I did was more than mere coincidence. It was providence. The reading, albeit primarily in service of preparing to write this foreword, shaped the way I experienced my engagement with United Methodist Christians in Liberia. I saw myself and my practice of ministry and that of sisters and brothers in Liberia with multiple new lenses. I am confident that the thoughtful, prayerful reading of the essays in this volume will assist you in trying on several new sets of lenses that will offer fresh clarity as you engage the mission of disciple making.

Hearing, seeing, and experiencing the mission evangelism practices of Christian churches in a wide array of political and cultural contexts is essential for any who would take mission evangelism seriously. It is essential if you happen to see yourself and your church as primarily an exporter of mission and evangelism. While I would hope and pray that such a parochial view is long since behind the church in the West in particular, the reality is it is not. In-depth exposure to diverse practices of disciple making in diverse contexts is also essential if we are to be faithful and effective in our disciple-making ministry right at home, wherever home is. Patterns of migration alone make more contexts than not more diverse and multicultural than they have ever been in recent memory. Add to this the flattening of the world through digital technology and it becomes obvious that effectiveness will depend in part on being prepared to understand and appreciate more cultures than the one that formed us.

I am haunted, chastened, and inspired by the Apostle Paul's self description of missional strategy and practice. "I have become all things to all people, so that by all means I might win some. I do all of this because of the gospel, so that I can be a participant in it" (1 Cor 9:22b–23). This book will help us all to more fully participate in the gospel and the world. Read it without delay.

Gregory V. Palmer, Resident Bishop,
The Illinois Episcopal Area, the United Methodist Church
Past President, Council of Bishops

Preface

MY FAMILY AND I HAD THE GREAT PRIVILEGE OF SPENDING TWO TERMS of mission service with the General Board of Global Ministries of The United Methodist Church on the continent of Africa. In Kenya I served on the faculty of the oldest theological institution in East Africa, St. Paul's United Theological College in Limuru, which celebrated its centenary while we were there. In Zimbabwe I helped to launch the Faculty of Theology at nascent Africa University in Old Mutare, teaching in the youngest theological seminary on the continent at that time. These proved to be two very distinct experiences, but the important lessons we learned during those years remain with us to this day.

The community of which we were a part in Kenya included people from every continent and dozens of different African ethnic traditions. Among the faculty were colleagues from Canada, England, France, Holland, Kenya, Korea, and the United States, with occasional visitors from Australia and Latin America. In the compound we lived shoulder to shoulder with students and staff who were Kikuyu, Akamba, Meru, Embu, Tharaka, Luo, Luhya, Taita, Maasai, Samburu, Kalenjin, Pokot, and Kipsigis, in addition to Dinka and Nuer from the Sudan, Tigreans from Eritrea, Ewe from Togo, Chagga from Tanzania, Tutsi and Hutu from Rwanda and Burundi, Baganda and Acholi from Uganda, and even Zulu from South Africa. Our experience at Africa University further expanded our horizons as we were befriended by additional Christian brothers and sisters from Angola, Ghana, Liberia, Malawi, Mozambique, Zambia, and Zimbabwe. What had been a rather monochromatic portrait of the Christian faith, up to that point, exploded into a kaleidoscopic vision of God's family. The most important lesson we carried away from this experience was the need to expand our horizons, open our lives to other perspectives, and embrace a global vision of Jesus' people. This is, in part, the reason for this volume.

Two immediate concerns gave rise to this project on making disciples in a world parish. First, leaders within the life of my own denomination, The United Methodist Church, have given increased attention in these opening years of the new millennium to our mission, which is "to make disciples of Jesus Christ for the transformation of the world." In the face of continuing decline and general malaise in the North American church, nothing could be more important than rediscovering our reason for being. Congregations have engaged in studies that touch in one way or another upon this topic, pastors have been encouraged to address this concern in cluster groups and in their own personal reflection and practice, bishops have renewed concern about "the Wesleyan way" and the need to "rethink church," and scholars have produced books and study guides to explore this terrain. At the same time, United Methodism, in particular, struggles to come to grips with its evolving identity as a truly global community. What I have longed to hear in the midst of this conversation are the voices of Methodists from around the world. The primary purpose of this volume, therefore, is to provide an opportunity for Methodists from the world parish to speak, affording their perspectives on mission and evangelism in the world today, and for those of us who read these pages to listen attentively.

Second, 2010 marks the centennial of the groundbreaking World Missionary Conference of Edinburgh. Methodists stood in the forefront of this amazing event that gave birth to the modern ecumenical movement and, in many ways, helped to define the modern Western missionary movement. The Methodist layman and ecumenical statesman, John R. Mott, set the tone for Edinburgh 1910, and the title of his best-known book, *The Evangelization of the World in this Generation*, became the watch cry for many in the opening decades of this past century. The world in which we live today is a different world from that of 1910—the center of gravity of Christianity has shifted from the global north to the global south, triumphalist attitudes have given way, at least in some quarters, to a spirit of partnership and mutuality, and a passion to participate in the *missio Dei* is slowly displacing the kingdom-building mentality of the twentieth century—but mission and global evangelization remain pressing concerns in our world today. My hope is that, in some small way, alongside the many celebrations linked to Edinburgh 2010, this volume will contribute to a rediscovery of the biblical call to mission, a passion to spread the good news of Jesus Christ, and a celebration of what God is already doing to restore the world through a truly global, multi-cultural community of faith.

The essays that follow are divided into six parts. The first five are grouped alphabetically by continent and the final section voices the insights and reflections of people in cross-continental appointments. In addition to their chapter, I requested that each contributor submit a list of resources related to disciple-making, mission, and evangelism that they have found helpful in their own context. From these recommendations I have culled twenty-five titles for each section and these suggestions for further reading come at the conclusion of each Part of the volume. Not only does this volume give us an opportunity, therefore, to hear the voices of the contributors from around the world, but these suggestions for further reading permit us to listen in on the conversations vicariously with nearly two hundred other people that have shaped their thinking and practice. Suggestions for further reading in the area of disciple-making in the Wesleyan tradition also accompany the general introduction. The bibliography at the close of the volume consists of all works cited in the essays themselves (nearly 200 titles).

Many people have supported me throughout the course of this project. I am grateful, first and foremost, to the amazing community of contributors who have joined their voices to create this resource. They are remarkable and have demonstrated their interest to experience God's gift of *koinonia* in one another. They have taught me much, not only about the specific focus of this volume, but, more importantly, about the meaning of life in Christ. While each has played a major role in shaping this volume, several deserve a special word of thanks for their work above and beyond the call of duty. Phil Wingeier-Rayo functioned, not only as a contributor, but also as a translator. Having translated one of the essays myself, I am fully aware of the complexities of this critical task, and especially appreciate his careful work. Helmut Renders provided assistance to me in securing contributors from Latin America. This proved to be a unique challenge. Whereas Christianity throughout Latin America continues to grow by leaps and bounds, Methodism remains a relatively small community in a sea of Roman Catholic and Pentecostal influence. Helmut helped me to navigate these waters carefully. Dr. Russell Morton, Research Librarian at Ashland Theological Seminary, provided invaluable assistance in tracking down full bibliographical information on non-Western titles. Throughout the course of this project, the editorial staff of Wipf & Stock have been both supportive and patient. Unlike typical publication endeavors, the path of a project of this nature inevitably includes unexpected twists and turns in the way. Charlie Collier and Diane Farley, in particular, extended grace to me on many occasions and kept my attention on the important signposts along the way.

Making Disciples in a World Parish addresses the two primary issues identified in the title, namely, the Spirit's work in the community of faith that enables people to fall in love with Jesus and walk with him in life and the global reality of the Christian faith and its Wesleyan expression. Rev. Elisha Kabungaidze, my good friend from our sojourn in Zimbabwe, exemplifies the best of both worlds. During the terrible drought in southern Africa in 1991-92, he incarnated mission and evangelism in the Wesleyan spirit. Grateful for his indefatigable witness to Jesus Christ, I dedicate this volume to him.

Paul W. Chilcote
The Conversion of Paul, 2010

Introduction: "Love, that never, never fails"

IN THE MIDST OF CONTROVERSY CONCERNING HIS VOCATION AND THAT of the movement of Christian renewal he had come to spearhead, John Wesley confided to a friend: "I look upon all the world as my parish; thus far I mean that, in whatever part of it I am, I judge it meet, right, and my bounden duty to declare unto all that are willing to hear the glad tidings of salvation. This is the work which I know God has called me to, and sure I am that his blessing attends it."[1] The world of John and Charles Wesley was actually quite narrowly circumscribed. It is hard to imagine that they ever would have conceived this "world parish" as something extending around the globe. We find their spiritual progeny today, however, on every continent—their influence extends, literally, around the world. The Wesleys rediscovered the importance of accountable discipleship and the biblical call to share the good news of God's love in Christ through a robust ministry of mission and evangelism. Making disciples of Jesus Christ constitutes the essence of their legacy, not only for those in the Methodist community, but as a gift to the wider church as well.

Contemporary Christian scholars and practitioners are rediscovering this same lesson, namely, that the primary mission of the church is to "make disciples of Jesus Christ." For those who stand in the Wesleyan tradition, in particular, this has led many to reclaim both the missional nature of the church and the missional heritage of Methodism. All of these efforts, from the highest level of church structure to the grass roots of the local congregation are to be highly commended. Only limited efforts have been made, however, to interface the global community and this all important practice of the church. If Christians today are serious about embracing God's mission in the world, then they must learn important lessons from all quarters of the global community of faith. This book provides an opportunity to listen to the voices of global Methodism as leaders speak to this issue and share their corporate

1. Wesley, *Works*, 19:67.

wisdom and vision of mission and evangelism from the perspective of a world parish.

The Changing Face of Global Christianity and Methodism

During the closing decades of the past millennium, the face of Christianity changed dramatically and the shifting terrain of the Christian world is reshaping Methodism worldwide. In his new book, *Invitation to World Missions*, Methodist missiologist and seminary president, Timothy Tennent, identifies seven megatrends that characterize the current situation:

1. The Collapse of Christendom
2. The Rise of Postmodernism: Theological, Cultural, and Ecclesiastical Crisis
3. The Collapse of the "West-Reaches-the-Rest" Paradigm
4. The Changing Face of Global Christianity
5. The Emergence of a Fourth Branch of Christianity
6. Globalization: Immigration, Urbanization and New Technologies, and
7. A Deeper Ecumenism.[2]

Of all these seismic events, none is more dramatic, perhaps, than the shift of the center of the Christian faith from the global north to the global south. Philip Jenkins popularized this historical fact in his bestselling *The Next Christendom: The Coming of Global Christianity*. The mounting statistical evidence, however, is nothing short of overwhelming. From the early predictions of the *World Christian Encyclopedia* and the later *World Christian Trends*, to the hard data of the *World Religion Database (WRD)*, the *World Christian Database (WCD)*, and the *Atlas of Global Christianity (AGC)*, all indicators mark the southward and eastward movement of the Christian religion.[3] Several comparative state-

---

2. Tennent, *Invitation to World Missions*, 15–51.

3. Two prominent missiologists, David Barrett and Todd Johnson, are primary forces behind the creation of these massive databases and religious demographic studies. See Barrett, *World Christian Encyclopedia* (1982); the expanded second edition of

ments suffice to register the magnitude of the transformation taking place. Whereas in 1900 over 80 percent of all Christians lived in Europe and North America, the proportion had fallen to under 40 percent by 2005. Most projections predict that in another quarter century, nearly half of all Christians in the world will be in Africa and Latin America. Less than one third will be in the global north. The situation in just one African nation, Nigeria, illustrates the meteoric rise of Christianity in the south, with a relatively small community of less than 0.2 million at the beginning of the twentieth century swelling to over 64 million by the end of the millennium.

Developments within global Methodism reflect the same trends. Assessing information culled from the *World Christian Database*, Timothy Tennent observes: "Between 1970 and 2005 the Methodists in Nigeria grew from 80,000 to over 2 million. As a point of comparison, it should be noted that during that same time period, the Methodists in the United Kingdom lost over half of their entire membership (2 million to 996,000) and the United Methodist Church in the United States lost 6 million members, dropping from 14 million down to 8 million members."[4] The most current statistics of the World Methodist Council, the Wesleyan ecumenical body which links over seventy Methodist and related United Churches in over 132 countries, reported almost equal numbers of church members in Africa and North America in 2007. But, whereas Methodist Churches in Africa grew by over 300 percent over the course of the previous decade, North American Churches lost nearly 100,000 members. During the same decade, 1997–2007, while Methodist Churches of the Western world lost 150,000 members, non-Western Methodist Churches grew from nearly 18 million to nearly 28 million. Nearly two-thirds of all Methodists live today in the non-Western world, mostly in the global south.[5] These radical changes in the landscape of global Christianity and Methodism will inevitably shape the missional practice of the church in this new millennium.

---

this work, Barrett, Kurian, and Johnson, *World Christian Encyclopedia* (2001); Barrett and Johnson, *World Christian Trends*; Johnson and Ross, *Atlas of Global Christianity*; and the two online resources Johnson and Grim, *World Religion Database* and *World Christian Database*.

4. Tennent, *Invitation to World Missions*, 291.

5. See *World Methodist Council Handbook (1997)*, 256 and *World Methodist Council Handbook (2007)*, 279.

Making Disciples, Mission, and Evangelism

John and Charles Wesley's rediscovery of a mission-church paradigm in eighteenth century England fueled the renewal of the church in their own age and offers a model of enduring significance for global Christianity today. They reclaimed mission as the church's reason for being and evangelism as the heart of that mission in the world. Further, they developed a holistic vision of making disciples of Jesus Christ that maintained the integral connection of mission and evangelism, faith and works, personal salvation and social justice, physical and spiritual needs. All three terms—disciple-making, mission, and evangelism—elude easy definition, but their integral relationship can be seen in the biblical and historical roots and the contextual routes of contemporary thinking and practice.

Biblical Roots

The Wesleys embraced the notion that scripture is the foundation of all Christian faith and practice. They believed that their own calling was rooted in the mission of God revealed in the Word. It is important in this regard, then, to note two critical rediscoveries related to mission and evangelism in the contemporary biblical reflection on these practices.

First, a missiological reading of the Bible has led to a renewed emphasis on the centrality of the reign of God in Jesus' ministry and that of the early church. As a consequence, numerous works on mission and evangelism reflect a more robust and biblical understanding of salvation that embraces the dual dynamic of personal salvation in Jesus Christ and social action related to the kingdom of God. This vision refuses the old dichotomies that separated mission from evangelism; while these practices are distinct, from a biblical perspective, evangelism and mission are inseparable.

Second, a close examination of Jesus' so-called "commission texts," within the larger context of the biblical witness, has led to a revision of thinking related to the church's missional task. Two problems have dominated the traditional interpretation of these texts: the legal nature of Jesus' command and the conception of mission "over there." Many today have challenged the "command-and-obedience" interpretation of Jesus' commissioning of the disciples—principally the "great commission" of Matt 28:16–20—arguing that the commission of Jesus is not so much an assignment to be fulfilled as it is an identity, a promise, a gift to be received. This more grace-oriented perspective transforms the motivation for disciple-making dramatically. Similarly, in his exegetical treatment of the great commission, as well as in the highly influential work *Transforming Mission*, David Bosch argues against the typical fixation on the participle "go" in Jesus' statement, as if that were the command, and redirects our attention to the proper structural and theological focus of the text, namely, the privilege to "make disciples."[6] He thereby mitigates the triumphalist and frequently imperialistic attitude that has accompanied mission from the Western world, emphasizing instead the communal, contextual, servant-oriented, and incarnational themes that constitute this process and characterize the church's central calling.

Historical Roots

Making disciples in the Wesleyan spirit. Methodist leaders have generated quite a lot of conversation in recent years about the way in which the Wesleys sought to make disciples in the context of the early Methodist Societies.[7] Whether described as "The Wesleyan Way," or faith formation in the Wesleyan spirit, or accountable discipleship, no one questions the fact that this "work" constituted the vital center of their mission. But this task and privilege was part and parcel of the larger movement of Christian renewal in Britain characterized by six primary emphases— rediscoveries of the living Word, saving faith, holistic spirituality, accountable discipleship, formative worship, and missional vocation.[8] Within the context of this larger movement of the Holy Spirit, the Wesleys structured Methodism to help people discover the faith, learn what it meant to be a follower of Jesus, practice their new-found faith, and resituate their lives in disciple-making communities—this was the Wesleyan way.

First, the discovery of faith among Methodists came primarily through a revised vision of God. To put it simply but profoundly, early Methodist people came to understand that the Triune God is a mission-

---

6. Bosch, "Structure of Mission."

7. Consult titles in Further Reading in Wesleyan Disciple-Making at the conclusion of this chapter.

8. See Chilcote, *The Wesleyan Tradition*.

ary God. The Wesleys preached that the nature of love is to reach out beyond itself, and so, God's mission in the world begins in creation, continues through redemption, and stretches out toward consummation, as God reaches out beyond God's self to establish and restore relationship. The Wesleys took their clue to making disciples, in other words, from the vision of a God as a community of love who moves out in the dance of creation and redemption. Discipleship begins through an encounter with this God in the living Word and in the joy of finding faith through relationships with companions in the pilgrimage of life.

Second, once captured by faith, faith must be learned. The primary purpose of the Methodist Society was to teach people how to love. This lesson began in the waters of baptism, that sacramental act of the church in which God establishes our primal identity as the children of God. Like Clement of Alexandria, the Wesleys believed that faith leads to knowledge, that knowledge leads to love, and that love leads inevitably to a union with the One who is loved. This type of learning as ongoing formation in relationship takes place through many practices, but most profoundly around the Table of the Lord, in the celebration of the family meal or Eucharist. The early Methodist people described this meal as the chief means of grace—that place where God meets God's people to nourish and sustain them as they engage in mission for the life of the world.

Third, they practiced this faith by means of a holistic spirituality that combined works of piety and works of mercy. The works of piety, or means of grace as they were also called, included prayer and fasting, immersion in scripture, Christian fellowship, and participation in the Lord's Supper. The more private aspects of these practices one might simply describe as the life of devotion; the most important public dimension of piety was participation in the worship of the community of faith. But it was also important, if disciples were to be fully formed or reshaped into the image of Christ, for them to engage in acts of compassion and justice, the private and public manifestations of mercy. The goal of this balanced portfolio of formative practices—in fact, the goal of the Christian life itself—was to cultivate the deepest possible love of God and neighbor.

Fourth, the Wesleys were wise enough to know that none of this could be done alone. Indeed, John Wesley said famously on one occasion that there is no such thing as a solitary Christian. Discipleship requires community, which is itself a profound implication of having been created in the image of a God who abides in perpetual relationship. Genuine Christian community, however, does not exist for its own benefit. Like God, the love that constitutes it compels the community of faith to reach out with glad and generous hearts to all. In this way, the Christian family becomes a disciple-making community as it bears witness to the good news by making room and creating safe space for the other (hospitality), by offering reconciliation and peace to the broken-hearted and the oppressed (healing), and by living in and for God's shalom-vision for all humanity and creation (holiness).

Mission in the Wesleyan Tradition. The Wesleys concluded that the central purpose of the church is mission—God's mission. Their study of scripture, particularly the Acts of the Apostles, shaped the vision of the church they sought to replicate in their own day. In their view, their beloved Church of England had exchanged its true vocation—mission—for maintenance; it had abandoned its mission alongside the poor and, instead, had become something that approached a chaplaincy to those in power. Their primary concern was to help the church reclaim its true identity as an agent of reconciliation and redemption in the world. The Wesleys firmly believed that God raised up the Methodists specifically for the task of resuscitating a missional church more consistent with the biblical witness. Perhaps they knew instinctively that a church turned in on itself will surely die, whereas a church spun out in loving service into the world rediscovers its true vocation daily.

Elsewhere I have written that "offering Christ," to use Wesley's own terminology for the work of mission, "involves both word and deed, both proclamation and action; it connects the gospel to the world."[9] The primary motif with regard to mission in the Wesleyan tradition, therefore, was the idea of becoming God's partners in the redemption of the whole world. Whereas Wesley hardly ever used the term "mission" in his voluminous writings, his conception of mission found expression in a word like "benevolence." Based upon gratitude for all that God has done for us in Christ and in us through the power of the Holy Spirit, the practice of benevolence consists of all efforts to realize peace and justice in the life of the world. Methodists incarnated this mission in different ways to address unique contexts—e.g., their vigorous protest against slavery in Britain—but outreach to the marginalized and resistance to

---

9. Chilcote, "Mission-Church Paradigm," 155.

injustice characterized all of their work in mission. They expressed both actions through works of mercy that bore witness to God's rule over life. In imitation of the mission of Christ, they sought to heal the sick, to liberate those who were oppressed, to empower those who stood on the margins of life, and to care for the poor.

Evangelism in the Wesleyan Tradition. One aspect of the Wesleyan genius was to hold mission and evangelism together without pitting personal salvation against social justice. The way in which the Wesleys envisaged this essential connection between evangelism and mission is, perhaps, one of their greatest contributions to the life of the church today. Dana Robert hits the nail on the head when she describes evangelism as the heart of mission; this is most certainly the Wesleyan view.[10] The heart and the body, evangelism and mission, are interdependent and interconnected, and this is the essence of the Wesleyan synthesis. The holistic paradigm for evangelism that emerged from this larger vision can be described as an interdependent network of missional practices, including faithful preaching, inspirational singing, accountable discipleship, authentic worship, and incarnational service.

- *Faithful preaching.* The Wesleys proclaimed the message of God's unconditional love to the people in sermons aptly summarized in the so-called "four alls:" all need to be saved, all can be saved, all can know they are saved, all can be saved to the uttermost. But their preaching addressed the social evils of their day with equal force.

- *Inspirational singing.* Four themes pervade the hymns of Charles Wesley and communicated the gospel to the singers: the nature of God's unconditional love, the all-sufficiency of God's grace, the all-embracing nature of inclusive community, and the missional vision of God's people. Methodists discovered their essential identity as gospel-bearers by singing it.

- *Accountable discipleship (small groups).* Evangelism took place most fully in the intimacy of the small group, where faith was born and awakened sinners were encouraged to grow in grace, to be channels of love for others, and to enter a particular, revolutionary path of self-sacrificing love for the world.

---

10. Robert, *Evangelism as the Heart of Mission.*

- *Authentic worship (Eucharist).* If evangelism has to do with heralding the good news, bearing witness to God's love, and servanthood in the life of the world, then worship, and the Sacrament of Holy Communion, in particular, is the supreme place where the community embodies this action on behalf of the world.

- *Incarnational service.* The Wesleys went to great lengths to specify the two-fold character of Christian service as integral to Christian evangelism: 1) the servant offers to others what he or she has freely received from God, namely, grace, mercy, and compassion, 2) to have the mind of Christ—to be a gospel-bearer—necessarily entails the care of the poor.[11]

From a Wesleyan perspective, making disciples, mission, and evangelism are constitutive practices of the whole people of God. Through them, the community of faith woos others into the loving embrace of God and then helps them to see that their mission in life, in partnership with Christ, is to be the signposts of God's reign in this world. Having any sense of what this will mean or look like in this new millennium will depend in large measure on the attention we give to the emerging contextual dynamics around the globe.

Contextual Routes

One of the purposes of this volume, therefore, is to listen to voices from within the world parish of the Methodist family as women and men reflect on questions related to the practice of disciple-making in their own contexts. In an effort to develop a sense of coherence in this volume, the contributors were asked to reflect on five questions that interface the task of making disciples with mission and evangelism:

1. What are the most critical challenges related to disciple-making in your context?

2. What images/stories from scripture are most pertinent to your context in this regard?

3. How do you envisage and practice evangelism/disciple-making, therefore, in your context?

---

11. A distillation of Chilcote, *"Evangelistic Practices."*

4. Where do you see signs of new life and vitality in the life of the church as a result of this vision and practice?

5. What do the lessons you are learning about disciple-making in your context contribute to the rest of the world parish?

These reflections are organized by continent and also include a final section of contributions by scholar practitioners who live in cross-cultural situations.

Every continent has its own stories of struggle and faithfulness. Indeed, each distinct community within any given region has a voice of its own that deserves to be heard. This makes the construction of a resource like this one all the more difficult. The issue of inclusion/exclusion looms large and this humble effort is anything but perfect. Nonetheless, the inclusion in this collection of so many voices marks substantial progress. Of the twenty-eight contributors, not including the editor, six are from Africa, six from Asia and Oceania, six from Europe, four from Latin America and the Caribbean, and six from North America. This represents a remarkable global spectrum, by any standards, and may be the most widely distributed group of Methodist authors to attempt a work of this nature. Women's voices, of course, must be heard as well as those of their male colleagues. Mindful of the importance of gender balance, therefore, a "preferential option" was exercised to secure as many female authors as possible. In some regions of the world, however, this presented serious challenges. In the end, one third of the contributors are women (nine out of twenty-eight), and this, as well, represents a substantial advance in relation to comparable multi-author studies. Whereas the majority of authors are United Methodists, other communities, such as the African Methodist Episcopal Church, the Free Methodist Church, and many autonomous, national Methodist and Wesleyan Churches are represented among the contributors.

Given the fact that disciple-making, mission, and evangelism are practices that engage the whole people of God, an attempt has also been made to include representatives from across the spectrum of church life. The vast majority of the contributors (sixteen) are professors and teachers with specialization in these missional practices, but they are complimented by five church leaders (bishops or presidents), four practitioners (pastors, missionaries, or evangelists), and three officials or directors of agencies or programs directly related to the topic of the study.

The high level of positive response to initial invitations—with absolutely no material incentive whatsoever—is a measure, perhaps, of the shared concern related to the church's primary vocation around the globe. Also impressive is the fact that most contributors went on to complete their work and only a few found it necessary to withdraw, one quite simply because he had no electricity for some six months! As this far-flung group of brothers and sisters in Christ commenced its work, something like a "parable of community" emerged. It is not too much to say, perhaps, that they became gospel to one another as they reflected on the meaning of gospel-bearing in our world. They prayed for one another in sickness and celebration, through the tragedy of the Haiti earthquake and the expectation of a new decade in this new millennium. The meeting of the World Methodist Council Executive Committee in Santiago, Chile, actually afforded the opportunity for nine of the contributors to meet face to face and reflect together on their tasks.

One of the primary challenges of the volume was to preserve the unique voice and approach of each contributor over against the value of cohesiveness and balance in terms of style and presentation. While the hope was expressed that each author would find it possible to respond to the five questions in the study, permission was freely given for them to approach this task in their own way so that the integrity of their context, culture, and style would be honored. The fact that the contributors are drawn from a variety of disciplines and carry strikingly different portfolios in the life of the church adds a certain kaleidoscopic ambiance to the whole as well, to say nothing of the fact that some are seasoned scholars and published authors, while others are new to the world of a more public discourse. Needless to say, participation in this exciting work necessitated sacrificial commitment on the part of many. The journey has not been easy, but the growth has been significant. Hopefully, the final product of this labor of love reflects the joy of those who have been with one another in community.

In consideration of an image or images that might frame the contributions from each region and knit together those from around the globe, the bodies of water that separate people from people in our world and the watercourses upon which we travel came to mind. For those in the Christian community, of course, water is a powerful baptismal symbol, representing both death and life, challenge and victory. African Christians who are experiencing exponential growth in their communities seem to be riding the flood tide. The context of Asia and Oceania is exceptionally diverse, both in terms of culture and religion, which necessitates navigating cross-currents with care and sensitivity. With the demise of Christendom in the West, European Christians find themselves persevering through ebb tide, whereas, in Latin America and the Caribbean, the Spirit is moving and blowing where it will, with the church tacking into the wind. Challenged by the eclipse of modernity and the birth of a nascent postmodern world, North Americans are exploring an uncharted ocean. Those privileged to cross boundaries, living and working in cultures and speaking languages different from their own, are learning what it means to value the confluence of streams. The world parish is diverse and complex; the good news of the love of God in Jesus Christ is translatable and can find a home in any heart and any community.

In a little-known hymn, Charles Wesley articulates a vision of disciple-making, mission, and evangelism rooted in God's love—a vision of truly global proportions:

> Love, which willest all should live,
> Love, which all to all would give,
> Love, that over all prevails,
> Love, that never, never fails.
> Love immense, and unconfined,
> Love to all of humankind.[12]

---

12. Kimbrough, *Songs for the Poor*, Hymn 1.

Further Reading on Wesleyan Disciple-Making, Mission, and Evangelism

Anderson, Gerald H., editor. *Christian Mission in Theological Perspective*. Nashville: Abingdon, 1967.

Chilcote, Paul W. *Recapturing the Wesleys' Vision: An Introduction to the Faith of John and Charles Wesley*. Downers Grove, IL: InterVarsity, 2004.

Cole, Charles E., editor. *United Methodist History of Mission*. 6 vols. New York: GBGM, 2003–2005.

Collins, Kenneth J., and John H. Tyson. *Conversion in the Wesleyan Tradition*. Nashville: Abingdon, 2001.

Gunter, W. Stephen, and Elaine Robinson, editors. *Considering the Great Commission: Evangelism and Mission in the Wesleyan Spirit*. Nashville: Abingdon, 2005.

Heath, Elaine A., and Scott T. Kisker. *Longing for Spring: A New Vision for Wesleyan Community*. Eugene, OR: Cascade, 2010.

Henderson, D. Michael. *John Wesley's Class Meeting: A Model for Making Disciples*. Nappanee, IN: Francis Asbury, 1997.

Hunter, George G., III. *To Spread the Power: Church Growth in the Wesleyan Spirit*. Nashville: Abingdon, 1987.

Jones, Scott J. *The Evangelistic Love of God and Neighbor*. Nashville: Abingdon, 2003.

Kennedy, Gerald H. *Heritage and Destiny: Wesley Commemorative Volume on the Evangelistic World Mission of Methodism*. New York: Board of Missions of the Methodist Church, 1953.

Kimbrough, S T, Jr. *Resistless Love: Christian Witness in the New Millennium: A Wesleyan Perspective*. New York: GBGM, 2001.

Kisker, Scott. *Mainline or Methodist? Rediscovering Our Evangelistic Mission*. Nashville: Discipleship Resources, 2008.

Knight, Henry H., III. *Transforming Evangelism: The Wesleyan Way of Sharing Faith*. Nashville: Abingdon, 2006.

Logan, James C., editor. *Christ for the World: United Methodist Bishops Speak on Evangelism*. Nashville: Kingswood, 1996.

Logan, James C., editor. *Theology and Evangelism in the Wesleyan Heritage*. Nashville: Kingswood, 1994.

Manskar, Steven W. *Accountable Discipleship: Living in God's Household*. Nashville: Discipleship Resources, 2003.

Matthaei, Sondra Higgins. *Making Disciples: Faith Formation in the Wesleyan Tradition*. Nashville: Abingdon, 2000.

Messer, Donald E. *A Conspiracy of Goodness: Contemporary Images of Christian Mission*. Nashville: Abingdon, 1992.

Nuessle, John E. *Faithful Witnesses: United Methodist Theology of Mission*. New York: GBGM, 2008.

Padgett, Alan G., editor. *The Mission of the Church in Methodist Perspective: The World is My Parish*. Lewiston, NY: Edwin Mellen, 1992.

United Methodist Church. *Grace upon Grace: The Mission Statement of The United Methodist Church*. Nashville: Graded, 1990.

Watson, David Lowes. *Accountable Discipleship*. Nashville: Discipleship Resources, 1985.

———. *Covenant Discipleship: Christian Formation through Mutual Accountability*. 1998. Reprint, Eugene, OR: Wipf & Stock, 2002.

———. *Forming Christian Disciples: The Role of Covenant Discipleship and Class Leaders in the Congregation*. Nashville: Discipleship Resources, 1989.

Watson, Kevin. *A Blueprint for Discipleship: Wesley's General Rules as a Guide for Christian Living*. Nashville: Discipleship Resources, 2009.

PART ONE

Africa
Riding the Flood Tide

Introduction to Part I

AFRICA BOASTS SOME OF THE MOST ANCIENT FORMS OF CHRISTIANITY in the world. We find many of these traditions, of course, in the north where they continue to exist as minorities in a majority Muslim world. The late twentieth century, however, witnessed an amazing burst of Christian activity in sub-Saharan Africa, fueled in large measure by the post-colonial dynamic after the Second World War. It is not too much to claim that African Christianity is riding the crest of a flood tide in these opening years of the new millennium. In 1900 less than ten million Christians resided in Africa, but by the end of the century, this figure had escalated to nearly 400 million. That kind of exponential growth still characterizes Christianity in Africa today, with some estimating that this number will double in less than half a century. Much of this growth is due to indigenous African efforts, so we have much to learn from our African brothers and sisters with regard to disciple-making, mission, and evangelism.

In the opening chapter of this African story, Lubunga W'Ehusha reflects on what it means to be a disciple of Jesus Christ in the African Great Lakes Region. All of us are painfully aware of the legacy of genocide that has shaped Rwanda, Burundi, and parts of the Democratic Republic of Congo in recent years. What does it mean to be a Christian in such a context? How does one restore trust in a community of faith in which Christians have perpetrated heinous crimes against one another? W'Ehusha explores the mission of the church against this backdrop of evil and violence.

The nation of Kenya has long been viewed by many as the African epicenter. Nairobi, its capital, functions somewhat like a central clearing house for pan-African and international Christian organizations that are engaged in service and witness across the continent. Nahashon Gitonga examines the way in which the history of Christianity in Kenya—including the dominant understandings and forms of evangelism that were part of the colonial era and the East African Evangelical

Revival—shaped Christian praxis in both positive and negative ways. He argues that a renewed understanding of disciple-making that takes conversion, nurture, and inculturation seriously offers great hope for the future.

Perhaps no nation on the continent inspires and challenges our imaginations more than South Africa. Dion Forster shares his vision of a church in South Africa shaped by the holistic vision of the Wesleyan heritage, combining vital piety and social witness. Approaching his task from both an historical and theological perspective, he engages the primary concerns of this country of contrasts, including the HIV/AIDS pandemic, pervasive poverty, and the legacy of apartheid. He demonstrates how "the Methodist emphasis on social holiness as a constitutive aspect of a Wesleyan theology of perfection exerted a strong influence upon the missional character and ministry of the Church."

Both of the concluding essays in this section come from Zimbabwe. Professor John Wesley Zvomunondiita Kurewa's name, in and of itself, illustrates his rootedness in Methodism and his native Shona culture. In an incisive narrative concerning the church in which he was raised, which takes the form of a case study, he discusses the necessity of understanding people where they are and walking with them in a *dzvikiti*— a journey with Christ that liberates people from fear and leads them to God's promised land. One of his protégés, Christinah Kwaramba, draws upon her cultural heritage to depict a disciple-making community that gives first priority to evangelism, rehearses the stories that create identity, and celebrates God's Spirit manifest in diverse ways among people of faith. Both identify "starting where people are" as the key to making disciples of Jesus Christ.

1

Being a Disciple of Christ in the African Great Lakes Region

Lubunga W'Ehusha

> By this everyone will know that you are my disciples,
> if you have love for one another. (John 13:35)

HAVING SERVED AS A PASTOR IN SOUTH AFRICA FOR FOUR YEARS, I know what it takes to make disciples in a post-apartheid democracy when scars of racial divisions are still noticeable. How do you integrate White, Colored, Indian, and Black into the one body of Christ without stepping on some people's boundaries? It is particularly difficult since hatred, exploitation, and violence accompanied racial discrimination in South Africa. This has been a great challenge to Christian ministry in South Africa and the easy answer but tough practice seems to be, "make disciples."

Now that I have moved to the eastern part of Congo, in the African Great Lakes region, torn by years of civil war, tribal conflict, and genocide on both sides of the lakes (Rwanda, Burundi, and Congo), I realize how challenging it is to be a disciple of Christ in the midst of mass killing. For many years, the nations of this region experienced a steady growth of Christianity to the satisfaction of several mission agencies. The current crisis, caused by years of tribal and ethnic conflict and poverty, reveals how fragile and shallow Christian faith can be. Very few church members were able to carry their cross as disciples of Jesus and stand firm against the call to pillage and murder.

If statistics are accurate, an estimated eighty-three million people live in this region (sixty-six in Congo, ten in Rwanda, and seven in

Burundi), out of which 70–80 percent of the population in each of these countries claims to be Christian. How then can the church account for the breakdown of moral and spiritual values in a region so densely evangelized? Here, as elsewhere on the continent, the same urge resonates: "Make disciples." Given the fact that crime, corruption, hatred, and bitterness continue to escalate in this part of Africa, despite the fact that Christianity permeates the nations of this region, what went wrong? How does one delineate between "believers" and genuine "disciples" of Christ in the church?

These are tough questions that need to be tackled as one reflects on making disciples in the context of post-conflict Central Africa. The scope of this article does not permit a full discussion of all the complex issues surrounding these questions, but it does provide an opportunity to examine relevant challenges and approaches to disciple-making, scriptural images that resonate with the context, signs of vitality, and recommendations to the global church.

An Evangelistic Approach to Disciple-Making

According to the Great Commission, Jesus sent his messengers with the mandate to preach the good news and teach believers to observe all things that he had commanded so that his disciples might be found throughout the whole world (Matt 28:19–20). This mission entails preaching, teaching, and demonstrating Christ-like attitudes as essential aspects of disciple-making wherever the gospel is spread. This process aims at the creation of a distinctive culture or way of life that cuts across the boundaries of nation, language, and tribe, recognized most fully in the life and witness of the disciples of Jesus.

Today, as so many denominations and groups compete in the religious market place, analysts often measure the success of evangelism simply on the basis of numbers of church-goers or attendants, regardless of the actual character of their lives. In some instances, success even consists in the ability of one group to "steal sheep" from other denominations. At such a time, obedience to Jesus' approach remains the best way forward for the health of the church. He concentrated on a few and invested time, knowledge, and life until they become his imitators. "Now when they saw the boldness of Peter and John and realized that they were uneducated and ordinary men, they were amazed and recognized them as companions of Jesus" (Acts 4:13). To have been Jesus' companions here means that they spent time learning from him, living with him, and sharing his food and his suffering until they knew him through and through to become his disciples.

We know the success of Methodist classes in the past and of cell groups today in church growth; this remains a powerful tool for making disciples. In these small groups people share the Word of God as well as their own lives and, thereby, become a source of support and encouragement to one another. We need to strengthen this approach by equipping cell group leaders and participants with the tools they need to discern sound, biblical teaching and to engage in current debates, both in the church and society. But despite the fact that pastors proclaim the Word faithfully, crusades draw new converts into the faith, and leadership training events seek to bolster biblical foundations, many Christians still find it a major challenge to demonstrate Christ-like attitudes when they face a crisis. What are the primary challenges that hinder church members to live out their faith?

Critical Challenges

As Christians, we believe that the living Word of God has the power to transform human lives anytime and anywhere. Change will not occur, however, until the church deals seriously with the crucial problems that tarnish her image and hinder genuine disciple-making in our society. In the African Great Lakes region, tribalism/ethnicity, poverty, and lack of trained disciplers stand out as critical challenges.

Tribalism/Ethnicity

"I lost faith," testified a survivor of the Rwandan genocide of 1994, "when I saw members of my family slaughtered by fellow Christians from a rival ethnic group inside a temple where they found refuge." The painful reality embedded in stories such as this one, typical in Congo, Rwanda, and Burundi today, undermines the role of the church in society. How could Christians have participated in mass killing and sided with people of their tribe, clan, extended family, or ethnic group to commit such evil? The answer is to be found, in part, in the fact that the tribe or clan for most Africans provides their primary sense of identity or belonging.

People are likely drawn by fear and duty to maintain kinship bonds so as not to forfeit their place in the communal life. The traditional African view of a person, "I am because we are," defines the strong tie that exists between members of different clans, tribes or ethnic groups. As John Mbiti argues, "In traditional life, the individual does not exist alone except corporately.... He is part of the whole. The community must therefore make, create or produce the individual."[1]

When one needs human support in time of deep crisis or crucial decision making, such as marriage, elections, conflict, sickness, and death, most Africans, including Christians, tend to turn first of all to members of their own clan, tribe, and ethnic group. Ethnicity can become a threat to discipleship in this context, therefore, as the tribe requires from its members more allegiance to its cause than to Jesus and his kingdom. People participate in evildoing and elect wicked leaders, both in the church and in secular settings, because they fear being rejected by their kin. The disciples of Jesus, however, are called to pay the price of forsaking brothers, sisters, and parents if those relationships hinder them from following the way of Jesus and becoming his disciples. The Gospel of Luke states clearly what Jesus expected from His disciples. "Whoever comes to me and does not hate father and mother, wife and children, brothers and sisters, yes, and even life itself, cannot be my disciple" (Luke 14:26).

Fortunately we have many examples of disciples who measured up to this standard, hiding and sparing the lives of persons from rival tribes and ethnic groups during mass killing in the region. Many regard them today as icons of the Christian faith in their ability to defy degrading, dehumanizing, and fanatic tribalism. But these brave disciples are few in comparison to the multitude of Christians who fell prey to tribal and ethnic pressure.

Poverty

"I could not share the good news with the family as I noticed the extreme deprivation in which they lived. It seems they had gone for two days without food, but I had nothing to offer for their immediate need;" so reported an evangelist after a door-to-door outreach in a suburban location in the region. How does one share the gospel with people who

---

1. Mbiti, *African Religions and Philosophy,* 106.

are starving to death if there is no bread to give them at the same time? "If a brother or sister is naked and lacks daily food, and one of you says to them, 'Go in peace; keep warm and eat your fill,' and yet you do not supply their bodily needs, what is the good of that" (Jas 2:15–16)? Many factors, including the HIV/AIDS pandemic, environmental degradation and poor political governance have exacerbated the problem of severe poverty throughout the region. This situation worsens whenever the people are forced to endure the recurrent wars and tribal conflicts that cause major displacements of the population.

Many roads have not been maintained for years and are in a very bad state. Economic infrastructures destroyed by war still await renewal and repair. The sexual violence and rape practiced by armed soldiers have led to a very high prevalence of HIV infection in the region. Men and women left jobless succumb to drunkenness, drugs, and violence in order to numb their pain and fight for survival. Others spend all their time in the simple quest for food, leaving no time for them to attend to the deeper needs of the spirit. In many cases women have become breadwinners for their households by spending hours trading on the street. This situation compels many of them to compromise their faith in order to provide food for the table. While we know that poverty per se is neither a curse nor a blessing, it often becomes a driving force that leads many Christians astray. George Janvier identifies economic struggle as an important barrier to discipleship in West Africa,[2] and it is no less a barrier in other parts of Africa and in this region. While it must be said that some have seen their faith strengthened as they have learned to depend on God in their situation of poverty, there is no question that the dehumanizing affects of deprivation stand as a perennial challenge to vital discipleship on the continent.

Lack of Trained Leaders

The church also suffers from the lack of well trained leaders in the areas of evangelism and discipleship, in part, due to the disruption of theological education. The deplorable conditions in which ordained pastors must live and under which they are called to serve continues to limit the number of persons who are willing to respond to the call of God, even

---

2. Janvier, *Discipleship*, 3–10.

when they hear it clearly. Often the church leaves the task of making disciples in the hands of members without experience or skill.

Scriptural Images

Scripture provides a number of lessons and images that bear directly on the most pressing needs of the African Great Lakes context. Mark 3:31–35 demonstrates the centrality of one's new identity in Christ—a self-understanding that transcends all other claims. The synoptic Gospels all record an incident in which members of Jesus' biological family disrupt one of his teaching and discipling sessions. The interruption elicits the question of kinship, something equally applicable to African cultures as we have seen. Jesus asks, "Who are my mother and my brothers?" He establishes a new criterion for the bond of kinship and family membership—a bond of fellowship rooted in God's rule and way: "Whoever does the will of God is my brother and sister and mother." Those who embrace the kingdom of God immerse themselves in a whole new set of kinship relationships that supersede all other modes of identification. Becoming a disciple of Jesus entails a transformation of primal identity. Baptism symbolizes this change and unites all who are grafted into Christ in a new family of love. The injunction of St. Paul simply articulates the ramifications of this new identity: "Let us work for the good of all, and especially for those of the family of faith" (Gal 6:10).

The parable of the Good Samaritan (Luke 10:25–37) demonstrates the proper attitude of the disciple of Christ towards the enemy. The story is well known. A Samaritan—hated and despised by the Jewish community—chooses to assist a Jew in spite of the animosity between their races. He goes far beyond the accepted norms of care, even within one's own community and kinship system, in an effort to save the wounded victim. The story encourages the disciple to turn questions like "who is my neighbor" around and to seek ways to act like a genuine neighbor to others. Jesus shapes his disciples into neighbors of all and even sets an example of this teaching through his own behavior in his interactions with the Samaritan woman of John 4:1–42. He breaks down the walls of hostility and opens the door of salvation to the woman and to other Samaritans. He accepts the hospitality of those who are hated and breaks through cultural barriers in order to reach out to all without discrimination. He calls upon his disciples to exemplify the same attitude.

In Matt 15:32, Jesus demonstrates his concern for the poor, saying, "I have compassion for the crowd, because they have been with me now for three days and have nothing to eat; and I do not want to send them away hungry, for they might faint on the way." The multiple roots and causes of poverty make it a complex problem with which to deal. Some people are so desperate that the only way to share the gospel with them is to accompany the word of grace with relief. Jesus taught his disciples to demonstrate compassion towards the poor and he urged them to feed those who came to hear his message. On the other hand, sometimes the poor need an incentive to work so as to build their sense of dignity and worth and to mitigate a form of dependency that is contrary to biblical teaching. Perhaps this was in the mind of St. Paul when he admonished others to "work with your hands as we directed you, so that you may behave properly toward outsiders and be dependent on nobody" (1 Thess 4:11–12). Two things are clear from Jesus' witness: Christians must be concerned about the poor and work for the dignity of all people.

Disciples of Christ ought to speak on behalf of the oppressed and the marginalized, refusing to participate in extortion or exploitation and exposing those who practice it. The prophet Amos elevated this concern for justice and identified commitment to the rule of God as a primary characteristic of the people of God. The Book of Amos functions as a manual for social change, teaching the disciples of Jesus how to become advocates for those who suffer under the yoke of injustice and oppression. The prophet condemns those who "sell the righteous for silver, and the needy for a pair of sandals—they who trample the head of the poor into the dust of the earth, and push the afflicted out of the way" (Amos 2:6–7). He proclaims woe to all those who accumulate wealth at the expense of the poor, "who drink wine in bowls, and anoint themselves with the finest oils, but are not grieved over the ruin of Joseph"(Amos 6:4–7)! The great houses of the rich "shall be shattered to bits" because they have not heard the cry of the needy (Amos 4:11). Disciples of Christ must have the courage to speak out and condemn the enrichment of a few at the expense of the many, to advocate the equitable sharing of wealth, and to declare the realization of God's Jubilee. As the Deuteronomist proclaims:

> If there is among you anyone in need, a member of your community in any of your towns within the land that the Lord your God is giving you, do not be hard-hearted or tight-fisted toward your needy neighbor. You should rather open your hand, willingly lending enough to meet the need, whatever it may be.... Give liberally and be ungrudging when you do so, for on this account the Lord your God will bless you in all your work and in all that you undertake. Since there will never cease to be some in need on the earth, I therefore command you, "Open your hand to the poor and needy neighbor in your land." (15:7–8, 10–11)

Christian communities have succeeded in making disciples of Jesus when generosity and compassion characterize the lives of those who name the name of Christ.

Christian Vitality

Youth and children demonstrate Christian authenticity and vitality in the African Great Lakes region, perhaps more than any other group. Worship bands and choirs draw many young people to church services. To retain the spirit and vitality of the youth, the church must continue to provide opportunity for nurture in solid, biblical foundations. The church has a unique opportunity to empower those who did not participate directly in genocide and are willing to become citizens of a world village. This may necessarily entail changes in the theological curricula of seminaries and Bible schools in order to empower new leaders who will make disciples among the youth and children. There is a critical shortage of Bibles and Christian resources in many areas, particularly those that have been embroiled in war and genocide; but the Church is alive. Thanks to the work of the Holy Spirit, the church continues to thrive despite the dearth of resources and the lack of skilled leadership untainted by the history of violence and pain. But how long can this continue? The situation must be redeemed before it is too late. New leadership must be identified and trained. Those who are in positions of power and influence must find ways to respond with sensitivity to the many needs of the African people and to proclaim the message of God's reconciling love in a holistic way that refuses to separate the physical and the spiritual yearnings of God's children. The church must shape a generation of new disciples who have the ability to heal the wounds of the past and envisage a new future of peace and love.

Global Contributions

There may be important lessons here, drawn from the experience of making disciples in a context plagued with poverty and genocide, conflict and exploitation, division and poor governance. The African Great Lakes region has no corner on the market of evil. Every nation faces some form of this challenge in one way or another, even as disciples pray for God to "deliver us from evil." But Tokunboh Adeyemo may have put his finger on something of importance when he raised the question a few decades ago: "Is Africa cursed?"[3] His ultimate conclusion was a resounding, "No!" Quite to the contrary, he claimed that Africa is a continent blessed with enormous resources, both natural and personal. The church in Africa, in spite of its multiple problems, continues to grow, to learn from its mistakes and painful histories, and to offer a vision of dynamic Christian faith to the world. Doors keep opening for evangelism in Africa as noted by Anne Coomes,[4] and communities, despite their limited resources, enable the Spirit to form new generations of faithful followers of Jesus. By preaching, teaching, and cultivating a Christ-like attitude, they continue to demonstrate to the world that they are disciples of Jesus and the people of God. The words of Kä Mana serve as a fitting conclusion: "If Christ is perceived, in the spirit which he extends to the heart of the world as the very substance of the ethics of our relationship, it is not only African life which will be completely transformed, but also humanity as a whole in its political, economic, social, moral and spiritual relationship."[5]

---

3. Adeyemo, *Is Africa Cursed?*, 290.
4. Coomes, *Africa Harvest*.
5. Mana, *Christians and Churches of Africa*, 106.

2

Making Disciples in Kenya

Nahashon Gitonga

A SURVEY OF THE DEVELOPMENT OF CHRISTIANITY IN KENYA FROM 1900 to 2000 indicates that "the Christian faith has been expanding in Kenya at a meteoric rate."[1] This phenomenal growth could be attributed to two main factors: 1) mission societies originating from various countries in Europe and America prompted by the evangelical revival that swept that part of the world in the eighteenth and nineteenth centuries, and 2) the East African Evangelical Revival which originated in Uganda in the 1920s and swept across East African countries. About three decades have elapsed since that survey was undertaken. It is appropriate at this juncture to review the current trend of disciple-making in Kenya in light of these movements and propose an evangelistic practice suitable for Kenya today.

Critical Challenges

Kenya is facing two major challenges in the process of disciple-making, namely, cultural insensitivity and a lack of Christian moral integrity. As it will be noted subsequently, these obstacles to disciple-making emanate from the manner in which the gospel was presented by the two movements noted above.

---

1. Barrett, *Kenya Churches Handbook*, 157.

Cultural Insensitivity

The Euro-American evangelical revival had its beginnings in England with the work of John and Charles Wesley and George Whitefield. Missionary societies were established to propagate the gospel abroad. Kenya, as other parts of the world, benefited from this arrangement. During the latter part of the nineteenth century, Kenya received a number of missionaries from various European countries such as Portugal, Spain, Italy, Germany, and Britain, sent by Protestant and Roman Catholic missions. The Protestant missions included the Church Mission Society (1844), Foreign Mission Committee of the United Methodist Free Churches of Britain (1862), and the Scottish Mission (1891), while the Roman Catholic missions included the Holy Ghost Fathers (1890) and the *Intitut de la Consolata* (1902). In their disciple-making, the missionaries adopted the approach of condemning African traditional religious beliefs and practices as "pagan," "primitive," and "devilish." African converts to Christianity were required to abandon their traditional religious heritage as a condition of being received into Christian fellowship.

Many Africans, however, accepted Christian faith while at the same time retaining their traditional religious heritage. On one hand, the convert was enrolled as a full member of the church and regularly attended Sunday worship services, while on the other hand, during existential crises such as serious illness, the same convert resorted to traditional medicine-persons and attributed misfortune to curses.[2] The legacy of this dualism poses a critical challenge to disciple-making since it denies the opportunity for Christianity to permeate the entire life of the convert, including traditional worldviews, beliefs, and practices. Consequently, Christianity is rendered superficial in the life of the believer.[3]

Lack of Christian Moral Integrity

The origins of this problem lie in the manner in which the East African Evangelical Revival presented the gospel. A fire of revival spread throughout the Anglican Church of Uganda in Baganda in the 1920s,

---

2. Nthamburi, *Pilgrimage of the African Church*, 41–42.
3. Eitel, *Transforming Culture*, 31–32.

and from there into Rwanda in Gahini where a mammoth revival meeting was held in 1933. From Gahini the fire subsequently swept across East Africa due to the devoted service of people like Nsibambi, Blasio Kigozi, Yosiya Kinuka, Joe Church, and William Nagenda. In their disciple-making, the leaders of the revival reduced this practice simply to preaching the message of repentance and salvation. Undergirded by a strong evangelical theology, they emphasized the experience of receiving salvation in Jesus Christ, a primary tenet of the movement captured in the term associated with Revival converts in Luganda—*Balokole* (saved people). Thus, the hallmark of the East African Evangelical Revival, not unlike the Second Great Awakening in the United States, was leading men and women to an experience of conversion.[4]

In Kenya, the East African Evangelical Revival penetrated all Protestant churches. Its emphasis on the attainment of a conversion experience played two significant roles: 1) the claim of spiritual renewal through conversion was a call to those in the church, who had not experienced conversion in the way they conceived, to receive it, and 2) this claim was also a call to those outside the church to experience conversion and become a part of the ongoing life of the faith community. The effect of the East African Evangelical Revival continues to be felt in Kenyan churches, where revivals are held in churches and in open-air meetings aimed at leading men and women to the attainment of a conversion experience.

Emphasis on the experience of conversion to the exclusion of Christian nurture, however, has produced Christians who are not well grounded on spiritual and moral principles. These converts—who stand perennially on the threshold of their Christian journey and are described, therefore, as "still-born babies"—lack Christian moral integrity and witnessing capacity.[5] This is demonstrated by the fact that over 80 percent of the population in Kenya consider themselves to be Christians, yet the country is riddled with corruption and ethnic conflict.[6] Reflecting on a similar problem in a different African context, Waruta poses the question: "Is there a possibility that the Church in Africa may still be a Church of the 'multitudes' with only a small num-

---

4. Ward, "Tuku tendereza Yesu," 113.
5. Outler, *Evangelism in the Wesleyan Spirit*, 22–25.
6. Barrett, *Kenya Churches Handbook*, 160.

ber having attained the level of true 'disciples'?"[7] Neglect of Christian nurture for those converted, leading to a dearth of moral integrity, continues to be a critical challenge to disciple-making in Kenya today.

How can these obstacles be addressed so that the full gospel might flourish in Kenya today? The Bible provides some significant clues in the quest to find solutions to these problems.

Scriptural Images

Several scriptural images come to mind corresponding to these challenges.

The Challenge of Cross-Cultural Evangelism in the Greco-Roman World (Acts 15:1–29)

The problem of cultural insensitivity or dualism is reminiscent of the challenge of cross-cultural evangelism that confronted the early church. When missionaries of the early church carried the gospel beyond the Jewish borders into the Greco-Roman world there was an influx of Gentiles into the church. Some Jewish Christians went into the mission areas teaching that the Gentile converts should be circumcised as a condition of salvation and acceptance into the fellowship of the church. Paul and Barnabas argued strongly against the demand, viewing this Jewish practice as an obstacle to the disciple-making. The matter was referred to Jerusalem, the epicenter of the church at that time, for a ruling (Acts 15:1–29). After careful consideration, the Jerusalem Council resolved that: 1) the Jews, as cross-cultural missionaries, should not make their custom of circumcision a condition of salvation and acceptance into the fellowship of the church and 2) the Gentiles, as recipients of the gospel in a cross-cultural setting, were counseled not to practice customs that were repugnant to the gospel. The ruling by the early church throws some light on the manner in which the problem of cultural insensitivity or dualism should be tackled.

---

7. Waruta, "Church as a Teaching Community," 80.

Degeneration of the Corinthian Church into Moral Decadence (1 and 2 Corinthians)

Paul had spent about eighteen months at Corinth proclaiming the gospel. He was later joined by Timothy and Silas, partners in the gospel who had come to support his evangelistic endeavors in that cosmopolitan center. The mission was successful. They won many converts to the way of Jesus, but those new Christians lacked adequate grounding in the practice of their new-found faith; they had no foundation in living as Christians. The glory of conversion was short lived. The converts soon degenerated into moral decadence.

The first letter of Paul to the Corinthians reflects a situation in which the converts had ceased to grow spiritually. Instead, they have reverted to the old life of sin. Paul admonishes them against a number of behaviors he considered to be sub-Christian: divisiveness in the church (1:10–17), envy and strife (3:1–9), pride (4:6–13), and sexual immorality (5:1–8). In his Second Letter, Paul is less polemic and more edifying, teaching them the manner of living the new life of Christian moral integrity. He uses various expressions to drive this point home. He refers to the Corinthian convert as a "letter written by Christ" (3:1–3), a new creation (5:11–19), and an ambassador for Christ (5:20—6:2). Paul's admonition and teaching to the Corinthian church on their lack of moral integrity and new life in Christ is relevant to the Kenyan situation.

Having reviewed the missionary and evangelical revival movements in Kenya, having noted their strength (the way in which their focus on the experience of conversion won many converts), and their weaknesses (evangelism devoid of Christian nurture resulting in a lack of Christian moral integrity and a cultural insensitivity leading to superficial faith), and having examined scriptural images that shed some light on how the early church tackled similar challenges, it remains to be seen how this contextual situation and the biblical witness should shape evangelistic practice in Kenya today.

Evangelistic Practice

In view of the foregoing, an evangelistic practice suitable for Kenya today should give attention to at least three critical components: an emphasis on the experience of conversion, Christian nurture in the community of faith, and a genuine inculturation of faith and practice. These three components will inevitably produce disciples who have committed their lives to Christ, attained Christian maturity, and rooted their Christian life in the traditional cultural milieu. Such mature and responsible disciples will effectively participate in the transformation of the society.

Conversion

The experience of conversion must remain an essential aspect of disciple-making because it is through this experience that the Spirit leads all people into an encounter with the Lord Jesus Christ to the end that they may have abundant life (John 3:16, 10:10). This experience involves a radical transformation of the person (John 3:1–10, Acts 9:1–22).

The preaching of repentance, forgiveness of sins, and personal commitment to Christ through conversion appeals deeply to Kenyans, as witnessed by the East African Evangelical Revival. Those who were already church members by baptism and registration heard the gospel afresh and committed their lives to Christ—they experienced genuine conversion in their lives. Open-air evangelistic rallies, targeting unchurched people, especially in urban centers, won many people to Christ and increased church membership. This is the first component of a three-pronged approach to evangelistic practice suitable for Kenya today.

Nurture

Christian nurture was central in the ministry of Jesus. He was a rabbi par excellence, who spent a great proportion of his ministry in teaching. Teaching was a component of the great commission: "Go therefore and make disciples of all nations, baptizing them . . . and *teaching* them" (Matt 28:18–20). The early church was keen on teaching new believers in the faith (Acts 2:42). Paul advises the young Timothy and Titus to make "teaching" their main task (1 Tim 4:6).

The teaching ministry has not received adequate attention in the Kenyan church. To be sure, the missionaries combined winning of converts with teaching. They went out preaching in the villages, and the new converts were admitted in mission stations where they received instructions on Bible and Christian living. The missionaries were, however, dealing with few converts; and therefore their impact was relatively limited. The East African Evangelical Revival, however, placed no emphasis on teaching whatsoever. It concentrated on winning converts and paid no attention to the instruction of those who were awakened by the gospel message. It is important for the church to recover the integral balance of conversion and nurture today or Christian converts will never grow into mature disciples of Jesus Christ. Christian nurture, therefore, is the second component of a three-pronged approach to evangelistic practice suitable for Kenya today.

Inculturation

Inculturation—the intentional interfacing of the gospel and the culture in which it is immersed—is also based on biblical teaching. The incarnation, first and foremost, provides the strongest rationale for its centrality to Christian practice, since in Jesus Christ, "the Word became flesh and lived among us" (John 1:14). The early church affirmed that the gospel could take root in the Greco-Roman culture of the Gentile world just as easily as it found a place in its original Jewish milieu (Acts 10:1–48, 15:1–29).

In their evangelization, the missionaries condemned African cultures and dismissed them as unworthy of the gospel. Instead, they transplanted the form of Christianity they knew in their own part of the world, with all of its cultural attachments, and failed to adjust it to suit the local environment. Though there are some pockets of inculturation in Kenya, the majority of the churches continue to propagate Western Christianity in terms of liturgy, hymnody, church discipline, and polity.[8] There is an urgent need for inculturation in the Kenyan church. This will help Christian disciples here to overcome the dualism caused by cultural insensitivity and lead to a vibrant church, deeply rooted in African soil. This is the third component of a three-pronged approach to evangelistic practice suitable for Kenya today.

This three-pronged approach to Kenyan evangelistic practice involving conversion, Christian nurture, and inculturation will not only overcome obstacles currently militating against disciple-making, but

---

8. Magesa, *Anatomy of Inculturation*, 29–42.

will also produce mature and responsible disciples who will serve as agents of new life and vitality in the life of the church and society.

Christian Vitality

The commitment and capacity of an organization's personnel determine its strength or weakness. Leaders of organizations develop strategic plans, utilize the resources at their disposal, and turn institutions around. Likewise, mature and responsible disciples precipitate new life and vitality in the church. In Kenya, Christian leaders must attend to the revitalization of two strategic areas of need: the quality of worship and the moral transformation of society.

The Quality of Worship

Currently, many Kenyan churches continue to worship in a Western liturgical style, the characteristics of which are irrelevant to the needs, challenges, and aspirations of the people. On a continent noted for its distinctive and spirited singing and dancing, the church remains entrenched in a language and style distant from the sounds and rhythms of Africa. The Kenyan people, who traditionally sing and dance in response to their needs and in expression of thanksgiving, bawl Western hymns, standing still, in a foreign tongue and in response to alien needs and aspirations. Many Africans sense that their worship is both irrelevant and boring.[9]

Mature and responsible disciples who will have received training on inculturation through seminars and workshops will now participate in developing African Christian liturgy and composing African Christian hymns and songs. Among other things, an authentic Christian liturgy for Africans will express before God: 1) various forms of suffering such as famine, floods, diseases, unemployment, poverty, and insecurity, 2) repentance and confession related to environmental degradation, social corruption, theft, and robbery, and 3) thanksgiving for family and children, government and leadership, rain and harvest. African Christian hymns and songs will 1) capture people's hopes and aspirations for deliverance from suffering, 2) offer thanks for God's sustaining

---

9. Gitonga, *Evangelization and Inculturation*, 88–91.

provision and bumper harvests, and 3) sing and dance, clapping hands and jumping, and using drums and other African music instruments. African Christian liturgy and African Christian hymns and songs will transform and improve the quality of worship in Kenya. They will unlock people's thoughts and emotions as they express their adoration, petitions, and thanksgiving to God in culturally appropriate ways. By interfacing their faith with indigenous cultural forms and practices, African Christian will experience transformed and vibrant worship as "a place to feel at home."

The Moral Transformation of Society

Currently, Kenya, like many of its neighbors on the continent, is riddled with corruption and ethnocentricity. Based upon the International Corruption Perception Index 2009 Report, an evaluative process conducted by Transparency International, demographic experts place Kenya's level of corruption at 2.2 on a 10-point scale.[10] Corruption permeates every sector of the society, resulting in a depressed economy, poverty, and unemployment. Ethnocentricity (sometimes known as tribalism) is equally widespread and pernicious. More often than not, employment and promotions are based on ethnic considerations. This causes tensions and conflicts between various ethnic groups. This scenario has continued unabated because a number of Christians are themselves involved in corruption or ethnic favors, thereby undercutting their capacity to witness with integrity to their Christian faith.

Mature and responsible disciples, who have been nurtured in such a way to value moral integrity, will act as light and salt for the transformation of the society. As regards corruption, they will champion justice and fair play through word and deed. Ethnocentricity will be tackled through the principle of love (a*gape*) and good neighborliness as demonstrated by the story of the Good Samaritan who extended sacrificial love to a person of a different ethnic group. Mature and responsible disciples will be agents of new life and vitality in the life of the church in Kenya; particularly in improving the quality of worship and in the moral transformation of the society.

---

10. *Daily Nation*, No. 16347 (November 19, 2009) 11.

Global Contributions

In conclusion, three insights drawn from this analysis of disciple-making practices in Kenya commend themselves as potentially beneficial to the world parish: the foundational nature of Christian conversion, the significance of Christian nurture in disciple-making, and the importance of cross-cultural evangelism in a pluralistic world.

The foundational Nature of Christian Conversion

The East African Evangelical Revival made a remarkable and enduring contribution in the Kenyan context that may benefit Christians in other parts of the world. Its emphasis on the experience of conversion to Christ Jesus as a means of salvation continues to bear measurable and monumental results. In the first place, it awakens nominal Christians to approach the altar in repentance, committing their lives to Jesus Christ as "born again" Christians. Secondly, open-air evangelical rallies attract many people who identify with Zacchaeus (Luke 19:1–10), Nicodemus (John 3:1–15), and Paul (Acts 9:1–19), and they too, come forward in repentance and surrender their lives to the Lord. In this way, the church of Jesus Christ continues to be renewed and to increase in number. Certainly, the challenge of nominal Christianity and the need to win new converts to the Lord, are global concerns. Through conversion the Spirit of God acts in both situations to transform lives that they may hear and understand God's promise: "Once you were not a people, but now you are God's people; once you had not received mercy, but now you have received mercy" (1 Pet 2:10).

The Significance of Christian Nurture in Disciple-Making

The East African Evangelical Revival failed to include Christian nurture in the process of disciple-making to the detriment of the church. This approach produced "first-level Christians" who have been ill-equipped to participate in the transformation of the society. Consequently, Kenyan society is steeped in corruption and tribal animosity despite a sizeable Christian presence. Local and international electronic and print media report similar social injustice around the globe rooted in corruption, ethnic and racial conflict, environmental degradation, and political oppression. The rest of the world parish can learn from Kenya's painful experience and recognize the critical place of Christian nurture in the process of disciple-making. Moses admonishes God's faithful: "Teach them the statutes and instructions and make known to them the way they are to go and the things they are to do.... and all these people will go to their home in peace" (Exod 18:20, 23).

Cross-Cultural Evangelism in a Pluralistic World

The failure of Western missionaries in Kenya to recognize and appreciate the indigenous culture of the people—their indifference to inculturation—produced Christians who live a schizophrenic religious existence. They are neither comfortable completely in their "native habitat," nor has their Christian faith penetrated deeply into their lives; they struggle to forge their identity as authentic African Christians. Many communities around the world, particularly in the Southern hemisphere, who first encountered the gospel from Euro-American missionaries, find themselves, no doubt, in the same predicament. The global village dynamic of the world—the cultural and religious pluralism that characterize life today—calls for greater sensitivity with regard to the relationship between the gospel and the cultures in which it is immersed. In this regard, both the missionaries and those who receive the gospel may want to learn from the painful experience of Kenyans and consider more seriously how inculturation shapes the process of disciple-making. Peter's words are just as relevant today as when he addressed them to the Jerusalem elders: "Now therefore why are you putting God to the test by placing on the neck of the disciples a yoke that neither our ancestors nor we have been able to bear?" (Acts 15:10).

3

Evangelism, Mission, and Discipleship in Southern Africa

How Hope is Overcoming Tragedy!

Dion A. Forster

SOME YEARS AGO WHEN I WAS THE DEAN OF THE METHODIST SEMInary in Pretoria, I commented to a class of final year students, "Unless your church develops a significant HIV/AIDS ministry it cannot be considered faithful to the gospel!" This statement generated a great deal of debate! I still believe it to be true. In Southern Africa the church cannot be Christian unless it is engaged in caring for persons who are infected and affected by HIV/AIDS. The tragedy of this pandemic is exacerbated, of course, by the prevalence of poverty in Southern Africa. What is the meaning of disciple-making in this context? In this chapter I will outline the theological impetus and contextual factors that shaped the character of mission and evangelism in Southern African Methodism. I will demonstrate how a strong Wesleyan grounding and an awareness of contextual factors in Southern Africa shaped the Church's approach to evangelism, mission, and discipleship.

The Roots of Evangelism, Mission, and Discipleship

What are the characteristics of evangelism, mission, and discipleship in Southern African Methodism? In order to establish this, one needs to trace the strands of Wesleyan theology that connect contemporary Methodism with the theology of the founder of Methodism, John Wesley. Most Methodist scholars agree that the "way of salvation" was central to John Wesley's theology. The following quote from 1746 shows what Wesley himself understood in this regard: "Our main doctrines, which include all the rest are three: that of repentance, of faith and holiness. The first of these we account, as it were, the porch of religion, the next the door; the third religion itself."[1] Within the way of salvation, however, Wesley regarded one element as more important than the others, namely the goal towards which all faith moves—Christian perfection. He believed that Christian perfection was a peculiar emphasis that had been given to the Methodist movement by God. In 1789, just two years before his death, he defended this conclusion: "This doctrine is the grand depositum which God has lodged with the people called Methodists; and for the sake of propagating this chiefly He appeared to have raised us up."[2] John Wesley believed that living in and for the vision of a restored humanity in holiness was the primary mission of the Methodist people. Sadly, Wesley's particular understanding of Christian perfection has been largely misunderstood—especially among those who adapted it in the various "holiness movements" of the nineteenth century—and forgotten in popular Methodist circles.[3] A rediscovery of Wesley's vision of Christian perfection, moreover, would cause similar reactions of disapproval and conflict among the overly spiritualized, highly individualized, faith communities of our day, as it did when Wesley himself defended his understanding of this doctrine. "There is scarce any expression in Holy Writ" he wrote in his Sermon on Christian Perfection, "which has given more offence than this. The word *perfect* is what many cannot bear. The very sound of it is an abomination to them."[4] For Wesley, Christian perfection was intrinsically linked to the concrete realization of the kingdom of God on earth, not just believing in Christ in order to live in paradise in the afterlife. What many found unbearable then, and still find unbearable today, was Wesley's emphasis on Christian perfection as *social holiness*. Social holiness is the practical expression of the gospel in everyday life that first led to the giving of the name "Methodist," and it is this same concern that lies at the very heart of Wesley's understanding of Christian perfection.[5] According to Wesley, the purpose of religion was to restore holiness of heart and life

---

1. Quoted in Rack, *Reasonable Enthusiast*, 286.
2. Quoted in Williams, *John Wesley's Theology Today*, 238.
3. See Forster, *Wesleyan Spirituality*, 4–5.
4. Quoted in Cox, *John Wesley's Concept of Perfection*, 11.
5. See Baker, *Practical Divinity*.

in the child of God, to renew the image of Christ in the believer to the fullest extent possible. Concerning true religion and true holiness (as opposed to false religion and false holiness), he declares: "the gospel of Christ knows no religion but social; no holiness but social holiness. 'Faith working by love' is the length and breadth and depth and height of Christian perfection."[6] He distinguished between holiness expressed in personal piety (love of God) and holiness expressed through social service (love of neighbor), always emphasizing the inseparability of the two.[7] In his view, no one could be truly "holy" or "perfect" as a disciple of Christ unless her or his life was characterized by holiness of heart *and* life. In other words, the follower of Jesus cannot be truly holy just by praying, attending church, and reading the Bible. True holiness impacts a person's whole life (how he spends his money, the choices she makes about where she works, which political party they embrace). This kind of holiness (a holiness that combines personal piety *and* social action), Wesley maintained, is described in scripture (scriptural holiness), expressed through interaction with others and the world (perfect love), and is the ultimate goal towards which we aspire (Christian perfection).[8] Wesley firmly believed that God planned and willed for Methodists to live out and proclaim this vision of the Christian life as their singular mission in the universal church. To express this insight in ecclesial terms, then, the purpose of Methodism was to shape Christians for whom the primary reason for their being was participation with God in the renewal and transformation of society. Wesley's hope was that the people called Methodists would function as a catalyst of renewal within the church, enabling the church to rediscover its true vocation as well. He believed that this was nothing other than the mission of Jesus extended throughout history. While personal piety deals with inner healing and transformation, social holiness seeks to heal and transform the larger society. Like Jesus' own ministry, it focuses on the realization of God's rule. Henry Rack argues that Wesley's balance of personal piety and social holiness took shape in response to the context in which he

---

6. John Wesley, *Hymns and Sacred Poems* (1739), Pref. 5, quoted in Baker, *Practical Divinity*.

7. See Heitzenrater, *Wesley and the Methodists*, 165–80, 199–241, 261–80; cf. Richardson and Malinga, *Rediscovering Wesley for Africa*, 161–72.

8. See Forster, *Wesleyan Spirituality*, 4–5 and Attwell, *What Wesley Believed and Taught*, 4.

lived. The needs of the poor and disenfranchised in eighteenth century England led him to formulate clear and pragmatic strategies for social development, practical transformation, and reform, while his experience within the Church of England led him to emphasize the need for personal piety.[9] Wesley's understanding of how he could participate with God in the *missio Dei* was thus strongly influenced by the context in which his faith was formed. From its inception Methodism had been an evangelical movement, seeking to share the gospel of God's kingdom with all, drawing particular attention to the need to honor God by striving to attain perfection in this life. There was never any question in the minds of the Methodists that this vision was God's desire and plan for all persons throughout the world. Not only the Arminian theology of the movement, but the burning desire for all people to experience true holiness, fuelled the great missionary movement of the nineteenth century following Wesley's death. As a consequence of this emphasis, Methodist missionaries carried their message of holiness of heart and life throughout the world and transplanted this core theology into new contexts with different challenges and opportunities from those faced in Britain.

The Developing Character of Evangelism, Mission, and Discipleship

The form of Methodism discussed above came to Southern Africa soon after John Wesley's death in 1791. According to Millard-Jackson, the very first record of a Methodist (lay person) in the Cape was that of an Irish soldier of the English Army, John Irwin, who held prayer meetings at the Cape as early as 1795.[10] Balia notes that the first record of a Methodist preacher in Southern Africa was that of a soldier of the 72nd regiment of the British army, George Middlemiss, who had been stationed in the Cape of Good Hope to secure British interests there in 1805 as a result of the war between Britain and France.[11] Middlemiss soon gathered a small group of Methodists in the Cape around himself for prayer and fellowship. This work quickly grew. By the time Sergeant

---

9. Rack, *Reasonable Enthusiast*, 72.
10. Millard-Jackson, "Who Called the Tune?" 31.
11. Balia, *Black Methodists and White Supremacy*, 14.

Kendrick, a Methodist class leader and lay preacher, arrived in 1812, the congregation numbered 142 persons, of which 128 were of British descent and fourteen were of mixed race.[12] By 1820, when the British settlers arrived at the Cape, Methodism was already well established in Southern Africa. In subsequent years missionaries were dispatched from England to establish and spread Methodist work throughout the sub-continent.[13] They did this with great courage, sacrifice, and faith. By 1860 there were 132 Methodist ministers and missionaries in the Eastern Cape and Natal, and their combined congregations numbered around 5,000 members.[14] From the very beginnings, Methodist work was multiracial and, while some other churches and mission organisations concentrated almost exclusively on one racial group (either working among the white settlers or indigenous African people), the Methodists established joint works. In part this led to the Methodist Church of Southern Africa having more black members than any of the other mainline denominations in Southern Africa. Moreover, de Gruchy notes that, at the same time, the Methodist Church became the largest English-speaking denomination in the country.[15] Methodism continued to spread and grow in Southern Africa throughout the nineteenth century. Even at this early stage, there was a clear sense of the need to inculturate the mission and identity of British Methodism, and particularly Wesley's emphasis on Christian perfection as social holiness, in this new African context. Thus the early missionaries placed a strong emphasis on the need to engage not only in the proclamation of the gospel and the fostering of personal piety, but also in the work of social transformation and development within the mission communities. Naturally some of the attempts at social transformation and development had a decidedly Western, and even blatantly colonial, slant to them, as was common among nineteenth century missionary thrusts.[16] The emphasis on social holiness (that was influenced by the missional identity of Christian work in England) can be seen in projects of these early years: establish-

---

12. Mears, *Methodism in the Cape*, 6.

13. See Magoba, P. Grassow, and J. Millard-Jackson in Forster and Bentley, *Methodism in Southern Africa*, 26–30, 13–25, 31–39 respectively.

14. See Attwell, *Methodist Church*, 3–6.

15. De Gruchy, *Church Struggle in South Africa*, 14.

16. See Grassow's chapter in Forster and Bentley, *Methodism in Southern Africa*, 13–25.

ment of schools and skills development projects translation of the first complete Bible into an African language (1859) offering medical care to all, and the establishment of hospitals establishment of homes for orphans and senior citizens development and publication of Christian literature facilitating racial reconciliation among the settler and the "native" population working for reconciliation and peace in areas that were subject to conflict. The social and political climate of the day played a significant role in the development and appropriation of Methodist theology on African soil. The racial ideology of "apartheid" was one of the most significant social and political forces that the church had to contend with in Southern Africa during the twentieth century.[17] This powerful social threat would be the most significant tool in reshaping Southern African Methodist identity and mission in subsequent years. In many ways apartheid caused Methodism in Southern Africa to take on new characteristics in its structure (e.g., Episcopal leadership), yet, in other ways, it helped Methodists in Southern African to hold more tightly to their true identity, namely, to be agents of Christian perfection, with a particular emphasis on social holiness. As the Nationalist government implemented this system of racial segregation and oppression from the early 1940s many native South Africans were forcibly removed from their ancestral lands; the land itself was expropriated and either put to use by the government or sold to white South Africans. In order to maintain this system of segregation, and force black persons to remain in the black homelands, various apartheid laws were employed to systematically oppress black South Africans. Black South Africans were disenfranchised economically through job reservation and Bantu Education, and health care, civil service, and even freedom of movement were all curtailed. The violent and systematic implementation of this evil ideology had considerable and damaging effects on Southern African society as a whole, and particularly on the individual South Africans who suffered under it. The effects of apartheid are likely to be felt for many generations to come. Neville Richardson has noted the influence and significant impact of this ideology of systematic oppression on the operation and identity of the South African Church:

> The church under apartheid was polarized between "the church of the oppressor" and "the church of the oppressed". Either you were for apartheid or you were against it; there was no neutral

17. Sparks, *Mind of South Africa*.

ground. Given the heavy-handed domination of the minority white government, those who imagined themselves to be neutral were, unwittingly perhaps, on the side of apartheid. This complicity was especially true of those Christians who piously "avoided politics" yet enjoyed the social and economic benefits of the apartheid system. . . . While young white men were conscripted into the South African Defence Force, many young black people fled the country to join the outlawed liberation movements that had their headquarters and training camps abroad. What could the church do in this revolutionary climate? And what should Christian theology say now?[18]

The Methodist Church of Southern Africa worked against apartheid in many ways between 1948, when the ideology was formally adopted, and 1994, when it collapsed. The Minutes of Conference throughout this period contain evidence of the Church's struggle to undermine the false theology that supported the apartheid system and to ameliorate the evil consequences that resulted from it. It is in this social context that the Methodist Church of Southern Africa sought to shape its mission and discipleship efforts, and to inform them with a concept of Christian perfection oriented toward both personal piety and social justice. The self-understanding and practice of Methodists would need to be changed and adapted from its roots in eighteenth century England in order to adequately and effectively address the needs of Southern Africans in the nineteenth and twentieth centuries. The situation required a measure of flexibility that allowed for a dynamic interaction between orthodoxy and orthopraxis; the emerging missiology both celebrated the truth of God's loving nature (personal piety) and expected Jesus' disciples to embrace God's rule for individuals and society (social holiness). Given this theological foundation, Arthur Attwell's conclusion that Methodism seemed peculiarly well-adapted to meet both the spiritual and social needs of a changing Africa makes perfect sense.[19] In the Southern African context, therefore, the Methodist emphasis on social holiness as a constitutive aspect of a Wesleyan theology of perfection exerted a strong influence upon the missional character and ministry of the Church.

---

18. Richardson, *God, Truth, and Witness*, 231–32.
19. Attwell, *What Wesley Believed and Taught*, 4.

Examples of Mission as Social Holiness

The two largest problems that loom over Southern Africa are HIV/AIDS and poverty. If this is the case, then the Church needs to engage in tangible and effective activities of mission to engage these challenges in a constructive and sustainable manner. A large amount of the Church's energy before the end of apartheid in 1994 was devoted to deconstructing the heresy and social consequences of that evil system. The Methodist Church of Southern Africa developed a very clear strategy in their efforts to dismantle the evil system of apartheid—a political agenda of their own that was both scripturally grounded and theologically informed. The Church saw these actions as an essential aspect of their mission. The leaders in the struggle against apartheid viewed their prophetic witness as a partnership in the *missio Dei* and an effort to realize the rule of God in South Africa.[20] Among these various prophetic acts, five stand out: the 1958 "One and Undivided" movement against segregation and racism the formation of the "Black Methodist Consultation" in 1975 the 1981 "Obedience" conference that informed the Church's civil disobedience against unjust apartheid laws the "Journey to the New Land" of the early 1990s that paved the way for racial reconciliation and social transformation leading up the 1994 democratic elections the "Mission Congress" of 2004 that shaped the Churches mission efforts in subsequent years. By the time of the 2004 Mission Congress, years after the dawn of democracy in South Africa, very little had changed in Southern African society. Poverty and segregation were still rife. Segregation was connected inextricably to economic disenfranchisement, a high rate of HIV/AIDS infection, and the slow pace of service delivery by the new government. Earlier, in 2003, the Church had adopted the vision of working towards "A Christ healed Africa for the healing of Nations."[21] Clearly, this statement was grounded in the understanding that African Christianity was both valid and valuable as an instrument for achieving God's mission in the world. This vision of mission embraced the fact that "God calls the Methodist people to proclaim the gospel of Jesus Christ for healing and transformation." It should not be surprising that the Church articulated its subsequent mission strategy in terms of social development, ministry, and

---

20. See Forster and Bentley, *Methodism in Southern Africa*, 70–99.
21. See *2006 Yearbook of the MCSA*, 3–22.

growth. These objectives found expression in the mission pillars of the Methodist Church of Southern Africa: a deepened spirituality justice, service, and reconciliation evangelism and church growth development and economic empowerment.[22] It is evident that these mission initiatives strike a strong balance of personal piety and social holiness. Through an examination of the priorities of this mission strategy, one can see how the Wesleyan concept of Christian perfection, conjoining vital piety and social action, found rich expression in the context of Southern African Methodism. Those priorities highlighted in the Conference of 2005 include: a mission consciousness shaped by the imperatives of spirituality, evangelism and church growth, justice and service, development and economic empowerment the liberation of the laity, to be facilitated by the clergy, that will enable their full participation in the life and witness of the church the revamping of our structures that they may serve our vision, mission thrust, and transformation strategies the eradication of racism, prejudice, and inequality in institutional life taking seriously the call to a healing ministry, especially in our response to the HIV/AIDS pandemic a clear understanding of Church/State relations within the socio-political realities of our time, and the jealous guarding of the duty to be ready to speak with a prophetic voice when necessary. The Methodist Church of Southern Africa still seeks to address the social and spiritual needs of Southern African society, working not only for the salvation of individuals, but also the healing and transformation of society as a whole. In the milestones discussed above, we can clearly discern the influence of an understanding of Christian perfection that includes social transformation. There is still much work left to be done in Southern Africa; the problems of HIV/AIDS, the collapse of the economy and the rule of law in Zimbabwe, and the slow pace of transformation and change in South Africa still loom large over the subcontinent. These complex contextual challenges confront the church in Southern Africa today and call for great courage and faithfulness on the part of the Christian community. But the Methodist tradition has much to offer in this context, particularly a theology of mission and evangelism—an approach to making disciples—rooted in the quest for Christian perfection and a vision of social holiness leading all people into God's shalom.

---

22. Ibid.

4

Local Church—An Arena for Making Disciples
A Case Study of Sherukuru United Methodist Church in Zimbabwe

John Wesley Zvomunondiita Kurewa

AS A PRE-SCHOOL CHILD, I STILL HOLD A VIVID PICTURE IN MY MEMORY of a worship service in my village church, Sherukuru United Methodist Church, seeing a woman who was in the spirit of rejoicing as she sang a song, going up and down the aisle of the church and raising her hands in praise, with tears coming down her cheeks. After we got home, I asked my mother, "Why was that woman singing and jumping up in church the way she did?" Mother explained: "The woman was giving her testimony. She was born with a twin brother. Prior to the coming of the Christianity to Zimbabwe, Shona (the largest ethnic group) tradition did not accept the birth of twins. They regarded the birth of twins as a bad omen. If a mother gave birth to twins, one of the twins was starved to death so that only one survived. When it came to the gender issue, some parents often sacrificed the girl-child. In the case of the woman you are talking about, it happened that when she and her twin brother were born, their parents had become Christians. The parents chose to keep their twins alive, instead of following the Shona tradition. So she was celebrating and rejoicing that she owed her life and her survival to the coming of the gospel in her village and to her parents' faith in Jesus Christ."

Sherukuru United Methodist Church is situated in the eastern highlands of Zimbabwe, in Chief Mutasa's area. It was founded in 1907, and its name is derived from the name of the Chieftess (a daughter or sister) of the area. Chief Mutasa was responsible for the introduction of the church. Having permitted the Methodist Church into his area in 1904, in 1907, Chakanyuka, the reigning Mutasa, in the company of some of his counselors and a handful of Christians, including Samuel Matimba (the first African Methodist preacher who was then based at Mutasa's royal court), visited the Chieftess, Sherukuru, at Mapfekera to introduce the same church to his sister and her people. The Chieftess, having accepted the new church, asked Kurewa (the author's grandfather), then headman of a community that was about ten kilometers away from that of the Chieftess, to receive the church in his community and guard the church that Chief Mutasa had introduced to her.

For all these years from 1907, Sherukuru United Methodist Church had been a part of other circuits. Due to its geographical location, being located in a valley surrounded by mountains and plagued by political, administrative, and transportation problems, in December 2007, at the time of its centennial anniversary, at the Seventh Session of the Zimbabwe East Annual Conference, Sherukuru United Methodist Church became a circuit, and was transferred from Makoni-Buhera District to Mutasa-Nyanga District.[1] The first pastor of the new circuit was a young man named Barnabas Chikuni. Prior to his appointment at Sherukuru, Barnabas had served as a Student Chaplain at Old Mutare and Murehwa missions—the two biggest mission centers of the Episcopal Area. With the appointment of Barnabas Chikuni, the new circuit has remarkably sustained its new status, meeting all its financial obligations, and above all, it has become a vibrant congregation in the Mutasa-Nyanga District. Sherukuru has developed a reputation similar to St. Paul's description of the Thessalonian church, when he wrote, "Your faith in God has become known everywhere" (1 Thess 1:8).

Good news about the ministry of Sherukuru Church has reached the ears of many people, both in the valley where the church is located and beyond the mountain boundaries of the valley itself. The Zimbabwe Episcopal Area has always cherished revivals as a way of evangelism. To talk of revivals in the United Methodist Church in Zimbabwe is to talk of evangelism; the usage of the two terms is almost synonymous. Hence, at every annual conference, pastors and district superintendents are either urged to or talk about holding at least four revivals in a year in their areas. Sherukuru United Methodist Church is unique in the sense that, for almost the entire year, the circuit has continuously witnessed

1. *Zimbabwe East Annual Conference Report* (2007), 23.

a transformation both within the congregation and in the surrounding communities that is tantamount to a continuous revival.

The purpose of this chapter is to share with the reader a vital ministry going on at Sherukuru United Methodist Church—a ministry that focuses on disciple-making by reaching out to all people in the valley with the gospel, emphasizing both evangelism that introduces people to Christ and education that enables those who have believed the gospel to understand what the Christian discipleship means. This ministry also exposes the falsehood of some messengers who claim to be prophets, when actually they are savage wolves among the people (Acts 20:29). Sherukuru has rediscovered the Matthean model of making disciples, where evangelism and Christian education go hand in hand (Matt 28:19).

Critical Challenges

In a conversation that we shared concerning these matters, Pastor Chikuni identified the primary challenge that he and the Sherukuru community face, namely, *the challenge of fear that comes in many forms*. There is *fear of violence* due to the political situation in the country. In the 1960s and 70s, Zimbabwe went through the horrible experience of a war of liberation that took the lives of many people, and the memory of those atrocities are still fresh in the minds of many. Similarly, violence also accompanied the re-run of the presidential elections in 2008 and planted the seed of mistrust in the community, leaving families and some churches divided. When people no longer trust one another, fear reigns in their hearts and minds.

There is also *fear about the future* due to the economic situation in the country. Towards the end of 2008, many families in the rural areas of Zimbabwe experimented on eating roots and fruits of wild trees that they had never eaten before because of famine. Many now fear that the situation will not change in their lifetime, doubting that a political solution can be found to transform the nation. Increasingly, skilled Zimbabweans leave the country for greener pastures elsewhere, increasing the anxiety and fear of those left behind.

One of the greatest fears people suffer in the rural areas has to do with *the influence of witchcraft*, which seems to thrive in times of deprivation. Most Christians consider witchcraft to be a great enemy in rural Africa, as many understand it to be a mysterious power that some individuals possess to outwit or hurt others. For example, Sherukuru falls in an area of the eastern highlands where some people are allegedly considered to possess power to cause lightning. Such individuals at times openly boast to others about their possession of such powers. There is a common saying, *tingosanga kwatikugunha*, literally meaning "we will meet when it starts thundering" during the rainy season.

Another kind of witchcraft that people fear relates to those who allegedly kill others by poisoning their victims through food or traditional beer drinking. These witches purport to travel long distances at night and claim powers to enter any homes at night to bewitch their victims. People believe this; hence, fear reigns in their minds. Thus every death in these villages is understood in the light of witchcraft. Even if a person has been declared by a medical doctor to have died of cancer or AIDS, rural people may still believe witchcraft is behind it all. Hence a saying *hapana rufu rusina muroyi*, meaning, there is no death without a witch. Fear of witchcraft still reigns.

Thus, the fear of being hurt or killed by the practice of witchcraft usually leads people to desire protection for themselves and their families. Often they seek a *n'anga*, a traditional healer or herbalist, for such aid. Others continue the practices inherited from their parents and their ancestors long gone. Traditional means of protection often involve dependence on some evil spirit or demon. Those who believe in and trust such spirits wear a charm or fetish or some special artifact, such as a special cloth, that is kept in a secret place in the homestead or in a small house not far from the homestead. Exorcism, therefore, is a normal aspect of the pastor's ministry and that of the church. For people in this area, exorcism is not an academic issue to debate; rather, it is a real pastoral challenge that the pastor and congregation at Sherukuru face frequently. Thus, people come to the church—members and non-members alike—seeking deliverance from the domination of evil spirits. Increasingly, they come from African Initiated Churches and some charismatic communities in which their leaders claim the ministries of "prophesy" and physical healing.

Persons suffering all these kind of fears, now find Sherukuru United Methodist Church to be a place where they are able to regain their senses, with all the fears dispelled by genuine faith in Jesus Christ.

Scriptural Images

An Old Testament image that has captured the imagination of United Methodists in Zimbabwe is that of the children of Israel as a congregation in the desert. This relates well to their own context and their ability to face the struggle of hard times. Moreover, as Browning has observed, "the people of Israel were considered as a group for *travel*" (Exod 16:1), a corollary image that relates so closely to African experience.[2] Zimbabwean United Methodists identify closely with the traditional Shona phrase *tiri parwendo*, meaning "we are on a journey." In other words, Christian discipleship involves participation in a journey of faith through difficult times—a journey not just for individuals, but for the whole community of faith.

Sherukuru United Methodist Church has embellished this theme by describing the journey of discipleship around Christ as *dzvikiti*, meaning "a journey on which all kinds of battles are being waged." In expounding the meaning of the image, Pastor Chikuni said that, as the children of Israel faced numerous challenges from their arch-enemy, the Pharaoh (conquest, enslavement, oppression) and the ordeal of Exodus (fear, lack of water, food, shelter, and stability), so the people at Sherukuru are facing similar challenges, all of which produce fear. But whereas there is fear of the political and economic situation, and the fear of witchcraft, the community boldly proclaims the gospel of victory and the assurance of reaching the "promised land" and teaches the people how to make the journey together.

For example, a person comes to the pastor saying, "Pastor, I can't sleep at night. There are people who are trying to choke me each time I try to go to sleep at night. I need your prayers, pastor."

Or, "Pastor, I had a quarrel with Mr. Chimuti, this week, and he said to me something will happen to a member of my family in the near future. Mr. Chimuti practices witchcraft, and is alleged to have bewitched some people in this community. I am afraid."

In our conversation, Pastor Chikuni said: "Try not to argue with such a person. The best thing to do is for both the pastor and the congregation to learn to enter the world in which such persons are living. It is futile to make pronouncements from the pulpit or make statements from 'another world.' Sit where they are living (Ezek 3:15) and, as Jesus,

---

2. Browning, *Dictionary of the Bible*, 76.

dwell among them (John 1:14), and then listen to them." We talked about how, as African churches or congregations, we have often posed as "the Western church" when we should be "an African church." The journey through difficulties upon which we embark is our own, shaped by our own culture, values, and view of the world. The fear of witchcraft in rural Zimbabwe is not all superstition. It is a world in which some people live, and it takes a courageous pastor and a congregation to believe there is such a world, enter it and listen to what is going on in that world. Believing that such a world exists for some people, and courage to enter that world of darkness, gives the pastor and the congregation an opportunity to speak and live the authentic gospel.

This is precisely what Pastor Chikuni and the congregation at Sherukuru are doing. They have expelled the fears that some people have had for years, because they have been willing to walk with the tormented in their oppressive world and have enabled these people to sojourn with them in a life of discipleship with Christ. Paul writes to the saints of Ephesus, "For our struggle is not against flesh and blood, but ... against the powers of this dark world and against spiritual forces of evil" (Eph 6:12). The reality of evil powers in the African context needs to be acknowledged, and the full armor of God, consisting of the belt of truth, the breastplate of righteousness, the shield of faith, the helmet of salvation, the gospel of peace, and the sword of the Spirit (Eph 6:14–18), must be put on in this *dzvikiti*.

Evangelistic Practices

The pastor at Sherukuru United Methodist Church is preaching the gospel of faith—having faith in God through Jesus Christ. Africans have always believed in God, but through their ancestors or ancestral spirits. The heart of the gospel, however, is faith in God through Jesus Christ who said, "I am the way, and the truth, and the life. No one comes to the Father except through me" (John 14:6). In the current African situation, it is time to proclaim Jesus Christ as the proto-ancestor through whom all have access to God the Father. By acknowledging the reality of evil powers that people face and by entering the world of those terribly frightened by these forces, the Methodists of Sherukuru are walking "through the valley of the shadow of death" with these terrified seekers. They demonstrate to them that they no longer need to fear evil because they now know their proto-ancestor is leading them, with his rod and staff comforting them (Ps 23:4). The secret is taking the gospel into the world in which the people live—there the gospel becomes flesh. The people can believe in this enfleshed gospel (Rom 10:14). The pastor and people of Sherukuru United Methodist Church communicate this gospel daily and weekly. They challenge the practice of witchcraft and other horrendous traditional evil practices in the community on the basis of the gospel. Through this gospel they bring certainty and hope to a people in the midst of a difficult political and economic situation, because the people have come to know they rest ultimately in the hands of the only One who can lead them on a journey to the "promised land." Several practices inform this gospel sharing.

First, *regular Sunday worship services* attract people of the whole valley, beginning with non-church members, back-sliders, and even those of other churches. The message of the pastor is Jesus Christ, and the sermons commonly embrace both the preaching of the Word and the teaching the Christian faith. His style often begins with the life situation of the people—the world in which they live. He attends funerals, not only of his church members, but also of those who belong to other churches or who have no church of their own. He attends family or clan ceremonies known as *nyaradzo*—prayer meetings intended to comfort a bereaved family, often held about a month after the burial of a family member. He also attends unveiling of tombstone ceremonies for all families in the community. Since African tradition often dominates these ceremonies, the pastor does not interfere with the cultural practices. Instead, he uses what he observes in such traditional rituals to reach out to the people who listen to his sermons, and through such practices, brings the gospel of Jesus Christ to the people, as if saying, "And now I will show you the most excellent way" (1 Cor 12:31).

Second, the pastor uses *visitation evangelism* extensively. A year before the current pastor was appointed, I conducted a "Two by Two Lay Visitation Evangelism Workshop." The church organizations, such as *Vabvuwi* (the United Methodist Men's Organization) and *Rukwadzano* (the United Methodist Women's Organization) and the United Methodist Youth Fellowship, consider themselves as the evangelistic arms of the church. They penetrate the surrounding communities to win people to Christian discipleship. On Friday, July 10, 2009, for example, I went at Sherukuru hoping to see the pastor. He was not there, but earlier in the morning, the *Vabvuwi* had gone to hold a prayer meeting in a home of a non-Christian about three kilometers from the church.

Third, as the *reputation of vitality* in both the young preacher and the congregation have spread all over the place, the sub-chiefs, headsmen, and councilors have invited the pastor and his congregation to conduct prayer meetings in their areas. The result is that in the past twelve months, four new preaching points have been opened in surrounding communities, and their distance from the main church range from eight to twelve kilometers. While local preachers are sent to these new preaching points, the pastor with some members of the church visit the same new preaching points during the week, holding prayer meetings with small groups in the homes. Despite the fact that the intention was for these to be small group prayer meetings held in homes, they have grown so rapidly that they are now outdoor or open-air meetings. Exorcism of evil spirits has become a common phenomenon in these meetings.

Christian Vitality

First, Sunday worship service attendance reflects the vitality of the church. The church building is fully packed every Sunday and one has to be there early enough to get a seat for there are always people sitting outside.

Second, congregational singing has become a blessing to everybody who participates in the worship service. Such singing is often accompanied by African instruments, such as drums and *hosho* (a small dried calabash). The youth seem to take a leading role in congregational singing which lifts the spirit of everybody participating.

Third, there is a noticeable change in the lives of many people. As one who often goes to my home village and attends church service from time to time, I see people who some years ago did not seem to have interest in the church; they are active members today. These are also people who seemed to be in "another world," but today they are Christian disciples, taking a leading role in the life of the church.

Fourth, the practice of sharing testimonies has always been a mark of African Methodism. The pastor and church leaders have helped people learn how to share the story of their journey of faith. The heart of their Christian testimony is the story of God's love shed abroad in their hearts—the story of God's grace, the undeserved experience of forgiveness, escape from damnation, and everlasting life with Christ.

At one of the workshops, a woman who had stopped coming to church for a whole year shared her testimony on the Sunday she returned, thanking those who had visited her in her home. She explained that she had stayed away from church so long because of a remark one the church women had made to her: "You always come to church with nothing to give. You are always eating other people's food. When will you begin to bring us something?" It happened that the woman who had said these words was present. The two women forgave each other and hugged each other in front of everybody in that church.

Testimonies like this have become a common aspect of almost every worship service at Sherukuru. Terence Ranger, a renowned historian, made a very interesting observation about African United Methodist testimonies. He wrote: "African Christian testimonies—made use of and interpreted in all these ways—constituted a major genre of both official and popular Methodism in eastern Zimbabwe and Mozambique. Nothing similar survives for eastern Zimbabwean Catholicism and Anglicanism. AMEC [American Methodist Episcopal Church] missionaries not only had a particular interest in testimonies, they also had a particular interest in sermons."[3]

Fifth, Sherukuru United Methodist Church has embraced a vision to transform the community. The pastor views the community of faith through the eyes of the prophet Isaiah who envisaged God's people as servants, called and molded to be a light and bring salvation to all the surrounding communities (Isa 49:6). He and the congregation seek to implement this vision in multiple ways: (a) They have approached government authorities to reclaim both the primary and high schools that go by the names Sherukuru Primary School and Sherukuru Secondary School. Churches controlled most of the schools in the country until the 1970s when they relinquished the responsibility to run schools to the government. Although these Churches retained the control of schools at major mission stations, today they seem to question the decision to abandon control of the other schools. Sherukuru United Methodist Church may be leading the way in an effort to reclaim these schools and restore the direct influence of churches. (b) The secondary school, in partnership with church people, embarked on a project of teaching

---

3. Blakely, *Religion in Africa*, 280.

people to raise pigs for meat consumption. Since bush meat is scarce, rural people today tend to rely on vegetables only and hardly have enough meat for protein. They have considered other horticultural and poultry projects as well. All of these efforts offer Sherukuru an opportunity to take a leading role in transforming the lives of people physically, economically, and spiritually.

Global Contributions

The experience at Sherukuru in disciple-making contributes significantly to the rest of the world parish in a number of ways.

First, Sherukuru United Methodist Church has rediscovered that it is a church established upon the solid foundation of Jesus Christ. Amidst all the new challenges that have come, particularly from charismatic groups who identify evidence of the Holy Spirit with speaking in tongues and prophesying, Sherukuru Church has demonstrated the truth of the gospel by connecting the work of the Holy Spirit directly with Christ—not as a manifestation of God apart from Christ, but as something inseparable from the glory of Christ (John 16:13, 14). Their whole approach is thoroughly grounded, both theologically and Christologically.

Second, Sherukuru Church has come to appreciate the God-given context in which it thrives—the cultural and social environment which must be understood first in order to discern God's mission. They employ the term *dzvikiti* to describe the path of Christian discipleship, a term that describes the journey of faith, the challenges and the battles to be fought and won within the cultural and social context that Shona people understand. This kind of contextualization of the gospel models a way in which every community of faith can realize God's potential for them in their own journey to the "promised land."

5

Disciple-Making in the Zimbabwean Church

Christinah Kwaramba

SOME CHURCHES IN ZIMBABWE TODAY LACK MOTIVATION, MEANING, and methodology to fulfill the great commission—to make disciples of Jesus Christ and "mature" them in the Christian way of life. Church members assume that evangelism is the preserve of the clergy, linked to Sunday services alone, and this attitude has hampered the spread and quality of the gospel in this generation. The Bible, however, provides a different vision of Christianity—a daily way of life for all the people of God. This resonates very closely with an African cultural perspective, articulated most clearly by the great African theologian/philosopher, John Mbiti: "I am because we are, since we are therefore I am."[1] Christians live for each other and with each other as a community of God's people. For John Wesley, the essence of faith was personal and inward, but the evidence of faith was public and social.[2] The biblical witness, African culture, and the Wesleyan perspective combine, potentially, to form a powerful vision of disciple-making.

Albert Outler, in his analysis of evangelism in the Wesleyan tradition, claimed that this important practice must issue in visible social effects or else its fruits would fade and wither. Outward witness in daily living is the necessary confirmation of any inward experience of faith. In Wesley's Societies, Methodists translated the word they heard into visible action in the world. These structures of early Methodism, therefore, became evangelistic agencies in their own right. Thousands may never have heard Wesley preach, but many were attracted to the

---

1. Mbiti, *African Religion and Philosophy*, 106.
2. Outler, *Evangelism in the Wesleyan Spirit*, 25.

Christian life and were actually evangelized (converted, born again, nurtured, and matured) by the outreaching and ingathering influence of the local Methodist people.[3] It was not only their preaching that impacted their world, but also their lives—on the job, in the market place, in their redemptive involvement in the social agonies of their times. For the Wesleyans, evangelism was more than conversion and regeneration. It was, instead, both initiation and maturation in Christ and in Christian fellowship. In the Zimbabwean context, two organizations in particular reflect this vision and practice, RRW (Rukwadzano Rwe Wadzimai) and MUMC (Mubvuwi we United Methodist Church). They have functioned historically as agencies of evangelizing, initiating, and maturing converts into the reign of God.

This is the background for the following reflections on the practice of disciple-making in the United Methodist tradition in Zimbabwe. An African perspective, such as that offered here, has much to contribute to the vision of mission and evangelism in a world parish.

Critical Challenges

One of the critical challenges in the Zimbabwean context has to do with the distinction between *making members of the church and making disciples of Jesus Christ*. Leaders of the church have tended to emphasize numbers over and against disciple-making, thereby elevating quantity over quality. This problem is exacerbated by the fact that many members do not read the Bible or know its message well. But the Word of God provides a clear vision of the way in which people ought to live—as citizens of a world parish. It proclaims that the faithful are the Body of Christ, regardless of our skin color, language, political affiliation, and culture. The Wesleyan tradition provides a healthy prescription given this situation. In this heritage of faith, quantity and quality must inform each other. Wesley's small groups met frequently for fellowship, prayer, Bible study, and to watch over one another in love. In Zimbabwe, small groups/sections and organizations within every Methodist congregation recruit and nurture people into disciples. These small groups organized in the neighborhoods provide a sense of belonging to the people involved. This sense of connectedness keeps people from feeling

---

3. Ibid., 28.

alienated and alone and mitigates the anxiety of separation they often feel. This leads to both growth in numbers and growth in faith.

The *socio-economic, political, and cultural situation* in Zimbabwe directly affects the lives of many people, and many have compromised their faith for sake of survival. Civil war in many African countries—a debilitating legacy of Western colonialism—has disrupted the processes of disciple-making that were once on the rise. Many Africans have fled into the Diaspora, leaving behind the elderly and impoverished who no longer have the energy or power to engage in evangelistic ministry.

Colonization also left Africans with an identity confusion or problem. Colonial masters often demonized the African way of living, so the majority of Africans have developed a double standard way of living, perpetually confused about the demands of the Christian way of life and how to integrate it into their larger world. Many Africans, therefore, no longer understand their own culture; but if they were to explore it more fully, they would discover a vision of life in which being a disciple of Christ makes sense to them.

The HIV/AIDS pandemic and the pervasiveness of other diseases, poverty, and starvation drain the limited resources of the church, stifle its mission, and make it difficult to mount effective evangelistic programs.

With regard to the broader social context, male domination and other cultural practices hinder women from being agents of evangelism and disciple-making in Zimbabwe.

One of the greatest challenges today, however, relates to the practice of discipleship in a *world that has rejected and is hostile to true love*? The Shona people of Zimbabwe embrace an understanding of love shared by many in the human family—"when you love someone, you cannot stand to see them suffer." The greed and selfishness of political leaders in Zimbabwe, however, has led to the untold suffering of so many. Love means doing everything possible to liberate humanity and, most importantly, to alleviate suffering and expose injustice. Justice demonstrates love in a public way. It gives love legs, arms, soul, and voice, bringing genuine love to life in every sphere. One of the most difficult realities in Zimbabwe, therefore, is the fact that women and children have suffered rape, beatings, and abductions at the hands of the people who should have been loving and caring for them as citizens and as children of God.

Scriptural Images

Jesus Christ, the prophets, and the apostles all talk about and demonstrate how to live as God's people. Mastering these basic fundamentals is essential to finding joy in practicing them. African Christians need to reconfigure evangelism so as to bring it in life with the methodology that Jesus implemented. Several biblical texts model the evangelism of Jesus at its best: Matthew 5:13–16; Mark 5: 18–20; and John 15. Perhaps none sums up Jesus' approach to communicating the good news better than his encounter with the Samaritan woman at the well (John 4:1–26, 39–42). Jesus restores the dignity on this woman and equips her to be an evangelist to the whole village. Viewed within an African context, this narrative demonstrates how women should be given the opportunity and freedom to be channels of the gospel to communities. Moreover, the story of Jesus' resurrection and women at the tomb demonstrates the effectiveness of women as evangelists. In the hands of these women, the gospel became contagious in their communities.

The primary characteristics of Jesus' own ministry provide a pattern relevant to any context. He seized every opportunity to share the good news. His ministry was a threefold matrix of teaching, preaching, and healing. In all his encounters he identified himself with the people in all towns and villages. Needy, marginalized, and rejected people surround the church on every side. In this situation, one question stands out with regard to the vocation of discipleship: "What have our congregations done for these people that Christ would have done had he visited them?" The biblical narrative centers on freedom, love, faith, and hope. Ministry in a world parish must be centered on and directed by the way of Jesus related to the "least of these." This is the primary image from the scriptures. Disengaged from this vision, the church will remain an idea and not a reality. St. Paul captured this vision and proclaimed a world community in which there is no longer Jew or Gentile, slave or free, male and female (Gal 3:28). The disciples of Jesus are simply the people of the way—his way. Such a theology of the Body of Christ can help frame what we mean by a "world parish" in a global perspective.

Evangelistic Practice

Jesus, indeed, shared good news with the poor. Disciples of Christ, therefore, are called to dine with the poor, lost, blind, lame, and all outcasts in the world. A Christian style of life, in other words, is an essential precondition of evangelism at every level. If the lives of Christian disciples do not attract people, no message that they proclaim will. This reflects the beauty and simplicity of New Testament Christianity. As Michael Green has observed, the earliest Christians showed tremendous practical love.[4] Likewise, George Hunter asserts that the crucial issue in evangelism is "the credibility of the witnesser."[5]

In the Zimbabwean context, the *local church is the best platform* from which to launch a program of evangelism into the whole community. This is where the people are, where the flock is fed, and hence where the disciples of Jesus Christ are made. Ministers or evangelists do not do this alone; they understand that to be a Christian necessitates bearing witness to Jesus Christ and, therefore, they involve all believers in faith sharing.

Secondly, *faith must be lived out* if it is to make any sense in an African context. When Christians meet people and talk to them about their need of faith, those people will immediately assess the believers' lives to determine if the faith they profess is authentic and real. Personal faith, in other words, is an absolute prerequisite to evangelism. According to Michael Green, early Christians overflowed with joy as they cared for the poor and the needy.[6] Their witness was persuasive because people could immediately identify with them. Whereas the Holy Spirit convinces people that Jesus is Lord, God works through lives that are compelling by virtue of their authenticity. African traditional religions place a high value on people who are truly caring. African people will ask: "Is she or he one of us or our kind of folk? Is he or she one with us? Are they trying to add members to the church roll, or are they genuine friends?" African communities need evangelists who share their real hopes and feelings with people who yearn for good news in their lives.

Listening to individuals and their context is the key to disciple-making. Faithful witness depends upon the ability to provide hospital-

---

4. Green, *Evangelism through the Local Church*, 326.
5. Hunter, *Contagious Congregation*, 78.
6. Green, *Evangelism through the Local Church*, 326.

ity—a space of safety and freedom—and the capacity to befriend any type of human being with the hope that they will accept Christ. This requires attentiveness. Sharing the faith with one person at a time, after listening intently to his or her own story, paves the way to genuine discipleship. Dr. John Kurewa, E. Stanley Jones Professor of Evangelism at Africa University, summed this up on one occasion by saying: "We need to pour water into glasses one by one to make them all full, rather than throwing water at them all one time." This presents a challenge to evangelistic practice today. The "one size fits all" method is no longer effective. It is essential to get to know people as individuals in their own homes and communities. African people open up to Christian witnesses, ask questions, and seek guidance for their lives when they become close to one another and live in solidarity in their settings. Evangelism in this context, therefore, must be incarnational, elastic, and indigenous—related to people where they are and as they are, rather than as Christians would like them to be. Individuals in the community can hear the gospel as good news, rather than as strange propaganda, when a space for listening and hospitality enables their response and provides a way into discipleship.

Another important aspect of mission and evangelism, related directly to this, has to do with *going to where the people are*. Experience in Zimbabwe teaches clearly that people come to Christ and to church through personal acquaintances. A personal testimony illustrates this dimension of the work. In 2001, I served as the pastor of Sunningdale UMC, a congregation populated largely by women. I rescheduled my pastoral visitation in the homes of members after the local bar had closed, remembering that Jesus went to where the people were. I met almost all the spouses to my female members. I decided to simply listen to them, chat, and, above all, befriend them as they were. In a month's time my church was full of men too and I accepted them as they were. Bit by bit we witnessed to them and nurtured them into the reign of God. A degree of trusting friendship had to be established before effective witness could take place. The evangelism I applied had to be indigenous, fitting the other person's context and culture, needs, and pattern of engagement. Evangelism, in that setting, involved sharing the love and mercy of God through Christ in a way that connected with the reality of their lives.

Finally, the political and economic situation in Zimbabwe, while negatively impacting the lives of many people, has also provided an opportunity for people to rediscover what is most important in life and to depend and believe in God for survival. The circumstances in Zimbabwe today simply produce *a yearning in people to rediscover their spiritual roots*. When asked, "How are you managing to stay alive in Zimbabwe at this point in time?" almost every Zimbabwean will testify: "*Tiri kurarama ngeNyasha dzaMwari*" (We are surviving by the grace of God). Christians can seize this opportunity to direct people to the God of unmerited grace and unfailing love. The circumstances simply provide an opportunity to recognize and testify to the love of God in the midst of these challenges and to make disciples of Jesus Christ who live by faith and are sustained in practical ways through the faith by which they believe.

Christian Vitality

In Zimbabwe, the women's and men's organizations remain the most vital centers of evangelistic witness and mission in the church, patterned largely after Wesley's own structures and methods. They function as "little churches within the church," caring for the souls of their members, nurturing new converts, and, as William Abraham emphasizes in his vision of evangelism, initiating them into the reign of God as revealed in Jesus Christ.[7] Despite the fact that the country continues to face monumental humanitarian challenges, or perhaps because of it, these devout disciples consider mission and evangelism to be their primary work. The MUMC and RRW specialize in individual, personal evangelism, but they also sponsor and support open air revivals that have been traditional in Zimbabwe for years. These events also remain a pillar of the evangelistic enterprise. Typically, each local church and each district sponsors at least one revival a year, and the Annual Conference often promotes two each year on the national level. These larger events are almost always held on camping grounds where the whole conference, including the bishop, spend as much as a full week in intense programs of preaching, praying, and singing in the African style. During these revivals, hundreds of people are converted, reconverted, and renewed in their faith Zimbabweans are excited about sharing their faith with each

---

7. Abraham, *Logic of Evangelism*, 95.

other and putting their faith into practice as they rely on the promises of God in troubled times. Paul's testimony in Rom 8:35 and 37 fills them with hope: "Who will separate us from the love of Christ? Will hardship, or distress, or persecution, or famine, or nakedness, or peril, or sword? . . . No, in all these things we are more than conquerors through him who loved us."

Global Contributions

The Christian future might lie in Africa or Asia. The "Christian heartland" has shifted from Europe and North America to Africa, Asia and South America.[8] As a Ugandan missionary to the United Kingdom, Stephen Tirwomwe, observed: "It was so depressing when I first arrived to find churches empty, and being sold when in Uganda there isn't enough room in our churches for people. There is great need for revivals in Britain—it has become so secular and people are so inward-looking and individualistic. The country needs reconverting."[9]

The global community of faith needs to hear the witness of the African churches and their experience of the living Christ. In Africa 37 percent of all baptisms today are of adults.[10] This demonstrates the importance of the evangelistic efforts of believers, since people are making deliberate decisions to convert from other faith traditions to become the followers of Christ. Christians on both local and global levels are challenged to identify God's mission in their own community and beyond, and to know that God has invested in them some talents to be utilized in reaching out to all people in their unique situations of need. Zimbabwean United Methodists have much to offer a world parish with regard to mission and evangelism.

Disciple-making begins where people are. This is the only way for the gospel to be truly relevant in people's lives. This strategy of the early church, as well as many African contexts, locates the point of contact between all people and the gospel in the needs, hopes, yearnings, fears, longings, and deepest motives of the people themselves. Every facet of the gospel matches every basic human need. A beautiful sermon, in most cases, will not get down to where people itch. Most evangelism

---

8. Migliore, *Faith Seeking Understanding*, 220.
9. Ibid., 205.
10. Jenkins, *Next Christendom*, 195.

happens outside the walls of a sanctuary in personal conversation and in the simple telling of the story of God's love in Jesus Christ.

Evangelism should be the number one priority. For Africans, evangelism is the spontaneous, natural chattering of good news that leads to the making of disciples. Originally, evangelism was a way of life, not a church program. Many churches today, however, tend to be inward looking and ministry nourishes the faithful rather than reaching into the chilly waters of contemporary unbelief to draw new members in. Many clergy and church members have never led anyone to faith. Faithfulness today requires going back to the New Testament vision of the church in which mission and evangelism were central.

Christianity is a communal, story-telling religion, not an individualistic quest. One of the most important contributions that Africans make to the current understanding of disciple-making has to do with their essentially communal vision of the church. From an African perspective, people want to belong first before they believe in anything. Making disciples, therefore, involves belonging to one another and listening to each other's stories. There are a number of ways to tell the truth about life, but no way is more common, yet powerful, than the use of story. Stories have always been the way people have kept their tradition alive and created identity. Africans know who they are by their stories. Africans have stories of faith to tell and they need a listening ear from the world parish. Many of their stories are rooted in suffering, and their vision of discipleship keeps them close to human suffering in a way that helps them discern and respond to a loving God who liberates and makes all things new. Africans offer a holistic vision of life in which HIV/AIDS, poverty, war, and hunger are necessarily integrated into the life of faith.

"Living the gospel means affirming diversity and celebrating God's spirit that falls on 'every nation under heaven.'"[11] These words of Harold Recinos emphasize the need to embrace God diverse creation and to look for the activity of the Spirit all around. Coming out of a context of such staggering diversity—one of the most diverse Continents on this globe—these words present a huge challenge. African Christians are learning to speak to the larger world of which they are a part, relating to it, working to make it better—this world that has so many needs and problems, so many faults and failures, and yet, is beloved of God.

11. Recinos, *Good News from the Barrio*, 14.

This requires developing relationships with global neighbors, countries, communities, and races so as to attract them all to Christ. How can we do ministry together? That is the pressing question of our time. All of God's people—African, Asian, American, European—need to be admitted into the broader debates about the global church and affirmed for the contribution they can make. When everyone is allowed to speak at the table, all can learn from one another and share their stories about what matters to them most with regard to making disciples in a global community of faith.

Further Reading on African Contexts

Bate, Stuart C. *Evangelisation in the South African Context*. Rome: EPUG, 1991.
Bediako, Kwame. *Christianity in Africa*. Maryknoll, NY: Orbis. 1995.
Beidelman, T. O. *Colonial Evangelism: A Socio-Historical Study of an East African Mission at the Grassroots*. Bloomington: Indiana University Press, 1982.
Byo, Yohanna. *Sheep Don't Follow Sheep: Administering Christian Education*. Jos, Nigeria: Ya Byangs, 2008.
Foli, Richard. *Christianity in Ghana: A Comparative Church Growth Study*. Accra, Ghana: Trust, 2006.
Gatwa, Tharcisse. *The Churches and Ethnic Ideology in the Rwandan Crises, 1900–1994*. Milton Keynes, UK: Paternoster, 2005.
Joe-Adigwe, Hypolite A., editor. *Women, Justice and Evangelisation*. Onitsha, Nigeria: Archdiocesan Secretariat, 1980.
Jules-Rosette, Bennette. *The African Apostles*. Ithaca, NY: Cornell University Press, 1975.
Kalilombe, Patrick A. *Doing Theology at the Grassroots*. Gweru: Mambo. 1999.
Kurewa, John Wesley Zwomunondiita. *Drumbeats of Salvation in Africa*. Mutare, Zimbabwe: Africa University Press, 2007.
———. *Preaching and Cultural Identity: Proclaiming the Gospel in Africa*. Nashville: Abingdon, 2000.
———. *The Church in Mission*. Nashville: Abingdon, 1997.
McGamy, Cecil, and Patrick Ryan, editors. *Inculturating the Church in Africa: Theological and Practical Perspectives*. Nairobi: Paulines, 2001.
Mroso, Agapit J. *The Church in Africa and the New Evangelisation*. Rome: EPUG, 1995.
Mugambi, J. N. K. *The Biblical Basis for Evangelization: Theological Reflections Based on an African Experience*. Nairobi: Oxford, 1989.
Muzorewa, Abel Tendekayi. *Evangelism that Decolonizes the Soul: Partnership with Christ*. Eugene, OR: Wipf & Stock, 2005.
Nyajeka, M. Tumani. *The Unwritten Text*. Mutare, Zimbabwe: Africa University Press, 2006.
Oduyoye, Mercy, editor. *The Will to Rise*. Maryknoll, NY: Orbis, 1992.
Ranger, O. Terence, and Isario Kimambo. *The Historical Study of African Religion*. Nairobi: Heinmann, 1972.
Robert, Dana L., editor. *African Christian Outreach, Vol 2. The Mission Church*. Menlo Park: Southern African Missiological Society, 2003.
Shorter, Aylward. *Evangelization and Culture*. London: Geoffrey Chapman, 1994.
Shorter, Ayword, and Joseph N. Njiru. *New Religious Movements in Africa*. Nairobi: Paulines, 2001.

Ukpong, Justin S., editor. *Evangelization in Africa in the Third Millennium*. Port Harcourt, Nigeria: Catholic Institute of West Africa, 1992.

Wheeler, Andrew, editor. *Land of Promise: Church Growth in a Sudan at War*. Nairobi: Paulines, 1998.

Williams, Walter. *Black Americans and the Evangelization of Africa*. Madison: University of Wisconsin Press, 1982.

PART TWO

Asia & Oceania
Navigating Cross-Currents

Introduction to Part 2

ASIA IS THE WORLD'S LARGEST AND MOST POPULOUS CONTINENT AND Oceania one of the most far-flung collections of islands and archipelagos. The image of cross-currents conveys the reality of millions of different people shaped by a staggering variety of religious traditions, ideologies, and cultures, among which Christianity represents, by and large, a minority perspective. The Philippines—the fourth largest Roman Catholic nation in the world—South Korea—which boasts the largest Protestant population in Asia—and Australasia—dominated demographically by Christianity, but in many ways nominal with regard to religious practice—stand out as exceptions to this rule. But the fact remains that most Asian and Oceanic Christians, even Koreans, Filipinos, and those "down under," must navigate the sometimes treacherous cross-currents of their contexts. The reflections of the Asian authors in this section reflect the agony and ecstasy of this calling.

Reflecting upon the task of making disciples in China, Lo Lung-kwong orients his vision around the famous words of Dietrich Bonhoeffer, "When Christ calls a man, he bids him come and die." He points to the costly nature of discipleship in this context and elevates the servant nature of the Christian community and the incarnational nature of its mission. "In short, for the Chinese," he argues, "being a disciple of Jesus Christ entails living intentionally in missional communities that embrace the necessity of sacrifice and life-giving service to others." In a context of oppression, evangelism must be nothing less than living out the life of Christ by word and deed, even to the death.

Lenita Tiong's reflection on the status of Christianity in Malaysia illuminates the amazing diversity of this region. The repressive policies of the Muslin state exacerbate the difficulties that accompany a radically pluralistic context. Due to the political changes in Malaysia's recent history, an impasse between the generations has developed along the fault lines of language and culture, in both family and church. Given this situation, it is not surprising that the story of Pentecost provides a helpful and hopeful paradigm for a renewed passion to make disciples of Jesus Christ.

The essay by Daniel Arichea reflects a very different context, that of the "most Christian" nation in Asia—the Philippines. With over 80 percent of the population identified with the Roman Catholic Church, this reality presents a completely different set of challenges and opportunities. After identifying the primary internal and external challenges to mission and evangelism, he advocates a vision of missional cooperation, examines the issue of pervasive poverty, and highlights important ministries to children. In response to these particular issues, the local church must incarnate the gospel in concrete actions in the life of the community.

While the Republic of Singapore is an island city-state—the smallest nation in Southeast Asia—it may be one of the most cosmopolitan Asian centers, with Chinese people forming an ethnic majority and four official languages (Chinese, English, Malay, and Tamil) serving the diverse population. In a context such as this, nothing is more important than religious sensitivity. Robert Solomon exegetes this context and prescribes a disciple-making model that reflects a deeper relationship with Jesus, a wider engagement with the poor and marginalized, and a higher commitment to partnership in the *missio Dei* for the sake of the world.

J. C. Park explores the formative role of "missionary congregations" in the evangelistic ministry of the Korean church. Using the mission narrative of Korean Christianity as his fundamental framework, he explores how the translation of the Bible led to a revolution of God, how the internalization of biblical language and the formation of faith communities through prayer shaped their vision of discipleship, and how participation in the liberation of suffering people through education and discipline reclaimed a holistic vision of life and ministry. He narrates the amazing journey of a people from a trail of tears to a highway for the gospel.

Tevita Siuhengalu's contribution related to the Tongan Diaspora in Australia completes this Asian/Oceanic tour. He explores the realities of "displacement" and identity crisis among those who seek to live their lives as Christ's disciples in the cross-currents of competing cultures and religions. In their effort to navigate these difficult waters, Tongan Methodists walk alongside a "torn generation" in imitation of Jesus and the Emmaus journey, and they reclaim the formative influence of small groups and family ministry—hallmarks of the early Wesleyan traditions. These practices exemplify a "there and back again" paradigm that sustains their communities in troubled times.

6

Making Disciples in China

"When Christ calls a man, he bids him come and die."

Lo Lung-kwong

Critical Challenges

ROBERT MORRISON, THE FIRST PROTESTANT MISSIONARY TO CHINA, launched the missionary movement in this part of the Asian continent. He left England in January and arrived at Macao on September 4, 1807 via New York.

While the number of Christians continues to decline in both American and European contexts, churches in Asia, in general, and China, in particular, are growing. Chinese Christians, however, are a minority in the society. They live in a context of political struggle for democracy. They also live in a context of economic growth so rapid that it has made the gap between those who "have" and those who "have-not" even wider. At the same time, globalization threatens traditional Asian cultures that have long and rich histories. Religious pluralism characterizes the reality of everyday life.

When all of the missionaries left mainland China after 1949, political leaders abolished the system of denominationalism inherited and imposed from the West. A church emphasizing the "three-self principles"—self-governing, self-supporting, and self-propagating—was established in 1950. The church in China experienced the test of fire during the Cultural Revolution (1966–1976).[1] Rather than decreasing, however, the number of Christians increased rapidly during that

---

1. See Barnouin and Yu, *Ten Years of Turbulence*.

period and onward. During the half century between 1949 and 1997, a Christian community of approximately 700,000 believers increased more than fifteen fold. In 2006, the number of Protestants in China was not less than twenty million.[2]

Why is the number of Christians growing so rapidly in China? How is it that Christians, who live as a minority group under a Communist government with a market economy, in a social and cultural context of religious pluralism and traditional values reaching back more than four millennia, have experienced such rapid growth,? This typifies the challenge for Christians in China.

Scriptural Images

According to Acts, disciples were first called Christians at Antioch (Acts 11:25). Thus, the terms "disciples of Jesus Christ" and "Christians" are synonymous. As I have discussed elsewhere, a vision of a community of disciples should be the primary image of the Church.[3]

Not only was discipleship important in the time of Jesus, it defined the emerging religion embodied by the early church. Luke-Acts functions as a bridge between the time of the Gospels and the early Christian community. Even though Matthew is the only Gospel writer to use the familiar term *ekklesia* to refer to the company of followers that Jesus gathered around himself, the community of disciples became a prototype of "the assembly of God's people."

Among the many images of discipleship spelled out in the Gospels, the following characteristics resonate most fully with Chinese Christians in the Asian context:

1. Jesus initiates disciples by calling them into a particular way of life; it is not something based upon their own motivation.[4] Jesus confronts those around him or traveling with him or even following him with the demand to submit their life totally to him. This sense of calling and the recognition of the lordship of Jesus are essential to becoming a disciple.

---

2. Ting, "Rationale for Three-Self," 66.
3. See Lung-kwong, "Ecclesiology."
4. Hengel, *The Charismatic Leader*, 72–73.

2. Jesus clarifies the conditions of following him. He demands a complete break with the past, and if necessary, the abandonment of families, vocations, and security (e.g., Mark 1:16–20; 2:14; Matt 8:21–22; Luke 14:25).

3. Jesus demands a radical renunciation of the control of one's own possessions. The disciple must share them with the poor, rather than hoarding material wealth for self, thereby becoming more and more possessive (Mark 10:21; Matt 19:21; Luke 18:22).

4. Jesus requires a serious denial of self among his disciples, admonishing them to take up their own crosses if they are going to follow him. This means to follow Jesus to death (Mark 8:34–35; Matt 10:38–39; 16: 24–25; Luke 9:23–24).

5. Jesus illustrates vividly that discipleship entails the desire to serve rather than to be served (Mark 10:41–45; Matt 24–28; John 13).

6. Jesus welcomes the disciple into a lifelong relationship with himself (Mark 3:14), something akin to "abiding" with him forever. Disciples of Jesus live in union with him in the same way that branches are engrafted into a vine, drawing their life from the stock and producing a special kind of fruit as long as they remain connected (John 15:1–5; 17:20–26).

7. Jesus commissions his disciples, not simply to follow him, but to proclaim the same gospel that he embodied in his life, death, resurrection, and ascension (Mark 3:14), to be his witnesses (Acts 1:6–8), and also to exercise his power (Matt 9:37–38; 10:5–15, 40; 11:21–23; 28:18–20; Mark 6:7–13; Luke 9:1–6).[5] Jesus prayed for his disciples and sent them out in the same way that he had been sent by God (John 17:18; 21:22).

8. Jesus invites his disciples to participate in his kingdom mission—to offer and to abide in the kingdom in it in the same way he made it known through his ministry.[6]

---

5. Ibid., 78–79.
6. Ibid., 73.

9. Jesus calls "individuals" to a life of discipleship,[7] but immediately gathers them into a "community" with him as their Master.[8]

Chinese Christians build their vision of discipleship and evangelistic practice around these primary images, demonstrating their faith in both word and deed in the specific context of their lives.

Evangelistic Practice

According to the Gospel of Mark, the good news is the gospel of Jesus Christ (Mark 1:1). For Paul, Jesus Christ himself is the content of the gospel (Rom 1:2–4; 1 Cor 15:3–4). Thus, the heart of evangelistic practice is living out the life of Jesus by word and deed (Rom 15:18); this means "making disciples" (Matt 28:18–20) rather than simply recruiting church members.

For Chinese Christians, making disciples forms the core of evangelistic practice. They cannot conceive of disciples living as isolated individuals; rather, they are drawn ineluctably into a community. Making disciples, therefore, involves extending an invitation to people to join a community of those following Jesus. The Chinese social, economic, religious, and political context stands over against the values and lifestyle of Christians in various ways. A Chinese community of disciples is composed of those who are willing and ready to follow Jesus to death together. This highly intentional vision of life not only helps the Christian community to survive, but it enables the disciples of Christ to find their true identity. These communities of Chinese Christians are a living entity—the "word in flesh"—a witness to the fullness of grace and truth in Christ (John 1:14) among people, the majority of whom are non-Christians. Through them, Jesus Christ continues to live in this world; they bear witness to his presence through their words and their actions, in their day to day lives that the world might believe.

Chinese people perceive and understood the Christians they have encountered in a variety of ways: as imperialist invaders, colonists, capitalists, preachers, educators, medical doctors, social workers, and activists. The Chinese are pragmatic people; they prefer actions rather than empty words. They prefer to see words-in-action rather than just

---

7. Ibid., 61–63, 71–72; cf. Dunn, *Jesus' Call to Discipleship*, 92.
8. Dunn, *Jesus' Call to Discipleship*, 92–94.

hearing words spoken or argued. Thus, for evangelistic practice to have integrity among the Chinese, it must be "infleshed"—the Word must be manifested by disciples of Jesus through "service-in-action" as well as in proclamation. With this understood, making disciples among the Chinese means calling people to follow the way (the lifestyle) of Jesus together, in humility and simplicity of life, to love one another and to serve the weak and the poor, to confront injustice and power with courage, and to resist pressures to conform to ancient tradition and family values, even unto death. In short, for the Chinese, being a disciple of Jesus Christ entails living intentionally in missional communities that embrace the necessity of sacrifice and life-giving service to others.

Christian Vitality

In China, this understanding and experience of the meaning of discipleship had been of utmost importance for the rooting and growing of the Church in China from its very beginning. Missionaries came to China in the nineteenth century when China was not yet ready to be open to the world. The blood of the missionaries was seed to the rise of Asian Christianity in the same way that the blood of the martyrs seeded the early church. The growing number of Christians in mainland China during the Cultural Revolution witnesses to this truth. Jesus' call to discipleship is costly, but demonstrates its power when the situation makes people feel powerless. Christians literally give their lives for something more valuable than life. As the Lutheran martyr, Dietrich Bonhoeffer, once observed: "When Christ calls a man, he bids him come and die."[9] Similarly, Confucius says: "One could die just as light as a feather, but one could die as heavy as Taishan (a famous big mountain in North East China near the native county of Confucius)"[10] Dying for Christ—an act of immeasurable value and meaning—elevates the life of the martyr, demonstrating to all the great love and truth to be found in a Christian existence.

When Christians take grace seriously and understand that God's invitation into the community of love entails serious responsibilities—when believers view grace as responsible grace—all people are deeply

---

9. See Bonhoeffer, *Cost of Discipleship*, 79.

10. A quotation from the famous Chinese historian Qian Si-ma, "A Letter sent to Ren On."

blessed. Likewise, Bonhoeffer's adage is just as true in the present age as in previous eras of persecution and testing: "Cheap grace is the deadly enemy of our Church."[11] The understanding of the Church as a community of disciples willing to die for Jesus has brought amazing vitality to Chinese Christians. When people no longer fear death, nothing can frighten them or shake them from the foundations of their life; rather, they are filled with power to live and to serve, and have the authority to call people to follow Jesus.

Global Contributions

What explains the declining number of Christians in both American and European contexts, while churches in China and other parts of the world are growing? It would be dangerous to think there is an easy answer to this complex question, but, from an Asian perspective, the church in the West seems to have lost a biblical vision of Christian discipleship. When it is easy to be a Christian, when baptism means little more than welcoming a newborn baby into the world, when there are few challenges associated with the life of someone who follows Jesus in a social and cultural context that purports to be Christian, the central meaning of the Christian life can easily be lost. The individual pursuit of religious experience, whether it is personal conversion ("new birth") or healing, the achievement of individual success, prosperity, and power, and the claim to some superior moral status or blessing at the hand of God, become the goals or the identity markers of many Christians.

The scriptural images, the witness of early Christians, and also the experiences of Chinese Christians, all point to an understanding of costly discipleship as the key to Christian vitality. The church provides an authentic witness to the world when the disciples of Jesus live out their lives in intentional communities of service and love, even if it means giving their lives for the life of the world. Bonhoeffer's words still ring true: "When Christ calls a man, he bids him come and die!" In fact, this was the model of those Western missionaries who sacrificed their lives in China and thereby became the seed of the church. This has been the life model for those Chinese Christians who have been willing to live out the life of Jesus in hardship and under the shadow of death with love, faith, and hope, and with a sense of mission and

---

11. Bonhoeffer, *Cost of Discipleship*, 35.

vitality. This model of making disciples in China has attracted many to follow Jesus, because it is real. They are able to way with St. Paul: "We are afflicted in every way, but not crushed; perplexed, but not driven to despair; persecuted, but not forsaken; struck down, but not destroyed; always carrying in the body the death of Jesus, so that the life of Jesus may also be made visible in our bodies. For while we live, we are always being given up to death for Jesus' sake, so that the life of Jesus may be made visible in our mortal flesh" (2 Cor 4:8–11).

7

Multi-Lingual Disciples

Lenita Tiong

"Malaysia, Truly Asia" is a commercial seen on cable TV around the world promoting lush tropical forests and interesting sights and sounds. Indeed, Malaysia is truly Asia. With a population of only twenty million but made up of at least more than eighty ethnic groups, finding a common language of communication is a daunting task. The major ethnic groups are Malays (52 percent), Chinese (30 percent), Indians (8 percent), and indigenous groups (9 percent). The main religions include Islam (55 percent), Chinese religions (28 percent),[1] Christianity (8 percent), Hinduism (7 percent), and other miscellaneous traditions (2 percent). Geographically, Malaysia is made up of the West Malaysian peninsula, which is the southern tip of the continent of Asia, and the two East Malaysian States of Sabah and Sarawak on the Island of Borneo. The South China Sea separates the two parts, but in reality there is more than the sea which divides the west from the east. Malaysia gained her independence from the British Colonial Government in 1957 and the East Malaysia States joined the federation of eleven States only in 1963.

Education and Language

The legacy left behind by the British colonial government includes the judicial system, infrastructure, health care, and education. The educational system naturally emphasized English as the medium of instruc-

---

1. In this article, the broad term of Chinese religions is used, encompassing Buddhism, Taoism, Confucianism, ancestor worship, and other folk beliefs.

tion with the vernaculars taught as additional languages to those who chose to study them. Prior to 1961, the management, the recruitment of teachers, and the enrollment of students at mission schools were all prerogatives of the schools and the supporting churches. These schools were set up by the early missionaries with funds from their home churches and in the early days many of the teachers were missionaries. But the Education Act in 1961 changed all that; the Ministry of Education thereafter reserved the right to hire and fire the teachers as well as set the scale of the salaries of teachers. At the same time, the Ministry also reserved the right to appoint three members of the Board of Management of the mission schools. Mission schools, then, were known as government aided schools, losing their autonomy in terms of management and development.

At the same time, the teaching of Bible knowledge was severely limited. Teachers on government payroll are no longer allowed to teach any religion during school hours. Pressure from parents who wanted their children to excel in major examination subjects further made Bible knowledge an unattractive subject. In 1969, the then Education Minister, Abdul Rahman Yacub, mandated that all schools change the medium of instruction to Bahasa Malaysia. This one common language, the Malaysian language, is meant to unite the different ethnic groups throughout the country. This language is basically the Malay language, but a more formal version. At the same time, the Ministry of Education implemented the integration of urban schools, which consist of large Chinese and Indian student populations, with the rural schools with largely Malay students. With this implementation, the student population of mission schools changed dramatically.

This change was implemented immediately in West Malaysia, but was only implemented in the late 1970s in Sarawak. The reason was that, when Sarawak joined the Federation in 1963, four areas of governance remained under state control—Immigration, Land Use, Education, and Health Care. The State government retained its autonomy in these areas and was able to delay the change of the medium of instruction in schools. Hence, in Sarawak, the use of English as a medium of instruction in schools continued until the mid 1980s when the switch was made after the state relinquished the governance of education to the federal government. In reaction to this change, many parents of Chinese descent were concerned about the loss of the Chinese language and culture and with the help of community leaders started Chinese schools. Only in these schools, the medium of instruction is the Chinese language with the study of the national language and English as optional subjects.

The Methodist Church

Methodism came to Malaysia as an outreach from Singapore. Rev. and Mrs. James Thoburn and Rev. William Oldham arrived in Singapore on February 7, 1885. All of them were based in India at that time. The first church had European membership, but gradually ministry began among the Chinese and Indian migrants. Outreach among the Malay was initiated by William Shellabear in 1887 and a small and growing Malay congregation resulted. But sadly, by 1896 the congregation disintegrated and thus ended the ministry among this major people group.

Integrated Evangelism[2]

From Singapore, missionaries were sent to West Malaysia (known as Malaya at that time) to expand the ministry of the church. Evangelism took the form of an integration of three aspects of Christian ministry, i.e., evangelism, social work, and education. Evangelism included street preaching, evangelistic rallies, distribution of tracts in vernacular languages, house to house visitation, and church worship services which were evangelistic in nature. Social work included ministry among orphans, widows, and the newly arrived migrants. With the establishment of Methodist schools in West Malaysia, both boys and girls of different races were given the opportunity of quality education. Ministry among these students provided the church with youth who would grow up to be the leaders of today.

Churches, Races, and Languages

As converts gathered to form congregations, they developed naturally along language lines with the formation of Tamil congregations for the largely Indian migrants from South India and of Chinese congregations among the Chinese migrants. In some cases, some congrega-

---

2. This term is used only by Yung and Hunt in *Christianity in Malaysia*, ed. Hunt.

tions used the dialects of the congregants such as Cantonese and Hokkien.³ English-speaking congregations were also started mainly for the European settlers and civil servants working for the British Government. With passing time, local children who were educated in English or had gone through their education in the mission school joined these congregations.

In Sarawak, the first missionary, Rev. James Matthew Hoover, came in 1903 after a group of Foochow Methodist settlers had arrived in Sibu and were in need of pastoral care. Hoover quickly learned the Foochow language and ministered among those who spoke it. His wife, like the missionaries in Malaya, focused on women's ministry and education. She was instrumental in founding the Yuk Ing Girls' School in 1908 and the Methodist English School in 1918. Churches in the larger Sibu area mushroomed among the Foochows with Sunday worship services held in the Foochow language. In 1910, work among the Hinghwas started similar to the Foochows. The migrants settled in a township outside of Sibu town and a congregation of Hinghwas, worshipping in their mother tongue, started soon after their settlement. The ministry among the Ibans, a large indigenous group of about 40 percent of the State's population, started in the 1930s. Churches in the Iban language immediately emerged.

Religion and Propagation

On January 20, 1874, the British signed the Treaty of Pangkor with the Malay rulers or sultans, an arrangement known as the Straits Settlement at that time. This treaty allowed the sultans to co-rule their States with the British authorities. Whereas the British were allowed to appoint advisors or "residents" for each State, religion and custom were specifically excluded from the British sphere of influence. By the time Malaysia gained her independence in 1957, Article 3(1) of the Federal Constitution declared Islam to be the religion of the state; but other religions could be practiced in peace and harmony in any part of the Federation.

Despite its title, "Freedom of Religion," Article 11 of the Constitution actually limits the practice of other religions. Although people are free

---

3. Chinese migrants came mainly from the southern part of China, from the Canton and Fukien provinces.

to practice and profess their religion and each religion's community has the right to own properties and establish and maintain institutions for religious purposes, the propagation of any religion other than Islam is limited by Sub Clause 4 of this article. It declares: "State Law and in respect of the Federal Territories of Kuala Lumpur and Labuan, federal law may control and restrict the propagation of any religious doctrine and belief among persons professing the religion of Islam."[4]

This sub clause has been at the center of many debates, discussions, and even court cases and has been subject to many different interpretations. Lee Min Choon argues, for example, that propagation means the free exchange of religious ideas and intellectual interaction of persons of different faiths.[5] To him, the right to propagate goes hand in hand with the right to profess the faith and includes the right to inquire of other religions and the right to change one's religion. However, to many, this sub clause specifically restricts the propagation of other religions among the Muslim community, whereas the right to propagate religious doctrines among the non-Muslims remains an absolute right.

Because of this ambiguity and the possibility of reading the Constitution in a more restrictive way, many church groups and individual Christians hesitate to share the gospel with their Muslim friends and contacts. At best, they only hint at religious belief and practice and, at worst, avoid it altogether as a taboo subject. For fear of repercussions, Christians are limited in their task of evangelization of other people groups when they cannot even evangelize their closest neighbors. While the church is able to talk and teach freely about the evangelization of all nations, disciples of Christ cannot even publicly pray for the salvation of Muslims.

In addition to the limits placed upon the propagation of the Christian faith, the Constitution restricts another freedom as well. Previously, a Muslim was free to renounce his or her faith and choose another religion, but in recent years, new laws in many of the States classify such a change of faith as an act of apostasy punishable under the law. Punitive actions differ from State to State, but range from fines and/or imprisonment to whipping to detention up to six months in Islamic Rehabilitation Centers. The harshest punishment is found in the State of Trengganu which gives the apostate an opportunity to repent, failing

---

4. *Federal Constitution of Malaysia*, Article 11.4.

5. Choon, *Freedom of Religion in Malaysia*, 83.

which, he or she is subject to a death sentence and forfeiture of his or her properties. There have been many high profile cases in recent years in which Muslims have renounced their faith and the courts have ruled in favor of punitive actions against them.

In a study of religious liberty in Malaysia, Crystal Kuek Chee Ying concludes that "the status and identity of a Muslim is no longer a matter of personal faith or decision."[6] She expresses concern that, if left unchecked, the restrictions of religious liberty, that many argue are guaranteed under the Federal Constitution, may lead to even more repressive action on the part of more extreme elements within the Muslim community. Regardless, the current practice in many parts of Malaysia makes it impossible for Christian people to fulfill the great commission (Matt 28:19–20), "teaching and baptizing" those who are drawn to the Christian faith. The boundaries set by the Malaysian Government inhibit the evangelization of all people.

Forms of Evangelization

In the past, street evangelism and liberal distribution of gospel tracts were employed by the church in its evangelistic ministry, but with increasing ethnic and religious sensitivity, such activities have been curtailed and prohibited in many areas. Public meetings and rallies need prior approval from the municipal or local government agencies, and the ease of obtaining these permissions varies widely. In Sarawak, however, we are grateful that most municipal councils are sympathetic to the outreach of the church and to public evangelistic rallies as well as worship celebrations. In major towns such as Kuching, Sibu, Miri, and Bintulu, the Associations of Churches in these towns have been able to organize Christmas parades around the town. Church members, led by the pastors, together with the bands from the Boys and Girls Brigade, sing carols and distribute gospel tracts to spectators as they walk around the town.

Religious gatherings, including worship services and evangelistic rallies, can no longer be held in schools, as the school property now comes under the jurisdiction of the government rather than the church. In the past, the administrators of mission schools were able to include all students in school assemblies where the chaplain shared a sermon.

6. Ying, "Religious Liberty," 79.

With the new ruling, only non-Muslim students can be required to attend such assemblies. In a multi-cultural and multi-religious society, these clear demarcations and restrictive regulations make it very difficult to build bridges and understanding among the races, let alone communicate the message of the gospel.

Making Disciples and Language

As discussed previously, the medium of instruction in government schools has changed from English to Bahasa Malaysia and people of Chinese descent have the opportunity for their children to retain their language and culture through private schools. The consequence of these changes is that students from government schools are neither proficient nor fluent in either the Chinese and English languages. Church members who are at least forty years old are able to communicate quite effectively in either of these two languages, but those younger find it difficult to express themselves meaningfully in either. Deeper matters of faith, theological insights, doctrines, polity, and even traditional hymns have lost their meaning, therefore, as the younger Christians are not familiar with terms and ideas that have been commonplace to older members.

Two distinct examples of this disjunction relate to the use of the Disciple Bible Study program, developed by the United Methodist General Board of Discipleship, and the No Apologies program of Focus on the Family. Youth find some of the terms used in these materials very difficult to understand. Even Bible study groups require materials that are expressed in simpler language. Given these circumstances, leaders are restricted to teaching on a very superficial level; instruction in the faith is limited and basic. Likewise, with regard to those within the Chinese community, there are many youth who are seriously deficient in the Chinese language, unless they attend Chinese schools, and yet they are members of the Chinese church. For some, even reading the Bible is an uphill struggle. The Iban churches struggle with the same challenges when the young people educated in Bahasa Malaysia find it laborious to use Iban in worship and the life of the church. Living within all of these constraints, the Malaysian church struggles to find a suitable language for disciple-making and feels fragmented in its life and work. Whereas older members are comfortable because the language through which they worship is the language of their education, the language of faith is not the language of education for the younger generations. They find themselves stranded between two linguistic worlds.

Logically speaking, the church could use the Malay language for worship and disciple-making, but cultural and ethnic sentiments run strong along these linguistic fault lines and there is an inherent resistance to use this language in the life of the church. There are some churches using Bahasa Malaysia in services of worship, but these are meant either for Indonesian migrant workers or for indigenous groups. No Chinese or Iban churches have worship services for these communities. The use of the language is also constrained by the policies of the Malaysian government. For example, the government protects Muslims in their exclusive right to use "Allah" in their naming of God. Christian literature containing this word is either banned or confiscated by Customs. In recent years, the Malaysian church realized that the Indonesian church had developed comprehensive and extensive literature for evangelization, disciple-making, and theological education. Their attempts to import such materials, however, have been blocked or restricted in such a way as to make it infeasible. The publishers of "The Herald," a newsletter of the Roman Catholic Church, have been taken to court for the use of the word "Allah" and the case is still ongoing.

Multi-Lingual Disciples

In Acts 1:8 Jesus promised the disciples that the coming of the Holy Spirit would bring them power to be witnesses and when the Holy Spirit came on the day of Pentecost, that power was first manifested in the ability to speak multiple languages by a group of Aramaic-speaking Jews. The earliest disciples—the Jewish Christians—were essentially mono-cultural, with limited exposure to the vast range of cultures and languages of the world, yet God empowered them to communicate the gospel to people of other languages and culture. Their power to heal and their ability to forgive in the most extreme circumstances resulted from the ministry of the Holy Spirit and came only subsequent to their ability to speak in languages other than their own (Acts 3–4).

In the contemporary church, often the gift of "angelic languages" is overemphasized while the gift of "human languages" is overlooked (See 1 Cor 12–13). In the context of the church in Malaysia, it may be time for us to reexamine Acts 1 and 2 and to seek power from on high to be able to proclaim the message of salvation in a multi-lingual context. The challenge to break through the constraints of our various languages can then be seen as an opportunity to see the power of the Holy Spirit rather than an insurmountable obstacle that restricts our ability to communicate the gospel in our multi-lingual context. Disciple-making can be reclaimed as an invigorating experience as one sees how God uses the weakness of "unschooled, ordinary people" (Acts 4:13) to share the faith with peoples of different ethnic groups who also long to know God's love in Christ. We can stand back and stand by as we allow the power from on high to bring a refreshing wind and a powerful flame that will usher the church into a new era as we echo the words of Zechariah— "Not by might, nor by power, but by the spirit, says the Lord of hosts" (Zech 4:6).

The World Is my Parish

These words of our founder John Wesley—"the world is my parish"— take on a new meaning in this context. While Malaysia may not quite be Asia, despite the TV ad, it is an amazing melting pot of cultures, religions, and people groups, not all that different from the situation we see reflected in the early church. The church thrived and grew by leaps and bounds despite the fact that it was a marginal community struggling against a hostile, ruling power. John's Wesley world was more geographical than cultural but if Malaysian pastors and church leaders can see the world as cultural, then we too can hold on to the vision of our founder and make the multi-lingual world we live in our parish.

8

Making Disciples in a Philippine Context

Daniel C. Arichea Jr.

MAKING DISCIPLES OF JESUS CHRIST FOR THE TRANSFORMATION OF the world is the primary mission of the United Methodist Church. How this is carried out would vary, of course, from one context to another. I am interested in exploring how the United Methodist Church in the Philippines is carrying out its mission in such a way as to be faithful to the gospel, on the one hand, and how it seeks to be sensitive and relevant to the actual situation of Philippine society, on the other.

Challenges

As we consider the ministry of disciple-making, we are confronted with internal as well as external challenges. Internal challenges come from within the church, and include (a) training of church leaders, (b) financial support for church workers and their families, (c) resources and facilities for education programs as well as for worship, and (d) participation in the ecumenical movement.

External challenges come from outside the church. Among these external challenges are the following:

Religion. The Philippines is a Christian country. It is one of only two countries in all of Asia with a population that is predominantly Christian, 80 percent of which is Roman Catholic.[1]

---

1. The other country is East Timor. The most recent statistics tell us that the Philippine population of about 80 million consists of the following: Roman Catholic (80%); Protestant-Evangelical (10%); Islam (5%), and others (5%).

Age of Population. The Philippines is a very young country. Recent statistics indicate that children (newborn to eighteen) constitute approximately 40 percent of the population.[2]

Poverty. The Philippines is a poor country. The latest government reports indicate that, while the annual per capita income is US$5,000, 26.9 percent of the population are below the poverty line which is set at Philippine pesos 15,000, approximately $320.

Filipino Diaspora. The Philippines is a country of overseas workers. Filipinos are scattered throughout the world working as caregivers, domestic helpers, doctors, nurses, musicians, teachers, construction workers, and crew members in ships.

Violence. There are two groups that are engaged in armed conflict with the government: the left-oriented National People's Army and various Islamic liberation groups in Southern Philippines.

Graft and Corruption. The Philippines is listed as one of the most corrupt countries in Asia. The government is plagued with anomalies, suspicious deals, and lack of transparency.

What does it mean to make disciples of Jesus Christ in such a context? Due to space limitations, I will concentrate on three challenges, namely, the predominance of the Roman Catholic Church, poverty, and the youthful nature of the population. The paper will end with a brief statement on the place of the local church in the ministry of making disciples.

A Predominantly Roman Catholic Context

Biblical Images

Psalm 133. The first verse says: "How wonderful it is, how pleasant, for God's people to live together in harmony!"[3] This Psalm is primarily concerned with the unity of God's people.

---

2. Recent statistics are as follows: Ages 0–14 (35.4%); 15–19 (4%); 20–24 (3%); 25–29 (2.5%); 30–39 (4.5%), and 40–49 (3.3%).

3. All Bible quotations are from Today's English Version (TEV), also known as *Good News for Modern Man.*

Ephesians 1:8–10, 4:4–6. In Eph 1:10, we are told that God has a secret plan for the world, and that is, to bring all things together in heaven and on earth, with Christ as head. This plan of God, while not yet fully fulfilled, is now demonstrated in the church, with its sevenfold unity, as expressed in Eph 4:4–6: one body, one Spirit, one hope, one Lord, one faith, one baptism, one God.

John 17:20–23. Unity is not self-serving, but missional; it is evangelistic. The unity of Christ's followers has as its main purpose the conversion of the world from unbelief to belief. Jesus prays that his followers "may be completely one, in order that the world may know that you sent me."

Strategy and Approach

How does one engage in the task of making disciples in a country that is predominantly Roman Catholic? It was so much easier in pre-Vatican II days, when Roman Catholics and Protestants were not on talking terms, when Catholics claimed salvation only for themselves and when Protestants did not regard Roman Catholics as Christians. In those days, conversion was usually understood as moving from the Roman Catholic Church to a Protestant denomination.

The Second Vatican Council changed all that. Roman Catholics began to regard non-Roman Catholic Christians as "separated brethren." But it was much more than that in the Philippines. It had to do with the place of the Bible in the Roman Catholic Church. Vatican II has encouraged, in fact required, Roman Catholics to make available the Bible in local languages. And so it was that in the late 1960s, the Roman Catholic Church in the Philippines entered into a partnership with the Philippine Bible Society in the translation of the Bible in the eight major languages of the Philippines.[4] Inter-confessional translation teams were organized for this purpose. So for the first time in the history of Christianity in the Philippines, Roman Catholic priests and lay people sat around the table with Protestants. Today, inter-confessional translations of the whole Bible are available in all eight major Philippine languages.

---

4. The eight major languages are (from North to South): Ilokano, Pangasinan, Pampango, Tagalog, Bikol, Cebuano, Hiligaynon, and Samareno (or Waray-waray).

The most recent development in this regard is a program called the "May They Be One" campaign, which is a partnership between the Philippine Bible Society and the Roman Catholic Church. The goal of the program is to distribute one million Bibles every year for a period of five years. Most of these Bibles are earmarked for poor families. For most Roman Catholics, this will be their first opportunity to own and read a Bible. The Roman Catholic Church is now conducting Bible orientation seminars for their own members, and also cooperating with the Philippine Bible Society in holding seminars in many parts of the country under a program called "Bible Relevance for Modern Times."

These developments have tremendous implications for Methodists as they carry out the mandate of making disciples of Jesus Christ. For one thing, they need to rediscover the primacy of the scriptures. Somehow, they have viewed all four parts of the Wesleyan quadrilateral (Scripture, tradition, experience, and reason) as equal, and sometimes even regard "experience" as the most important, when, in fact, scripture is the most important of the four, and authenticates the other three. If this is so, then there is a need to promote Bible knowledge and Bible use in local congregations. Corollary to this is the need for church leaders who are knowledgeable in biblical scholarship and capable of providing leadership in the utilization of the Scriptures for individual and congregational development.

Additionally, Methodists need to have a different mindset in their attitude towards Roman Catholics. The general attitude has been that Roman Catholics are people to be won over to the true church. To be sure, this still has its place. It is always true that making disciples involves inviting people to join a particular faith community. In fact, United Methodist churches are growing in many parts of the country, and most of those joining on profession of faith come from the Roman Catholic Church. The Roman Catholic leadership has acknowledged their inability to provide adequate nurture for all their members. Their own statistics show that less than 20 percent of all Catholics attend mass regularly. A goal of evangelism then is to reach the unchurched and provide them with the opportunity to be part of a worshipping and nurturing faith community. It is logical to conclude that many Roman Catholics who are exposed to the Scriptures will find a home in many non-Roman Catholic faith communities. But while this is the case, this is a small victory compared with the transformation of The Roman

Catholic Church into a Bible-focused church and of Roman Catholics into Bible-focused Christians, that is, people who own, read, and live the Scriptures. What would happen in the Philippines if those who call themselves Christians begin to take seriously the written word? Isn't it possible that many of them would be led from the written to the living Word? As in the words of the popular hymn: "Beyond the sacred page, I seek thee Lord, my spirit pants for thee, O Living Word!"

What then is the proper attitude towards these developments? For one thing, Methodists should encourage Catholics to participate actively in the programs of Bible formation in their own local congregations. Furthermore, they should take every opportunity to join with the Roman Catholics in ecumenical programs, especially those that have as their primary aim the enthronement of the scriptures in Filipino homes. This is simply to say that, when dealing with Roman Catholics, the primary goal is not to make them leave the Roman Catholic Church, but to encourage them to discover as Catholics what it means to be disciples of Jesus Christ. Of course if they express a desire to join a United Methodist congregation, then they should be welcomed with open arms.

Poverty

Biblical Images

One of the most significant events in the Gospels related to material need is the feeding of the five thousand, a story found in all four Gospels. The account in John 6 bears in a special way upon missional concerns, that is, in the participation of a young boy in the episode.

"Another of his disciples, Andrew, who was Simon Peter's brother, said, 'There is a boy here who has five loaves of barley bread and two fish'" (John 6:8–9a, TEV).

Barley is the grain, not of the rich, but of the poor.[5] The mention of barley bread identifies the young boy as belonging to the poor and not to the wealthy. That this unnamed young boy becomes the means of meeting the needs of thousands of people opens up this story for appropriate application to our present situation.

---

5. See Achtemeier, *Harper's Bible Dictionary*, 97.

Very often, Christians define people as either givers or receivers. The givers do things for others, while the receivers benefit from the good deeds of others. The givers are the "haves," those who are prosperous and have much more than they need. The receivers are the "have-nots," those whose daily existence can be described as from hand to mouth, and nothing more. The givers are subjects, the receivers are objects.

The young boy with five loaves of barley bread changes all that. He is not the recipient but the source of abundant blessings. His story reminds us that the poor have dignity and value; they are not simply objects of charity, but sources of love as well. Poor people also know how to give, they know how to be concerned for others, and they know what it means to be generous. The poor are equally capable of receiving love and giving love.

Strategy and Approach

Working with and among the poor opens up huge possibilities. At the outset, it should be affirmed that the proclamation of the gospel is still primary. The poor among us need to hear the gospel as it is, namely, good news for them. However, for this to happen, the gospel needs to touch not only their minds and hearts, but also their bodies. In other words, the poor need to see the gospel as relevant, not only for their spiritual well being, but for their physical and material well being as well. To achieve this, there is a need for a holistic understanding and application of the gospel. As John Wesley puts it, there is no holiness except social holiness. The gospel message should be for the whole person.

Examples of this holistic approach abound in the Philippine church, mentioning a few of which will have to suffice.

MODELO. This program, which young adults started and developed, illustrates clearly the holistic approach to the gospel. It was first known as MODE, which stands for medical, optical, dental, and evangelism. Then it became MODEL, with L standing for livelihood. And presently, it is known as MODELO, with O standing for Organization. How does MODELO work? A volunteer group is formed consisting of doctors, opticians, dentists, social workers and church workers. This group visits isolated villages, provides medical treatment for people, especially children, and in the evening proclaims the gospel through songs and worship. The volunteers stay only for two or three days in one village. Before the team leaves, they gather those who have responded to the call to faith in Christ and organize them into a Bible study group or a worshipping congregation. The young professional volunteers are truly incarnating Christ and demonstrating through this program their love of God, and their concern for others.

Mary Johnston College of Nursing (MJCN). Mary Johnston College of Nursing (MJCN) is a United Methodist school now connected with Philippine Christian University. An excellent school, 100 percent of its graduates consistently pass the annual board examinations for nurses. MJCN is located in the district of Tondo, which is the most densely populated part of the city of Manila. The college is in fact surrounded by huts occupied by families who otherwise would be homeless. There have been suggestions for MJCN to relocate, but instead, the college decided to relate itself in a relevant way to the communities around it, in order to demonstrate the school's commitment to the gospel of Jesus Christ. MJCN chose as its pilot project the community closest to it. This is known as Barangay 39, Zone 3, District 1, Tondo, Manila. Activities in the barangay include the organization of a mothers club, feeding programs for children, seminars on infant health care, including breast-feeding, and recreational community activities like a beauty pageant for pregnant women and a barangay-wide Christmas program. While there are no organized worship services, there are Bible study groups especially among mothers. People are also invited and encouraged to attend a nearby United Methodist Church. Through this program, the barangay people have developed a very positive attitude toward the MJCN and a deeper appreciation of the gospel, which has become incarnate in their midst.

Kapatiran Kaunlaran Foundation Incorporated (KKFI). An excellent example of holistic ministry is that of Kapatiran Kaunlaran ["Brotherhood-sisterhood Progress"] Foundation Incorporated (KKFI), formerly known as the Methodist Social Center. KKFI "was born as a response to the challenge to work among and with the poor in their struggle for genuine human development." Two of its most important ministries are The Ethelou D. Talbert Shelter for Street Children (Girls), which was opened on April 12, 1999, and the Gilead Center for Children. The ministry of these centers includes both the physical and spiritual care of the children. KKFI also works with local churches, helping them to be involved in their own communities. As a result, many local churches have become centers of holistic ministry, not only for their own members but for the communities around them. Local church programs include livelihood projects and community cooperatives.

Holistic ministry is, indeed, a very appropriate strategy of mission in the context of poverty and want.

Ministry to Children

Biblical Images

A close reading of the gospels clearly reveals the exalted place of the child in society. A Jew from the obscure town of Nazareth (Can any good come out of Nazareth?) demonstrates great wisdom. When some irresponsible and uncaring adults prevented children from coming to Jesus, Jesus rebuked them with this statement: "Let the children come to me, and do not stop them, because the Kingdom of God belongs to such as these. I assure you that whoever does not receive the Kingdom of God like a child will never enter it." The passage then continues, "Then he took the children in his arms, placed his hands on each of them, and blessed them" (Mark 10:14–16). At another time, when the disciples were arguing about who was the greatest among them, Jesus made a little child to stand in front of them, put his arms around the child and then said to his disciples: "Whoever welcomes in my name one of these children, welcomes me; and whoever welcomes me, welcomes not only me but also the one who sent me" (Mark 9:37). Jesus made one's attitude toward children a litmus test of faithfulness to the rule of God!

Strategy and Approach

Engaging in the ministry of disciple-making in the context of a young population means putting emphasis on children. What are the goals of ministry to children? One answer is to make sure that every child that is born into this world (or in this case Philippine society) is wanted, planned for, cared for, and loved as a human being worthy of the love of God himself. If this is so, then how does one even begin to talk about ministry to children? The challenges are so tremendous. The needs are so great and the resources are so scarce.

Despite the scarcity of resources, there are expressions of concern for children especially in the faith communities. There are homes for orphans. An interchurch body known as the "Ecumenical Bishops Initiative for Children and Families" (EBICF), established in 2001, promotes the interest of children and families. Similarly, the Philippine Interfaith Network for Children (PHILINC) advocates the rights and needs of children.

The United Methodist Church, in particular, embraces this ministry in several ways. First, there is a program of making local churches child-friendly. This program includes making sure that in every local church, there is no hungry child, no unschooled child, and no unwanted child. To state it positively, every local church should ensure that the material and medical needs of the children are taken care of, that every child in every Methodist family is in school, and that there is adequate education and counseling for parents and prospective parents. Making the church child-friendly also includes the implementation of attractive Christian education programs for children, in order to ensure that the needs of children are taken care of in so far as Christian nurture is concerned.

Second, many local churches have programs of early childhood education through their kindergarten schools. Most of the teachers of these kindergarten schools are commissioned deaconesses. In these schools there is a happy blending between secular and religious concerns. The quality and standards of early childhood education are enhanced as they are molded together with a healthy spiritual emphasis, and all of these are done without a spirit of sectarianism. It is no surprise then that these schools are positively regarded by the community, as indicated by the fact that the majority of children attending come from other faith communities. This situation creates an opportunity for Christian leaders in the schools to live out the gospel message for children and on behalf of children. They demonstrate Christian virtues, and children and their parents are exposed to what Christian faith is all about. Although evangelism is not the main purpose of these kindergarten schools, it is not unusual for children and their parents to become members of local Methodist churches as a result of their children's participation. It is not also unusual for many adults who have attended these schools to speak about how their attendance in these schools has played a very positive role in their lives.

The Place of the Local Church

A very important question to ask is what is the place of the local church in the ministry of making disciples? The local church is the starting point and locus of mission. One reason for the increase of local congregations in the Philippines is the basic understanding that a vital part of the mission of every congregation is the need to start new congregations and to plant new churches.

But the ministry of the local church goes beyond church planting. It is the place where the gospel is incarnated, and where people are nurtured and enabled to incarnate the gospel in their own contexts. Thus, while the growth in the number of organized congregations is very encouraging, there is also a great need to strengthen existing congregations and to enable them to more adequately fulfill their mission. How is this done? There are many necessary ingredients, including properly trained church workers, active lay leadership, and adequate financial resources. Strengthening local congregations is in fact the greatest challenge for the Philippine church.

Conclusion

The ministry of making disciples of Jesus Christ for the transformation of the world is a challenging task indeed. In the end, this ministry is closely linked with Jesus Christ himself. Making disciples of Jesus Christ includes incarnating Christ in the midst of society. To incarnate Christ is to follow his example. He prayed for the unity of all God's children. He identified with the poor, the sick, the forgotten, the outcasts, women, and even prostitutes. He fed the hungry; he healed the sick; he raised the dead; he comforted the sorrowing. He loved children and considered them as most important in the kingdom of God. The church is Christ's body and can do no less.

9

Making Disciples in Singapore
Challenges and Opportunities

Robert M. Solomon

AFTER HIS RESURRECTION, BUT BEFORE HIS ASCENSION INTO HEAVEN, Jesus identified the salient characteristics of Christian discipleship and articulated the missionary task of the church. He left critical instructions with his disciples in Matt 28:18–20 and Acts 1:8. These two passages contain important principles that form the backdrop for disciple-making in Singapore.

Firstly, *Jesus commissions his followers to make disciples.* His command establishes the central purpose of the community gathered around his name. Christians cannot be satisfied in producing converts only, but must proceed to make disciples. This calling involves evangelism (reaching out to the lost), baptism (incorporating converts into the church), and teaching (with a view to urge obedience that will lead to a life of holiness and love). This principle stands at the heart of the Wesleyan missional imperative.

Secondly, *the initiative to make disciples belongs to the triune God.* It is the Father who sent his Son and Spirit to save the world and reconcile the world to himself. The Son gave himself on the cross to save the world so that whoever believes in him will be saved. It is the Spirit who indwells and empowers believers to embrace their mission to make disciples.

The story of how Methodism began in Singapore illustrates this wonderfully. A party of four led by Bishop James Thoburn arrived in Singapore from India on February 7, 1885. They were surprised to find a stranger, Charles Philips, waiting for them at the dock when they disembarked. There had been no opportunity to send advanced notice to anyone in Singapore concerning their arrival. Thoburn was perplexed and asked Philips how he knew they were coming. He testified to the fact that he had seen them the previous night in a dream. He saw their steamer coming into the harbor, and the mission party just as they were at that moment. He was at the dock, therefore, waiting to welcome them and invited them immediately to stay with him at his home.

Thirdly, *God makes disciples through the witness of his children.* Witnesses do witnessing; disciples make disciples. The foundation of the Christian life is one's identity as a child of God redeemed by Christ. Everything that Christians do derives from who they are. Witnesses are those who have and are experiencing the grace of God. Disciples are those who are obeying Christ and living a life of holy love for God and neighbor. A living relationship with God—a vibrant interiority—and a developing, transparent, Christ-like character are constituent parts of disciple-making. Without these qualities of authenticity, techniques, programs, material, and campaigns are useless.

Fourthly, *the scope of the great commission is global.* Truly, the "world is our parish," for Methodists (all Christians, in fact) are called to go to the whole world with the good news of Jesus Christ.

Background Statistics

The Methodist Church in Malaysia and Singapore became autonomous in 1968, at which time the number of Methodist adult members in Singapore totaled almost 9,000. In 1976 this Church became two autonomous Churches, at which time the adult membership in the Methodist Church in Singapore (MCS) was about 10,000. Today, in 2009, the membership has grown to more than 36,000. This significant growth in membership follows the pattern of the growth of the churches in Singapore, in general, where the proportion of Christians in the nation was 6.8 percent in 1970 and 14.6 percent in 2000.

There are many reasons for this spectacular growth: evangelical emphases in the churches, effective ministry among young people, evangelistic parachurch organizations working alongside churches, intentional evangelistic programs, and the evangelistic enthusiasm of converts who formed a significant part of the church. But numbers do not tell the whole story, and disciple-making is not just about numbers. Whether there has been effective disciple-making depends on answers to other significant questions. What is the quality of discipleship among the members? Are they growing in holiness and love for God and neighbor? Do they show evidence of "faith expressing itself through love" (Gal 5:6)? Do they care for the poor and needy in society? Are they making disciples themselves? Significant evidence supports a positive response to deeper questions such as these. Many members are deeply committed disciples who practice genuine faith and are actively involved in discipling others. This does not mean, however, that there are no serious challenges to faithful discipleship in Singapore. Several challenges are immediately apparent.

Challenges in Singapore

Living in a Multi-Religious Society

Singapore is a radically pluralistic society with multiple religious traditions in the following proportion: 42.5 percent Buddhists, 14.9 percent Muslims, 14.6 percent Christians, 8.5 percent Taoists, 4 percent Hindus, and 14.8 percent with no religion.[1] While this profile immediately presents Singapore society as a mission field for evangelism and disciple-making, it also shows the difficulties that exist in this multi-religious society.

Firstly, *religious sensitivity*. There is ongoing (and increasing) sensitivity about evangelism when people of other faiths complain, from time to time, about proselytizing and aggressive forms of Christian evangelism. Church leaders have to give assurances that the church does not promote coercive forms of evangelism, while also pointing out that evangelism is an integral part of Christian discipleship. In this respect, 1 Pet 3:15 provides a model in which evangelism is essential to Christian witness, but in which the evangelist is called to be sensitive, wise, and winsome. It is best, as the Methodist missionary to India, Stanley Jones, pointed out, to focus on preaching Christ instead of running down other people's religions.

There are times when some Christians forget this, and get into trouble. Recently a Christian couple was charged in court for sedition; they were accused of sending evangelistic tracts (considered to be offensive) to Muslims. These tracts were published in America and had such

---

1. Based on the national census in 2000.

provocative titles as *The Little Bride* and *Who is Allah?*[2] This incident points out the danger of importing methods and material from other cultures and using them indiscriminately. As a general rule, evangelism should be done winsomely and by pointing to Jesus rather than aggressively taking an adversarial stance. In any particular multi-religious society, greater sensitivity is needed, and relations with other religious communities have to be managed well.

Secondly, *finding culturally appropriate methods*. In such a context, friendship evangelism is particularly necessary and effective, rather than big rallies. In 1978, a Billy Graham Crusade was held in Singapore at the National Stadium, attracting a crowd of 60,000 every night for a week. Thousands of people came forward to receive Christ or dedicate their lives to him. It is interesting that thirty years later, in December 2008, the Billy Graham Association had another nation-wide evangelistic campaign ("My Hope Singapore"), but this time, it was not a big rally, but a totally different approach. Churches were encouraged to get families and small groups to invite their friends and relatives to their homes to show specially produced videos, share their testimonies, and present the gospel. This change in approach reflects the changes that have taken place in society—greater postmodern influences and increased sensitivities about Christian evangelism.

Thirdly, *avoiding a superficial vision of faith*. The fastest growing religion in Singapore is Buddhism. This is in part due to a shift among the majority Chinese from the more traditional Taoism to the increasingly modernized forms of Buddhism. Being adapted to the modern life, Buddhism has a growing and confident presence in Singapore. It seems to cater to the needs of stressed out working people and professionals by offering meditation and other forms of stress relief. Publications and other educational programs have enhanced confidence among Buddhists.

A personal story reflects a central concern. Several years ago, a young undergraduate in a local university told me about his experience in reaching out to his Buddhist friend. When asked why he did not want to become a Christian, even though he understood the key concepts about the Christian gospel, his friend told him, "I find your gospel too simplistic. In Buddhism there is a more elegant and well-developed

---

2. "Couple found guilty of sending seditious tracts," *Straits Times* (May 29, 2009) A10.

psychology that explains what goes on within us. Why should I give that up to embrace your faith?"

This statement reveals much. Some Christians have portrayed their faith, simplistically, as a means of salvation from hell. A Wesleyan theology of salvation, however, seeks to grasp the entire purpose of salvation, not only the removal of our guilt through forgiveness, but also the healing of our sinful nature. It focuses more on the process by which God restores authentic life, makes the believer more and more like Christ, and perfects the disciple in love. Unfortunately, the modern church seems to have forgotten the importance of discipling, which takes all this into consideration. Many people today are seeking a way that has depth and substance, and the Wesleyan tradition has much to offer in this regard, particularly its holistic spirituality that entails life-shaping practices and the intimate sharing of deep questions about life. Some are recovering this vision, engaging in small group instruction, retreats, spiritual formation groups, and other disciple-shaping activities. More of this is needed.

Worldly Consumerism

It may be easy to take people out of the world, but it is much more difficult to take the world out of people. The global patterns of consumerism and individualism that increasingly influence people all over the world present a serious challenge to disciple-making. The pursuit of "the good life" can threaten the pursuit of Christ. Scripture demonstrates how godly knowledge and deep insight are necessary to discern what is best (Phil 1:9–11), whereas the pursuit of the good life often inhibits interest in the best life, "the life that is truly life" (1 Tim 6:19).

Part of the problem may be the preaching of an inadequate or distorted gospel. It is true that many become Christians because they are healed or their immediate problems are solved (and there is a place for what has been called "power encounter"). It is important to go beyond this, however, for the gospel really addresses the core human problems of sin and death. Disciples of Christ must learn how to present the Christian answer to these profound questions in such a way, therefore, that people experience the liberation from sin and death made possible through Christ's redemptive work. This means that discipleship involves surrender and consecration. Jesus taught that unless people are willing to trust him deeply and follow him wholeheartedly, they cannot be his disciples (Luke 14:26, 27, 33—he emphasized this three times). This call to discipleship comes as a big challenge to a world of individualistic consumers. Several implications spill out of disciple-making that attends to these kinds of issues.

Firstly, there is a call to *a deeper relationship with Jesus*. John Wesley preached that self- denial requires embracing God's will over our own.[3] It leads to a self-forgetfulness in the glorious and majestic presence of God. Those who relate to Christ more deeply experience a growing freedom from self-imposed prisons; they are freed to love and serve. This also entails a serious concern about the presence of indwelling sin and the desire to live free from habitual, intentional, and conscious sins—a Wesleyan emphasis. In addition to preaching and teaching about this deeper walk with Christ, churches encourage small groups that promote mutual encouragement and accountability, annual "church camps" where church members gather together for teaching, encouragement, and extended times of deeper fellowship—something reminiscent of the early Wesleyan camp meetings.

Secondly, Christians are encouraged to become aware of *the needs of the poor and marginalized* in society, and to be involved in ministering to them and walking with them. This is another key Wesleyan emphasis. Concern for those in need demands that Christians embrace a simpler lifestyle, that they overcome the temptation to pursue consumerist addictions and assist the poor actively. In 1981, the Methodist Welfare Services (MWS) was formed in the MCS to help bring together Methodists in their efforts to reach out to the poor and needy. The MWS now has thirteen services ranging from nursing homes for the elderly to family service centers that help families in crisis or distress. Organizational platforms and programs alone are insufficient. Helping others who are less fortunate should become second nature to all disciples of Christ.

In Jesus' parable of true friendship (Luke 10:25–37), the Good Samaritan was probably a frequent traveler on dangerous roads—perhaps even a fellow victim to the evils of that day. If that is so, his own personal experience of pain and victimization would have helped him to become empathetic to others. He also seems to have carried a "first aid kit" which he readily used to minister to the wounded man.

---

3. See John Wesley's sermon, "Self-denial" in Wesley, *Works*, 2:238–50.

He had a habit of doing ministry and lived in such a way that he used his resources to help others. Engaging in God's mission and ministry and embracing personal sacrifice are not so much programmatic aspects of church life as they are a lifestyle that the disciple chooses to live. This life in Christ can be exhibited in simple ways. For instance, when visiting poorer countries, why not bring some extra money to bless the people there, instead of seeking for bargains and haggling over the price when purchasing things?

Thirdly, discipleship entails *involvement in God's mission*. The disciple who seeks to bring the gospel to other places and is personally involved in the process learns to go beyond himself or herself. In this regard, the MCS established the Methodist Missionary Society in 1991 to bring together Methodists in mission. Over the years, the work has expanded to embrace six countries in the region, where churches are being planted, people are being discipled, leaders are being trained, and social needs are being met through orphanages, and educational, agricultural, and health initiatives. A surprising number of churches, families, small groups, and individuals have become involved in this work. Many mission teams visit the Church's mission fields; people are deeply affected and many of their lives are transformed. Embracing this global parish and recognizing the needs of others near and far goes a long way in helping people to become faith disciples of Jesus.

Another noteworthy reality is the significant presence of workers from overseas. There are about a million such workers in Singapore bringing the total population to 4.8 million. The church has been quick to recognize the opportunities that exist as the world is brought to our doorstep and into our homes. Churches have launched ministries that include the provision of medical and legal help to the workers. They offer meals and other kinds of material assistance in addition to finding ways to share the gospel with them. As a result, many come to know Christ. In one church, every month, about thirty workers from China are baptized. Many of these people return home and carry the gospel with them. Others find opportunities to pursue theological education and become fulltime Christian workers in their homelands.

The Centrality of Grace

Discipleship has to do essentially with relationships—our relationship with God and with others. In a world that has come to worship techniques, methods, and skills, it is important to remember this as Christians are discipled. David Gill has warned against the "Technical Trinity": the quest for quantifiable growth, measurable success, and rational efficiency.[4] It is in such contexts that we need to nurture disciples over and above our methods and programs.

The early Methodists had a clear method of Christian living. John Wesley believed in a practical Christianity—a life lived out in Christ in a disciplined way. He talked about works of piety (prayer, scripture reading, fellowship, Eucharist, fasting) and works of mercy (almsgiving, visiting the prisons, ministering to the sick, social action) as basic methods of Christian discipleship, besides the General Rules to do no harm, do good, and observe the ordinances of God. Rediscovering the heart or goal of Wesley's method provides a helpful foundation for disciple-making today. In *The Character of a Methodist*, Wesley defines a Methodist as "one who loves God with all his heart and loves his neighbor as himself." He encouraged disciples to strive for Christian perfection, understood as perfection in love. In other words, the spiritual methods of Wesley were means to an end; the goal toward which they moved was the fullest possible love of God and loving relationships with all people. It is dangerous to pursue or to become fascinated with methods as ends in themselves, as this can lead to the worship of the tools and techniques marketed today in the globalised Christian marketplace. How easy it is to become slaves to fads of the age.

In reality, the spiritual life can only be managed up to a point. Ultimately, it is God who gives growth (1 Cor 3:6). Amid the many versions of managed spirituality in the world today, it is crucial to rediscover God's grace. Heaven cannot be moved by spiritual techniques alone, if at all. People cannot even change themselves in fully satisfying ways; rather, the grace of God changes the lives of those who open themselves to its transforming power. This grace is received, not by pressing some spiritual buttons, but by waiting with faith for the Lord. Contemporary Christians face the temptation of trying to increase their control on themselves, others, and especially heaven. This danger calls

---

4. Gill, *Opening of the Christian Mind*, 43.

for a paradigm shift in which the Spirit of God shapes and controls all aspects of the disciple's life. As people shift their trust in technology and techniques to the grace of God, they will be transformed. In stillness and silence, they encounter and receive this grace. In the noisy urban environment in which most people live today, they need to rediscover silence, solitude, and stillness, which are part and parcel of classical Christian discipleship—disciplines urgently needed today.

The wrong use of spiritual methods makes people ask the technical question, "How?" rather than the moral question, "Why?" or the spiritual question, "Who?" The notion that spiritual progress is achieved by mastering spiritual techniques and tools becomes dominant whenever people fail to realize that the heart of all the spiritual methods is a wholehearted love for God. Genuine Christianity, in other words, is thoroughly relational in nature. Those who come to this realization stop looking breathlessly for the latest method that "works" and start opening their hearts to God. They learn to discover God on the roads less travelled, guided by the signposts of countless saints who have completed their journey in Christ. After all, in growing a relationship, methods are limited. There are some places methodical roads just can't go.

> William Stafford's poem puts it very well.
> They want a wilderness with a map
> but how about errors that give a new start?
> or leaves that are edging into the light?
> or the many places a road can't find?[5]

For Wesley, the process of making disciples was not technique, but relationship, not an achievement or performance, but a love. Spiritual methods are like servants who escort seekers to the door of the king and quietly leave them there to enter. They are like vehicles on roads from which one must alight, in order to walk in love with the Lord in a world that he is reconciling to himself.

---

5. Stafford, *Glass Face in the Rain*, 65.

10

The Spread of Missionary Congregations in Korea

Jong Chun Park

From the Land of Morning Calm to the Land of Evangelistic Power

FROM TIME IMMEMORIAL KOREANS HAVE BEEN A PEACE LOVING people. During the long history of five thousand years, Korea has been invaded numberless times by others, but never invaded any countries themselves. How many times the white linen clothes of the Korean people have been soaked with blood! What a destiny! And what a divine dispensation! How long, Lord, had Koreans waited for vindication? How long, Lord, had Korean people yearned for the atoning blood of Jesus Christ!

From the end of the nineteenth century to the middle of the twentieth century, the suffering of Korean people reached its peak. When the cruel rule of the longest Confucian regime in world history was over, the imperial powers of the West and of Japan took hold of Korea. Korea stood at the geo-political crossroad of four big nations; China, Russia, Japan and the United States of America. Certainly, Korea was a most uncomfortable and dangerous place. Yet it was the very place of the divine presence, God healing the wounds of the broken-hearted people.

The history of modern Korea is a history of thorns and thistles. It has gone through the loss of national sovereignty, Japanese colonial rule, the division of the nation by the United States and the Soviet Union, and the Korean War. Nevertheless, it is precisely through this history of suffering that God has been leading this nation with the grace and truth of the gospel. About a hundred years ago, the flame of an amazing revival rose up in this land—the Great Revival launched in 1903 at Wonsan by a Spirit-filled Methodist missionary named Robert Hardy. And the movement exploded in 1907 from Pyungyang to all over Korea.

Presbyterian missionary William Blair testified with great passion how God had prepared the Korean people for the gospel in their history of suffering and shame:

> The simple truth is that the Koreans are a broken-hearted people. . . . Now with respect to this world, at least, they know just where they stand. They know they are despised and rejected. The arrow had entered Korea's soul. Her spirit was broken. For years now she has been sitting in the dust, mourning not only her present misfortunes, but her past sins. Over such a stricken people has God so often stretched out his hands in blessing? By brokenness of spirit, Korea has been prepared for the Gospel, and when a further work of God's Spirit was manifested the Scripture was again fulfilled: "the sacrifices of God are a broken spirit; a broken and a contrite heart, O God, thou will not despise."[1]

A broken-hearted people! God wanted to save such a people. In his sermon "The Circumcision of the Heart," John Wesley also mentioned that a broken-hearted people are alive unto God, and dead to the world.[2] Indeed the broken-hearted Korean Christians of a hundred years ago must have been alive only unto God, and dead to the empires of the world.

My father who passed away many years ago was an excellent tenor. He used to sing his favorite hymn "The Bright, Heavenly Way" (*Korean-English Hymnal*, 545) at every funeral service of his church members. When I was a small boy, I thought the hymn was only useful for funerals. Recently I learned that the hymn, just like every other great hymn, was composed at a significant historical time. Korean Christians loved to sing this hymn from the time Korea lost her sovereignty to Japan in 1905. The hymn well describes a broken-hearted people who were dead to the empires of the world, but alive to the kingdom of God.

> The bright, heav'nly way, before me, lies clearly in my sight;
> And though sorrows sore beset me, and troubles black as night,

---

1. Blair and Hunt, *Korean Pentecost*, 25.
2. Wesley, *Works*, 1:401.

> At the splendor from the skies, Ev'ry darkling shadow flies,
> While we trust the grace of Jesus, and look ever to that Light.
>
> When I think on all the troubles, which in my world I see,
> Inner fears and outer trials seem nigh too much for me;
> But the precious blood of Christ, Overcomes my fears and trials,
> While we trust the grace of Jesus, and shall ever victors be.
>
> Drawing nearer to that city, yet seen by faith alone,
> Longing for the Father's mansions, and rest before the throne,
> All unworthy though I be, there is welcome there for me,
> For the King is our own Jesus, Lord and Savior of His own.

The kingdom on earth disappeared. The true kingdom, however, that glorious kingdom of God, was right there in heaven. And the king was there as well. Therefore, the Korean Christians believed they had lost nothing. This hymn expressed their understanding of history according to faith.

By the grace and power of God, this land of "Morning Calm" has turned into the land of "Evangelistic Power." The suffering people of Korea traveled the trail of tears from Manchuria and Vladivostok to Siberia and Central Asia, from Incheon and Pusan to Hawaii and Mexico. The gracious God has turned the trail of tears into a highway for the gospel. The Korean Diaspora around the world has become the frontier of global mission for the Korean church. The formation of missionary congregations in the history of the early Korean church consists of three stages: first, the translation of the Bible by both missionaries and their Korean helpers and the propagation of the Bible by Korean colporteurs and Bible women (1893–1910); second, the internalization of biblical language and the formation of faith communities through the collective experience of repentance in the Great Revival (1903–1907); third, Korean Christians' participation in the liberation of the suffering people through the education, the discipline, and the nation-wide networks of the churches (1919–1945). A theological interpretation or analysis of these paradigmatic experiences of the early Korean church provides a window into the nature of disciple-making in this context.

The Korean Bible and the Revolution of God: "Calling Out" Missionary Congregations

The significance of the translation of the Bible into Korean cannot be compared to that of the Protestant reformers' translation of the Bible into German or English. The appearance of the Korean Bible caused the "Revolution of God" in the history of Korean religions. No classics of Confucianism and Buddhism were translated into Korean and almost all Koreans suffered illiteracy. The early Korean Christians learned the Korean script while they read the Korean Bible. Through the koinonia of the saints who shared the Bible, they acquired communicative competence in socio-ethical discourse with their fellow men and women. The nationwide propagation of the Bible by the colporteurs and the Bible women broke the ground by new local faith communities all around Korea.

In East Asia, the Buddhist classics were owned and read exclusively by the elite monks. The lay Buddhists belonged to a popular Buddhism amalgamated with shamanism. The Confucian classics were also the properties of the literati class who considered Chinese characters the true script while they looked down on their own vernacular script which was used by women and common people. The Korean translation of the Bible helped the vast majority of people break away from ignorance and age-old bondage to seek autonomy and maturity.

The Great Revival in 1907 was achieved by the *sakyunghoe* (Bible examining meeting), which was a collective Bible class combined with a prayer meeting. This meeting incorporated into the open community of faith the countless people who were excluded from the privileged Confucian or Buddhist communities that owned and interpreted the traditional religious classics. The emergence of this unique Christian community of interpretation was the starting point for a universal community of love and justice open to all regardless of class, sex, and race. One of the remarkable aspects of the early Korean church was its collective reading and interpretation of the Bible. The missionaries' reports about the Great Revival usually described the collective confession of sin and the outpouring of the Holy Spirit. It is worthy to note that any open confession of sin was an alien practice for East Asians. Unless the early Korean Christians had encountered the Word of God in the Bible, it would not have been possible for them to be convicted of sin in front of God.

Korea became a Japanese protectorate in 1905. A resistance movement of the "righteous army," mainly consisting of Confucian scholars and their peasant followers, grew to its peak in 1907. The enormous sense of helplessness and hopelessness prevalent in those times may have made the early Korean Christians spiritually poor so that they could become open to the message of the kingdom of God. Through reading the Gospels, they encountered the compassionate heart of Jesus Christ. Jesus had compassion on a large crowd (*ochlos*) who were like sheep without a shepherd (Mark 6:34). The Korean *minjung* who were described by J. Z. Moore, Methodist missionary, as "lazy, shiftless, and purposeless," became the "dynamos of evangelistic power" when they were adopted as the children of God by their faith in Jesus Christ, the Son of God.[3]

The scandal as well as the power of the gospel in the early Korean mission was derived from the father-son relationship rooted in the Bible. It is impossible in Confucianism to think of God as a Father who has a Son. The father-son relationship was strictly confined to the most basic ethos of human relationships in Confucian ethics. In the eyes of Confucians, the Christian claim that Jesus is the Son of God "tends to undermine the significance of familial relationships."[4] The surprising discovery of God the Father awakened the early Korean Christians to an awareness of their adoption as the children of God. This awareness was given by the Holy Spirit's witness together with their own spirits in crying "Abba, Father!"

The conversion story of Sun-ju Kil, the most prominent leader of the Great Revival, is a good example of the typical experience of the gospel. When his Christian friend asked Kil to pray to God the Father, long-time Confucian Taoist Kil said, "How could man call God the Father?" Three days later, "while Kil was praying to God to let him know that Jesus is the true savior, . . . he heard a mysterious voice from above three times "Kil Sun-ju, Kil Sun-ju, and Kil Sun-ju!" He feared, trembled, and could not raise his head. Then he prostrated himself in prayer and cried out, "God the Father who loves me, forgive my sin and

---

3. Moore, "Great Revival Year," 118.
4. Wei-Ming, *Confucian Thought*, 123.

save my life." His body became like a ball of fire and he continued to pray earnestly.

The religious revolution that the gospel brought about did not mean a mere substitution for Buddhism and Confucianism; rather, it meant a creative transformation of traditional religions without losing the essence of the gospel. The essence of the gospel, that God the Father gave us his only Son, so that whosoever believes will have eternal life, shocked the religious and cultural sensitivities of the Korean people. Through calling God the Father, they challenged the age-old oppressive ties of familism, classism, and ageism; the arbitrary rule of many fathers in family, clan, and power structures was overthrown by the gospel of Jesus Christ. According to Confucian tradition, one "could not bypass his social relationships in order to establish an intimate connection with Heaven directly."[5] This Confucian ideology of gradual development from self-cultivation through family and state to world peace stops short at Confucian Pelagianism which could never have imagined the in-breaking grace of a heavenly Father from above.

The primary question that these new discoveries pressed was not whether God existed or not, but what characterized the nature of the true God? The primary discovery for Koreans was that this crucified God was not the "Wholly Other" who ruthlessly controlled and dominated the created world. Instead, the true God of Jesus Christ is the God who humbles or empties himself to go to the far country of this fallen world. The true God of the gospel justifies sinners whom he calls out of the world into his kingdom of light. Missionary congregations, therefore, are *ecclesia* in the truest sense of the word—communities called out of the plural forms of religions, including nominal Christianity! The gospel of the true God, revealed in Jesus Christ and written in the Bible, must be proclaimed by the missionary congregations to the people of other faiths. Missionary congregations as *ecclesia* face the possibility and the reality of persecution in every place of our world today.

---

5. Ibid., 127.

Tonsung Prayer and the Formation of Faith Community: "Up-building" Missionary Congregations

Tongsung prayer—collective audible prayer—is a typical form of Korean prayer and has been spreading all over the world. This style of prayer originated in the Great Revival of 1907. The missionaries' reports of the Great Revival described the early Korean Christians' experience of the gospel in terms of "the outpouring of the Holy Spirit," "the descending of the Spirit," "the infilling of the Holy Ghost." Despite their intentional effort to transfer the anger of Koreans who lost their nation into the consolation of a personal relationship with the Lord, it is still possible to discern the signs of a crisis consciousness in the Korean converts' collective experience of the Holy Spirit. Many Korean Christians internalized the national crisis and carried this burden into the depth of their own sense of guilt. This "hidden guilt" emerged in *tongsung* prayer and was dramatically expressed in the groans of the Spirit of God present among the people crawling over the hill of suffering. As G. S. McCune observed in his report of "the Holy Spirit in Pyengyang:"

> After Mr. Hunt's sermon Mr. Lee said a few words. The latter said, "Let us pray," and immediately the room full of men was filled with voices lifted to God in prayer. I am sure that most of the men in the room were praying aloud. It was wonderful! No man prayed with a loud voice, and yet if you would listen, you could distinguish between the different ones. Some were crying and pleading God's forgiveness for certain sins which they named to Him in prayer. All were pleading for the infilling of the Holy Ghost. Although there were so many voices, there was no confusion at all. It was all subdued, perfect harmony. I cannot explain it with words. One must sure witness such to be able to understand it. There was an absence of the sensational, the "emotional" (in the sense in which the word is so often used), and there was perfect concentration in the prayer of each one.[6]

A superficial observer would miss the deeper unity of such prayer which looked as if it were a mere collection of individual prayers. Each and every praying person sighed, pleaded, and cried out before God in a profound sense of unity. It is not uniformity erasing individuality, but unity affirming individuality. Such prayer neither robbed individuals of their community nor reduced individuals to uniformity. Instead it

6. McCune, "Holy Spirit in Pyengyang," 1.

helped an individual keep his or her concentration without confusion and in perfect harmony with the community. *Tongsung* literally means the communication of voices. In *tongsung* prayer one's voice comes out of oneself and one is surrounded by many other voices at the same time. In this regard *tongsung* prayer is the prayer of the Holy Spirit. In *tongsung* prayer, to listen to the others' prayers is as important as to raise one's voice in his or her prayer because the Spirit intercedes for him or her "with groans that words cannot express" (Rom 8:26). For Koreans, *tongsung* prayer manifests a unity-in-diversity within the community through the power of the Holy Spirit.

The early Korean Christian communities were literally the communities of both free and slave, of both man and woman, of both Westerner and Easterner. Sung-chun Park, a butcher who was considered part of the lowest class in traditional Korea, became a Christian in 1895.[7] For him to become a Christian meant to become a human being! In traditional Korea, butchers could not have jobs other than butchery. They were the outcasts of society and the scum of history. S. F. Moore, a missionary with love and courage, helped Sung-chun Park form the first community of Korean butcher Christians. Park later became an elder, a top lay leader of his integrated church along with another lay leader who belonged to the Korean royal family. One of the most important characteristics of Korean Christianity, in other words, was the way in which it enabled believers to realize their full humanity in Christ.

Moreover, the gospel of Jesus Christ reveals the true humanity of God. Using Karl Barth's phrase, it was God who went to the far country of the fallen world, but it was the human being who came home, being welcomed by the compassionate Father.[8] In Jesus Christ, God became human so that the human could become a partaker of the divine nature (2 Pet 1:4). The Spirit of God incarnate sanctifies the children of God. In sanctification we do not become God but we become fully human along with our fellow humans. And this makes possible the up-building of the missionary congregation in solidarity with all different kinds of suffering people for the sake of the Kingdom.

In the up-building of the missionary congregation there is no dichotomy between evangelization and humanization, or between personal faith and social witness. Neither faith devoid of love nor love

7. Huntley, *Caring, Growing, Changing*, 70.
8. Barth, *Church Dogmatics* IV.2, 21.

disconnected from faith, but "faith filled with the energy of love" (Gal 5:6) can build up the missionary congregations in solidarity with the groaning creation.

Evangelistic Praxis and the Liberation of People: "Sending" Missionary Congregations

Rev. Jung-do Sohn was the first missionary sent by the Korean Methodist church to China in 1909 right after the Great Revival.[9] He was converted to the gospel during the Revival when he heard the good news on the way to the government examination. He received the mandate of mission from the Holy Spirit at the Namsanhyun Methodist Church of Pyungyang as he read Acts 1: 6–8. Deeply meditating on the Word of God, Jung-do Sohn asked God, "Lord, are you at this time going to restore the Kingdom to Israel (or Korea, he might have easily thought)?" But Christ said to Sohn, "It is not for you to know the times or dates the Father has set by his own authority." Then he immediately understood the famous text of Acts 1:8 as the commandment of God for his contemporary churches: "But you will receive power when the Holy Spirit comes on you; and you will be my witness in Jerusalem, and all Judea and Samaria, and to the ends of the earth." For Sohn, Jerusalem and all Judea meant Pyungyang and all Korea, and Samaria and the ends of the earth symbolized Manchuria and China.

Rev. Sohn committed himself to a national independence movement as well as to ministry in China and Manchuria. One early morning, during his time of prayer, Sohn had a vision of the compassionate and faithful Savior, Jesus, who appeared to him with tears streaming down his face. He wept with Jesus. Immediately, he saw his twenty million male and female compatriots standing in a long line. He realized that Jesus gave him the mission to save and liberate those fallen in death and enslaved by the power of sin. In 1912, Sohn was arrested by the Japanese police and charged falsely of conspiring to assassinate the governor-general, Katsura. In prison he was brutally tortured by the Japanese. On one occasion, he was very near to death, having been tortured while hung upside down. Yet even in the very moment that his life-line became thinnest, he prayed continually. Then, once again,

---

9. Cf. Lee, *Rev. Jung-do Sohn*.

the crucified Savior, Jesus, appeared to him, filling the dark prison with light. Jesus said to Sohn, "Oh, my little son, as I know you, do not fear and do not be down cast." Sohn was moved with tears and filled with joy. Though groaning and moaning in the prison, he still danced and sang to the Lord.

Rev. Sohn trod the paths of exile in China and Manchuria. He was the first chairperson of the Parliament of the provisional Korean government in Shanghai. In 1924 he moved to Manchuria and established a Christian cooperative for Korean immigrant farmers. During his ministry in Manchuria he took care of a young orphan who later became the founder of the People's Republic of Korea, namely, the former president of North Korea, Kim Il-sung. When the youth was imprisoned for his radical socialist views, Sohn took pity on him for the sake of his late father, who was his friend. He helped liberate Kim Il-sung from the prison and cared for him, demonstrating his grace and generosity to all people. In the winter of 1931 when he returned to Manchuria after visiting his family in Beijing, and died from the consequences of the torture he had endured years before. Rev. Sohn interfaced the vertical pole of evangelism and the horizontal pole of liberation. He danced this "cross-shaped life" with the Lord and with suffering people.

God still commands the missionary congregations in Korea: "Be my witnesses in Jerusalem, and in all Judea and Samaria, and to the ends of the earth." Where is Jerusalem today? Most Christians in the Korean churches, that have been sending their missionaries all over the world and to the ends of the earth, think Seoul is the contemporary Jerusalem. They would also suggest that South Korea is Judea, one fourth of the whole population being Christian. Then where is Samaria today? Why does the Holy Spirit command that the missionary congregations have to go from Jerusalem and all Judea, not directly to the ends of the earth, but only by way of Samaria? Is Samaria a stumbling block or a stepping stone for mission?

According to the fourth chapter of the Gospel of John, Jesus Christ first reconciled Jews and Samaritans who had hated each other for many hundreds of years. When the early Christians of the New Testament viewed Jerusalem as the center of global mission, Samaria remained a stumbling block. But Jesus turned that obstruction into the stepping stone for God's mission in the world. This means that the missionary congregations in Korea today must not conceive their mission in the world apart from their neighbors to the north. The church in North Korea has survived in the midst of enormous hardships. Though the churches in the North are small in number, they are no less faithful than others who have suffered greatly. One Korean American pastor testified that she worshipped God with them in tears and even hand in hand with grey haired ladies in the North. "In Jesus Christ the whole building is joined together and rises to become a holy temple in the Lord" (Eph 2:21). When these words were written, there were no church buildings. There were no grand, gothic cathedrals, no luxurious, megachurches. Nevertheless, the true church, the true body of Christ, the true missionary congregation flourished.

The wind of the Holy Spirit blows over and beyond the walls of division. However high and thick the walls of ideology may be, the truly missionary congregation will dare to seek peace and reconciliation, something Jesus Christ has already accomplished through the hard wood of the cross. This gospel of reconciliation is not something that the church possesses; rather, it is a treasure to be offered freely to all. Only when the missionary congregation discovers its true posture in a ministry of service to the world will it be empowered by God's Spirit to be the church for the sake of God's kingdom.

11

Making Disciples in the Tongan Diaspora

Tevita M. Siuhengalu

Forty years ago, a trickle of Pacific Island people were beginning to form a small community in Australia and assembled regularly at Wesley Central Mission, Sydney, under the leadership of Rev. Dr. Alan Walker.[1] Since then, a consistent influx of Islanders invaded the east coast of New South Wales when new immigration regulations were more open to Pacific countries. As the Pacific Island Community (PIC) rapidly grew, major issues challenged this new settlement. I will focus my attention on the Tongan community and the understanding of disciple-making in this Pacific Island group.

Challenges for the Tongan Diaspora

Eagerness to leave the homeland for a better place was a major driving force causing Tongans to immigrate to places like New Zealand, Australia, and the United States. The majority of the people who wanted to leave their homeland were not well informed about their destinations and seldom checked into the harsh realities reported back by those who went before them. International news on the wireless in the Islands was not as accessible then as it is now through television and the internet.

This great wave of emigrations in the 1970s and 1980s brought a majority of highly motivated fortune hunters driven by the urgent need of a better material life. The quest for the necessities of life in a new country drove some to strip off their familial ties with home quite quickly. As they strove to settle in the new land, they were confronted with the chal-

---

1. Siuhengalu, "In Search of a New Identity," 13.

lenge of communicating in a language with which they were unaccustomed, a cold climate, and complex systems and infrastructures. Hence this transition period inevitably weakened the connection with family, culture, and religion. So, the clash of cultures and lifestyles raised serious questions of identity, family orientation, religion, and social status with which the second generation are now wrestling at school, in their families, and within the community at large. These fragile connections with their homeland compelled them to form their own communities within the new land, often very insular and ultra conservative, which then became the source of major challenges related to discipleship initiatives within their churches.

By the end of the 1970s, in this Tongan Diaspora in Australia, the desire to stay connected to the homeland, while weak, was still prevalent within the leadership of the Tongan community in New South Wales. In many cases, being perceived as outsiders and foreigners in the new land was unavoidable. The characteristic reality for most of the immigrants was that of "dis-placed persons," as Walter Brueggemann calls them, i.e., people without a place.[2] This was their experience because they had chosen to leave home, assigned their inheritance to others, and declared their homeland an unproductive place in which to live. Certainly, foreigners are almost always perceived as people who do not belong to the society at large. Simple but profound aspects of their new culture created a keen sense of disconnection from their roots, cultural traditions, and religious values. For example, they had been used to observing Sunday as a sacred day of worship when all stores and offices were closed. Now, in a much more secular habitat, they witnessed the majority of people around them playing sports on Sundays and living life like any other day.

The issue of language led to the breakdown of communication within families, between parents and children, home and school. On Sundays, a new generation of young people began to wander between the church building, where the worship service is conducted in the vernacular, and the church hall where the Sunday school was conducted primarily in English. As a consequence, many young people feel out of place in a totally Tongan-speaking fellowship and above the educational programs designed primarily for children. Their sense of being lost is poignant. Now claiming English as their first language, this wandering

---

2. Brueggemann, *Interpretation and Obedience*, 294.

generation is torn between two worlds and the tensions they experience and create reveal the deeper problem of identity crisis within the community.

During the initial phase of their time in Australia in the 1970s, those who immersed themselves in the Tongan Church were involved in the worship and ministry of Wesley Central Mission and enjoyed experiencing their cultural traditions and speaking the Tongan language. This actually precluded the attendance of non-Tongans in their services and gatherings and inadvertently inhibited their children from learning and understanding their faith. Few parents managed to cultivate an appreciation for the Tongan customs and language among their children. Many hours spent in English-speaking schools every day soon made their native tongue sound like a distant sound. The marked vulnerability of this wandering generation, yearning for a greater sense of belonging and "in search of a new identity," became the impetus for them to explore; but in which direction would they turn in this quest?

A New Community: The New Evangelism

In an effort to maintain a vital faith community, the Tongans have employed three main models for or approaches to disciple-making. While none of them is wholly new, it is worth exploring how they have been adapted to accommodate the geographical, cultural, and generational transitions. All of them have a strong foundation in pastoral evangelism within the setting of the home. They also emphasize the importance of networks for communication, nurture, and care.

The Emmaus Journey

This model is based upon Luke's account of the two disciples who walked from Jerusalem to Emmaus and the way in which Jesus joined them on the way (Luke 24:13–35). The story reveals a "there and back again" understanding of the journey from Jerusalem to Emmaus and from Emmaus to Jerusalem. In the account there is also a constant interplay among the elements of contextual experience, story-telling, reflection, and action in which Jesus and the disciples were deeply engaged. Obviously, this is not a closed circle but a *spiral* which always welcomes new situations along the way and new pilgrims or fellow travelers. The educational insights of the South American, Paulo Freire,[3] and the pastoral cycle of Laurie Green, which entails "Experience–Exploration–Reflection–Response," inform this model based in the Emmaus account.[4] This is an educational/evangelistic/discipleship model with dynamic pastoral aspects and applies particularly well to situations where Christian faith is not foreign.

Jerusalem was where the event took place and where the *experience* of the disciples took initial form. It was there that faith rose and fell, as it were. The two disciples moved slowly from the center of the faith back to an uncertain and doubtful future. On their way they never ceased talking about what they had seen and heard. Meanwhile, Jesus came and walked with them. Jesus allowed them to tell their story, which led to further *exploration and interpretation*. The evening meal they shared affirmed them and confirmed their faith. The breaking of the bread opened their eyes on multiple levels, enabling them to accept all that had happened, but also to affirm the living presence of the risen Christ in the whole process. Deeper levels of *reflection* began as their eyes opened and their hearts continued to burn. So in *responding* to all of this, the disciples got up and returned to Jerusalem with a different story. Jerusalem became for them, not simply a place where faith began and ended, but a place where they rediscovered life, where they shared hope—where faith began anew.

The second generation Tongans do not view Christianity as a foreign or unfamiliar phenomenon. Most, if not all of them, were brought up in Sunday School and their parents were adherents of their ethnic church communities. They reflect what Alan Tippert has described as a "nativistic" movement.[5] This phenomenon occurs in various forms, but is most common to second generation Christians whose spiritual experiences are not as dynamic as those of the first generation. Those who stand in the shadow of the elders can be described as a "torn generation," victim to the clash of cultures, the identity crisis, and the disillusionment that are part and parcel of their unsatisfied longings. Consequently, some are walking slowly away from the church, perhaps confused about their misplaced expectations.

---

3. See Freire, *Pedagogy of the Oppressed*.
4. Green, *Let's Do Theology*, chapter 2.
5. Tippett, *People Movements in Southern Polynesia*, 7.

More than anything else, making disciples among this torn generation means walking alongside them. They need to tell their stories and be enabled to see those stories from a different, biblical perspective. Both telling and hearing these stories requires vulnerability. They may be stories of fear, bitterness and pain. In this situation, the missional question in the midst of their own Emmaus journey is clear: Where is Christ in their story, and what is the best way for them to meet Christ?

This kind of question invokes a need for a close encounter with Christ and a willingness to share the experience with a new group of pilgrims. This Emmaus Journey Model begins where people are, in their present level of engagement. In John Finney's approach to "new evangelism," he states that the traditional approach of moving from doctrine to spirituality may need to be reversed today—a movement from experience to faith might be more appropriate.[6] This approach places a high value on the importance of mentoring and spiritual direction. Instead of being a distant guide, one rather walks alongside as a fellow traveler. Those on the journey together share hospitality, realized most fully in the discovery of Christ's presence.

Reformed Class Meeting

The Free Wesleyan Church of Tonga for many years struggled to revive the traditional form of the Methodist class meeting (Society Class).[7] This had been the source of power for the "Pentecost of Tonga" in 1834 and was also an effective instrument of evangelism.[8] More recently, however, the class meeting devolved into a class *misinale* (offertory) and was simply used as fundraising tool in the life of the churches.

But the Holy Spirit never leaves the society in darkness without a body of witnesses. Mass evangelism of the 1960s and 1970s, especially in the organized rallies of Allan Walker, Eddie Fox, and others, revived the youth movement in schools and local churches. Following these awakenings, a "Decade of Evangelism" impacted congregational outreach in the Islands dramatically during the 1990s. Open-air rallies became the norm for church mission outreach in public settings such as Nuku'alofa, the capital, in market places and on main streets.

6. Finney, *Recovering the Past*, 38.
7. Davies, *Methodism*, 73–74.
8. Siuhegalu, "Renewal of All Things," 4.

The Wesleyan Church engaged in this ministry in collaboration with other Christian communities and ecumenical agencies. The Director of the Department of Evangelism of the Free Wesleyan Church of Tonga met regularly with other church leaders for prayer and planning mission outreach, working closely with local churches. It was not unusual for congregations to organize rallies for visiting ministry teams from overseas, as well as Billy Graham's televised crusades. These endeavors led to the inauguration of a Christian television and radio station in Tonga, totally dedicated to providing Christian programs and music. This also spawned an immense and thriving "house group movement" across the country.

The house groups sprang up out of spiritual hunger for renewal and growth. At this time, the prayer groups developed, not on the basis of clerical initiatives, but from the pews. Those seeking renewal met at government houses, schoolrooms, churches, businesses, stores, parks, and homes throughout the week. My wife, Meleane, and I visited groups that met at 5:00 a.m. at a hotel, in the back room of a supermarket, at the sea front for prayer walks, and at homes in the evening where children were a part of the fellowship. This awakening infused new life and offered new focus for *kava* clubs and turned them into study groups for lay and local preachers. This also greatly influenced the lives of young people and rugby players who were "exported" to play in New Zealand, Australia, Japan and Wales. Those immigrants became great assets for house group planting and church growth in the host countries. These rugby players were a huge influence on Tongan young people, great role models, and powerful agents of evangelism. In most meetings, hospitality was provided to create a more comfortable, informal, and relaxed space for study, sharing, and prayer, totally different from the traditional setting of public worship.

Connectional Approach

I believe in God because I was brought up in a believing family. I have no doubts about my faith. My parents' home was the birthplace and the laboratory for my faith in the early years of my life. The Australian-born children may sing, "Jesus loves me, this I know, for the Bible tells me so." But those within my generation sang, "Jesus loves me, this I know, for my parents told me so." God created human beings for friendship and for fellowship and places everyone in a family and speaks through people. The network of extended family has always been a big advantage for building and strengthening relationships. Moreover, the effort to recover and maintain these connections has a way of restoring confidence and faith. Utilizing all of these connections is important to the rising generations.

Family ministry influences the lives of young people greatly. Parents who take their children to church and Sunday School should not underestimate their impact on the future. They encourage and praise them with regard to their involvement in the *Faka-Me* (Sunday School annual celebration), junior band/choir, drama, family camps, and worship. Children learn from these events that ministry is a joint, community effort, rather than an optional, individual service assigned to a few. The church and the family must work together to foster faith, offer direction, and strengthen the links with young people in their early age. The Tongan people deeply appreciate many of their pastors because the witness they provide through their families. They work as a ministry team in leading worship. Together, they sing, dance, read, pray, and receive communion. The children are also involved in junior church and youth activities.

Children in church feel secure and confident when they are properly introduced and warmly welcomed into the fellowship. They see things in a broader perspective as they grow up and become involved in larger Christian conventions on state and national levels. The increasing number of the "2 Gens Tongans" who grew up in the faith was evident in the number of participants at the National Christian Youth Convention (NCYC) of the Uniting Church in Australia, which met in Melbourne in January 2008. The Convention was just over a thousand young people and approximately 4 percent were Pacific Islanders.

It is a whole new world for many of these young people, living in a multi/cross-cultural context and worshipping in a more creative and reflective style. These new practices come as a breath of fresh air to their souls and are very different from the traditional worship of their ethnic churches. They celebrate diversity, rather than viewing it as a threat to their growth. For them, the world is a fusion of colors and variety is God's will for the creation. They are growing up as young people of faith, and most see education as a pathway to a tremendous variety of vocations that they are capable of undertaking.

This is the dawn of a new era and the Tongan Church leaders should no longer take their members' loyalty to the Church for granted. Rather than exhibiting a critical spirit and asking questions that call their people's faith into question, they need to think creatively about how to move from a hierarchical mentality to a networking mindset, to use the language of Eddie Gibbs.[9] The leaders need to release the people from the confinement of a church culture to exercise their God-given gifts fully in responding to their God-given calling. If one thinks biblically, a multicultural context is the ideal setting for the church of the future, where diversity is perceived, not as a threat, but as a gift from God. In this context, the most effective means of communicating the gospel of life is by living like Christ in the network of human community.

The three approaches mentioned in this essay attempt to meet people where they are and listen to their stories within their own contexts. The pressing need to belong, to be accepted, and to stay connected to the community is a perennial challenge, particularly for those who endeavor to live Christ-like lives in the world. But what Jesus commands, he always provides. His encounter with the crowd in Mark's Gospel provides a paradigm for faithful ministry in his name: "As he went ashore, he saw a great crowd; and he had compassion for them, because they were like sheep without a shepherd; and he began to teach them many things. When it grew late, his disciples came to him and said, 'This is a deserted place, and the hour is now very late; send them away so that they may go into the surrounding country and villages and buy something for themselves to eat.' But he answered them, 'You give them something to eat.' . . . And all ate and were filled; and they took up twelve baskets full of broken pieces and of the fish" (Mark 6:34–37, 55).

Today the church grows not just by offering the truth of Christ's life and practice, but also by caring for the people's needs in the most ordinary ways. In its efforts to be more inclusive and to communicate the faith in a way that connects with people where they live, the church remains faithful to Christ's message for the world.

---

9. Gibbs and Coffey, *Church Next*, 70.

Further Reading on Asian and Oceanic Contexts

Amaladoss, Michael. *Making All Things New: Dialogue, Pluralism, and Evangelization in Asia.* Maryknoll, NY: Orbis, 1990.
Asedillo, Rebecca, editor. *Rice in the Storm.* New York: Friendship, 1989.
Crocombe, Ron, and Marjorie Crocombe, editors. *Polynesian Missions to Melanesia.* Suva, Fiji: Institute of Pacific Studies, 1982.
Doraisamy, Theodore R. *Forever Beginning: One Hundred Years of Methodism in Singapore.* 2 vols. Singapore: Methodist Church, 1985, 1986.
Fernando, Ajith. *Reclaiming Friendship: Relating to Each Other in a Frenzied World.* Scottdale, PA: Herald, 1993.
Frost, Michael, and Alan Hirsch. *The Shaping of Things to Come: Mission and Evangelism in the 21st Century.* Peabody: Hendrickson, 2003.
Goh, Robbie. *Sparks of Grace: The Story of Methodism in Asia.* Singapore: Methodist Church in Singapore, 2003.
Hedlund, Roger E. *Evangelization and Church Growth: Issues from the Asian Context.* Madras, India: McGavran Institute, 1992.
Hinton, Keith W. *Growing Churches Singapore Style: Ministry in an Urban Context.* Singapore: Overseas Missionary Fellowship, 1985.
Huntley, M. *Caring, Growing, Changing: A History of the Protestant Mission in Korea.* New York: Friendship, 1984.
Im, Mi-Soon. "Role of Single Women Missionaries of the Methodist Episcopal Church, South, in Korea 1897–1940." ThD diss., Boston University, 2008.
Kavunkal, Jacob. *To Gather Them into One: Evangelization in India Today.* Indore: Satprakashan Sanchar Kendra, 1985.
Kiong, Tong Chee. *Rationalizing Religion: Religious Conversion, Revivalism and Competition in Singapore Society.* Leiden: Brill, 2007.
Kochuparampil, Xavier. *Evangelization in India.* Kerala, India: OIRSI, 1993.
Lau, Earnest. *From Mission to Church: The Evolution of the Methodist Church in Singapore and Malaysia: 1885-1976.* Singapore: Armour, 2008.
Munro, Doug, and Andrew Thornley, editors. *The Covenant Makers: Islander Missionaries in the Pacific.* Suva, Fiji: Institute of Pacific Studies, 1996.
Neave, Rosemary. *Gossiping the Gospel: Women Reflect on Evangelism.* Auckland, New Zealand: Women's Resource Center, 1992.
Niles, D. T. *Upon the Earth: The Mission of God and the Missionary Enterprise of the Church.* New York: McGraw-Hill, 1965.
Park, Jong Chun. *Crawl with God, Dance in the Spirit! A Creative Formation of Korean Theology of the Spirit.* Nashville: Abingdon, 1998.
Park, Jong Chun, et al. The *Korea Mission Field, 1905–1912: Beyond 1907, Reawakening, Renewal, Revival.* Seoul: Methodist Theological University Press, 2006.

Sng, Bobby E. K. *In His Good Time: The Story of the Church in Singapore, 1819–2002.* Singapore: Bible Society of Singapore, 2003.

Solomon, Robert. *A Feast for the Soul: Growing in Holiness.* Singapore: Armour, 2005.

Tangunan, Wilfredo Hidalgo. "Social Transformation in the Philippines: Three Methodist Contributions." PhD diss., Drew University, 2007.

Thangaraj, M. Thomas. *The Common Task: A Theology of Christian Mission.* Nashville: Abingdon, 1999.

The People Called Methodists: The Heritage, Life and Mission of the Methodist Church in Singapore. Singapore: Methodist Church in Singapore, 2003.

PART THREE

Europe
Persevering through Ebb Tide

Introduction to Part 3

FOR WELL OVER A MILLENNIUM, WESTERN CHRISTENDOM—THE HEGEmony of Christianity over religious and cultural life—dominated the European world. The towering gothic churches of the great European cities bear witness to the age of faith in which they were constructed, but now cast a dwindling shadow across the landscape. In the late twentieth century, Christendom collapsed in Europe and all of the structures and practices built upon this paradigm of authority and power lost their viability. In this part of the world, where knowledge of and commitment to the Christian faith was one time assumed, the gospel itself must now be rediscovered and translated for those who live in a very different world. Christians in Europe are learning how to persevere through ebb tide. In the following essays, two primary concerns surface clearly: the debilitating influence of the years of Soviet ideology and occupation in the eastern part of Europe and the radical secularization of nations previously dominated by Protestant state churches.

Estonia represents an interesting synthesis of both developments. Kaja Rüütel provides an incisive historical analysis of Christianity in this Baltic nation and demonstrates how the early imposition of colonial Christianity and the subsequent oppression under Soviet occupation alienated many from the faith. She prescribes a new model of disciplemaking that recognizes the importance of teaching the gospel to those who have never encountered it fully, the need to engage in holistic mission, and the Christian mandate to reach out to all people in a context of religious and cultural pluralism.

Lena Kim, a fourth generation Russian-born Korean, reflects some of the same concerns from the perspective of someone who has traveled extensively throughout Eurasia. Reflecting on her experiences in countries such as Belorussia, Ukraine, Kazakhstan, and Tajikistan, but with attention fixed primarily upon Russia itself, she describes the current crisis moment of the church in which danger meets opportunity. She examines five particular signposts into the future—quality of ministry;

education; self-sufficiency; mission, evangelism, growth; and social service—all of which will shape disciple-making in the coming years.

Achim Härtner employs the metaphor of "spaces" to explicate a theology of mission and evangelism appropriate to the postmodern and post-Christian sentiments of contemporary Germans. In this context, he argues, the Christian congregation must function as a space of healing for the weary, a space of immersion in story, and a space of growth in grace. Orienting disciple-making practices around the *missio Dei*, he believes the most helpful approach is to be found in an emphasis on the "positive, life-giving aspects of the gospel, not in a retreat into Christian fundamentalism or moralistic critique."

Of particular interest, perhaps, are Graham Horsley's reflections on the task of making disciples of Jesus Christ in Great Britain, the original home of the Methodist revival. Unlike the age of the Wesleys in which their movement of renewal aimed at recovering lost aspects of a known faith, the post-Christendom context today requires a recovery of confidence in "mission on the margins in alien cultures." British Christians, who once conceived mission through a paradigm of power from the center, must discover fresh expressions of an incarnational faith that is "whole-life and world-changing."

In his chapter related to the Eastern European contexts of the Slovak and Czech Republics, Pavel Procházka organizes his reflections around the issue of "identity" and how communities shape Christian identity in a time of rapid social change. His direct conversations with Methodist practitioners, and his use of surveys related to actual missional practice in the life of the church, make his contribution unique. As one of this colleagues confessed, "We go to people with empty hands, with no power, a short history, and cultural hostility from the majority. Jesus is fulfilling our daily needs in evangelism and discipleship."

12

Making Disciples in Estonia

Kaja Rüütel

The United Methodist Church in Estonia is a small church in a small country with ministry to two culturally and linguistically distinct communities, traditionally Lutheran Estonians (68 percent) and traditionally Orthodox Russians (25 percent).[1] In a country of only 1.3 million, the United Methodist Church in Estonia has twenty-six congregations and over 1,700 members. It is defined by its unique past, from which it has learned much, but also faces the challenge to be a missional church in the twenty-first century and to emerge from a period of decline during the past fifteen years. Church leaders are pouring a lot of effort into defining the church's vision and mission today. Given the present situation of the church, understanding where it has come from and what it has gone through are essential to discerning how best to face the challenges that confront believers today and in coming years.

The 2005 Special Eurobarometer Survey showed that Estonia is the most secular country in Europe: sixteen percent of respondents said that they believed in God, 54 percent stated that they believed in some sort of spirit or life force, and nearly a quarter (24 percent) were atheists or did not believe there was any sort of spirit, God, or life force.[2] According to the Eurobarometer Survey of the previous year, Estonia had a meager 4 percent of the population attending church services once a week.[3] The signs of secularization were visible already during the first independence period of Estonia (1918–1941). Several factors

---

1. Republic of Estonia, *2000 Census*.
2. *Special Eurobarometer Survey* (2005).
3. *Eurobarometer Survey* (2004).

contributed to this development, and they must be explored in order to understand the mind-set of Estonians today.

Mass conversion of Estonians to Christianity began in the thirteenth century as part of a Danish and German effort to colonize the region. Estonians remained as bond slaves to Baltic German landlords up to the middle of the nineteenth century, after which Germans still remained the ruling class both on the land and in the church—the Lutheran clerics were all of Baltic German origin up to the middle of nineteenth century when the first few Estonians entered the ministry and promoted the development of Estonian language and identity. However, up to this point Christianity had not been completely alien to the Estonians. The Moravian revival movement within the Lutheran Church during the eighteenth and early nineteenth centuries had a great impact upon the Estonian peasants. Through the democratic nature of Moravian meetings and the encouragement of literacy, the Moravian revival prepared the ground for a national awakening that developed during the second half of the nineteenth century.[4] The church leadership, for the most part, did not support the Estonian aspirations for freedom.

Therefore, both an anti-German and an anti-church sentiment pervaded the movement for independence.[5] The Estonian intelligencia created a new national identity by equating the colonization and the Christianization of Estonia, ignoring the peaceful Christian missionary activity that took place for two hundred years among Estonians before the thirteenth century colonization.[6] This led to a popular understanding of Christianity as something alien to and imposed upon Estonian people. The intelligencia also turned to France for their ideas and adopted the naturalist, liberal, and leftist views. This included opposition to religious education in public schools. The debates were fierce, continuing after Estonia gained its independence in 1918. In 1923 these debates culminated in a referendum that approved religious instruction; while the majority supported it, nearly a fifth of population opposed this educational policy. It was subsequently taught on a voluntary basis. This action demonstrates that the population at large, especially outside the cities, was keen to continue with the traditional Christian faith. Yet

---

4. Altnurme, *Estonian Culture*.
5. Altnurme, *Kristlusest oma usuni*, 54–56.
6. Gnadenteich, *Kodumaa kirikulugu*, 9–12.

the understanding that Christianity was brought to Estonia "by sword and fire" gathered strength and became increasingly popular. The later communists built their propaganda against the church upon the foundation constructed during the national awakening. The view is still alive today and used as the main argument against Christianity.

The fact that the church never became a truly indigenous movement during Estonia's first independence also fueled the spirit of secularization. Although the clergy were all Estonian by the end World War I, the theology they learned and taught was thoroughly rationalist and far removed from the people. By the end of 1930s it was clear that Christian identity and national identity had grown apart, and the church faced an even greater challenge of survival with the coming of the communist regime. During the Soviet occupation (1940–1941 and 1944–1991) most Estonians withdrew from the church entirely. In the beginning many did so out of fear, but increasingly they embraced the atheistic propaganda and the teaching of a scientific-materialistic worldview even while rejecting the other aspects of communist ideology. Religious rites of passage were quickly replaced with secular rituals.[7] A small percentage of the population continued to go to church and was persecuted for this. Faith, for most, became a strictly personal and private, even secretive matter. The free churches, those traditions that stood outside the Lutheran Church, although small, were deeply committed and fared better. During this period some, including the Methodist Church, even grew.

During the Soviet occupation, some regarded going to church as an opportunity to demonstrate their disagreement with and defiance of the system, but there were few who dared to undertake that step. In the search for alternative worldviews, some turned to Eastern religions as related publications were allowed.[8] When the winds of freedom started to blow in Eastern Europe in 1988, a new interest in the church appeared and people flocked in with mixed motives. Some were serious seekers, while others came (as there was no longer any serious threat) to protest against the ruling polity and its ideology. Unlike the situation in the nineteenth century, the churches across the nation supported the aspirations for freedom that swept the country. Soon after, however, when Estonia regained its independence in 1991, the interest faded

7. Ibid., 79.
8. Ibid., 76.

away. Churches that were used to keeping their activities inside their walls failed in the new situation to fill the ideological and spiritual void in the public arena left after the collapse of the Soviet Union. Next to the Eastern religions, New Age and all sorts of esoterica spread quickly and filled the religious marketplace.

The negative stereotypes, doubts, and fears related to church and Christianity in general have carried over from the nineteenth century to the Soviet period and again into the post-Soviet era. This became especially clear, again, in the public discussions about the necessity of compulsory religious education in the schools since 2002. Currently the schools are required to offer non-confessional religious education when there are at least fifteen students at the proper age who request it. In 2009 only about 10 percent of schools offered religious education and about 1–2 percent of the total number of students in Estonia participated in this instruction.[9] The children growing up today are already the fourth generation who have no connection to the church, neither do they have any knowledge about Christianity so as to be able to understand works of literature, art, and music rooted in the Christian tradition.

From 1945 until the 1980s, the Russian-speaking population in Estonia grew by leaps and bounds, primarily as a consequence of Soviet immigration policy. The Russian-speaking population is culturally different and also more religious as Orthodoxy is a part of their self-identity.[10] One study demonstrates how, between 1991 and 1998, the percentage of Russian speakers in Estonia who declared belief in God rose from 41 to 68 percent. Moreover, among Russian women, not one person declared herself to be an atheist. At the same time, however, the belief in palingenesis and astrology was about as strong as the belief in God, meaning that there is some overlapping as those who are nominally Orthodox can also have other beliefs.[11] This is in keeping with some of the broader trends across many European societies. While secularism dominates the cultural landscape, this is not to say that the people are devoid of religion or spirituality. Rather, their religious life is characterized by a personal, individualized eclecticism driven by the values of a postmodern, post-Christian, and post-communist culture.

---

9. Personal interview with Einar Värä, Estonian Ministry of Education and Research, September 11, 2009.

10. Liiman, *Usklikkus*, 107.

11. Ibid., 50, 56, 107, and 110.

The Estonian Methodist Heritage

The roots of the United Methodist Church in Estonia lie in the revival movement of 1907 in which there were two Estonian preachers, one a Moravian brother and the other a member of the St. Petersburg Methodist Episcopal Church in Russia, who started to hold evangelistic meetings on the Island of Saaremaa.[12] Soon the tensions between the converted and the local Lutheran church grew and this led to a separate gathering where the Sacrament of Holy Communion was first celebrated in 1908. From the very beginning, indigenous leaders have shepherded the Estonian Methodist Church, making it possible for them both to be understood and to live close to the people. The church has also maintained the marks of a revivalist movement with a strong emphasis on conversion and personal holiness. Up to 1940 nearly every monthly record of the church's work reported about revival weeks or rallies where people "found peace under the cross" or "responded to the altar call."[13] By the start of the Second World War there were fifteen congregations scattered across the country. With deep roots in the revivalist tradition, there tended to be little emphasis on the importance of social witness and service, except for some notable exceptions. Tartu Methodist Church, for example, participated in the temperance movement and had an effective ministry among the poor.[14]

During the Soviet occupation, several free churches were banned, including the Moravian Church, the Pentecostal Union, and the Salvation Army.[15] Methodists, by the grace of God and under wise and bold leadership, maintained their presence and work in the country. After losing half of its membership through two waves of intense persecution, 1940–1941 and 1944–1956, however, the church started to grow again. Several people from banned churches joined the Methodists, but the majority of the church members had no previous church affiliation, as seen in the study of the pastor of the Tallinn church in 1962.[16] Evangelistic meetings (allowed only in the church building) were held and people responded. Birthday parties were used for informal prayer

---

12. Ritsbek, *Mission in Estonia*, 56; see also Pajusoo, *The UMC in Estonia*, 10.
13. Ibid., 57–58.
14. Ibid., 69.
15. Ibid., 84.
16. Ibid., 92.

meetings and weddings were a good time to present the gospel to non-Christian relatives. At the end of 1960s and in the 1970s, charismatic renewal together with attractive rock music ministry brought young people to the church. After the collapse of the Soviet Union in 1991 the United Methodist Church in Estonia also had to adapt to the changing society. The most rapid growth centered on children's ministry. In 1993, when there were seventeen Methodist congregations with a total of 1,868 full members, the number of children in Sunday Schools was 1,269. Non-Christian parents were happy for their children to go to Sunday School or Christian kids' clubs, even when they themselves were not interested.

A Russian language ministry started in the 1950s when Ukrainian and Byelorussian immigrants, fleeing famine and persecution, joined the burgeoning Russian-speaking work force, primarily in the cities. The Tallinn church leadership realized the challenge, and in 1957 they started worship services in Russian. The ministry proved very successful and soon it became a growing community that attracted non-Christians as well. At the end of 1980s, when there was more freedom with regard to the open proclamation of the gospel, the Russian congregation developed an active youth outreach and was also the first in all Estonia to start visiting the prisons in 1989.

The number of congregations has grown over the past twenty years: six Russian and five Estonian churches have been planted, but four have closed. Since 1993 the total membership has been shrinking little by little. In 2008 there were only three Estonian and three Russian churches that were growing. Given this situation, the church is clearly going through a challenging time. There are signs of new life and vitality, however, and this can be seen primarily in three areas.

Discipleship in the Community Setting

The revivalist legacy of Estonian Methodism has emphasized the importance of a conversion experience. In today's society where people often do not have any previous knowledge of Christianity (or have a distorted understanding), conversion—at the heart of which stands the experience of God's unconditional love and grace—must be viewed as a process that takes more time and involves a true reorientation of one's life. Catechetical instruction, therefore, must be a part of this process from the very beginning of the Christian journey and must introduce the potential believer to the very basics of the Christian faith. Teaching of this nature that goes hand in hand with getting involved in practical service and the worship life of the community gives the sense of belonging and being valued and helps people to fully comprehend the Christian way of living. The context of the church today reflects a situation similar to that of the earliest church. Jesus' first disciples not only learned through the teacher's words, but through practical engagement and getting involved in what he was doing. This model of active engagement and learning by doing, under the guidance of the biblical story and Christian community, resonates well with the cultural dynamic that confronts the church today.

On the practical side, several congregations are running an *Alpha Course*, but leaders are beginning to realize that this often serves only as an appetizer and it needs to be followed by further catechesis and teaching. *Disciple Bible Study* immerses the participants in the biblical narrative and moulds their lives into a pattern of faithful, biblical discipleship. This is especially important when people are no longer compelled to follow or are convinced by authoritative "do's and don'ts."

Tartu St. Luke United Methodist Church is one of the six growing churches in Estonian Methodism today. It is intriguing that they have set the expectations for church membership higher than usual. Those wishing to undertake the catechetical course are also required, on the minimum level, to participate in the community's worship life on a weekly basis. In Estonian society, this is no easy road, for the person who goes to church every Sunday can be easily labeled a religious fanatic by those outside. Yet the more stringent requirements are bearing fruit and the vast majority of those who start their journey through catechesis later become not only committed church members, but genuine disciples of Christ who wish to learn and to grow further.

Discipleship in the framework of community is also important for children's ministry. When Sunday School teaching is coupled with participation in the life and service of the church, the children are more likely to remain in the church as they mature. Those congregations that took discipling children and youth seriously in 1990s are still experiencing growth today. In 1994, Võru United Methodist Church started with six adults and about twenty non-Christian children in the kids club. In essence, the children were the church and were involved in all activities. Those children are now the dynamic leaders of the church.

Engagement in Holistic Mission

One of the strengths of Estonian Methodism is its focus on personal commitment and holiness which, in the most difficult of times, made its fellowship warm, vigorous, and attractive. In today's society the witness of the church is more credible when the experience of God's grace is expressed not only in personal piety but also in the love of the neighbor and engagement in relevant social concerns. This is a view of the Christian life deeply imbedded in the Wesleyan heritage which has always espoused the view that there is no religion but social religion, no holiness but social holiness. This holistic mission and ministry finds perfect expression, of course, in the ministry of Jesus who cared not just about the lost souls, but for the whole persons, body and spirit. Prostitutes and tax collectors sat at his table and lepers and the demon-possessed were healed and restored to society. Yet the basic overarching story of the Bible is that through Jesus Christ, God desires to restore all things to himself—individuals, relationships, whole nations, and the rest of creation—for "through him God was pleased to reconcile to himself all things whether on earth or in heaven, by making peace through the blood of his cross" (Col 1:20). This holistic mission of the church, therefore, makes a claim upon Christ's disciples in terms of their care for the whole creation—what could be described as an "environmental holiness." And this must be seen as a part of evangelistic mission as well.

In reality, the shortage of specialists and financial resources restricts the practice of social holiness in a situation where even most pastors have to hold secular jobs to support their families. When churches launch projects, it is usually possible to run them only with foreign aid or in collaboration with the local government. The newest such initiative comes from Jõhvi which is in a poorer area of Estonia. The Jõhvi United Methodist Church has been running a soup kitchen for several years. The church provides the staff, who proclaim the gospel to their guests through both word and deed, and the city government provides the finances. In 2008, with the help of Norwegian friends, some members of the Jõhvi congregation, who were living in the neighboring industrial town of Sillamäe, began to provide lunches in a dormitory for those who had lost their jobs. As a result of sharing the gospel in this concrete way, people started to become Christians. Now there is a small church plant with twenty new people, some of whom have become helpers in the project. As the economic depression hit hard in 2009, the number of people in need started to grow. The town officials, after being rather skeptical during the first year of their ministry, finally acknowledged the work and started to finance it as well.

Another way to address relevant social concerns is to partner with other churches. The Christian churches make up only a small percentage of Estonia's population, and if every church would operate only on its own, the impact they could make would be minimal at best. The realization of this, as well as the common suffering during the Soviet period, brought the churches closer together in effective ecumenical relationships in the form of the Estonian Council of Churches (ECC). The ECC has become the main link between the state and churches. It has become a voice piece for the Christian community and speaks out concerning ethical issues in the society and engages in the practical work of ecumenical chaplaincy and rehabilitation. Currently the Methodist Church has two chaplains working in the defense forces and four in prisons and in the area of social rehabilitation.

The part of holistic mission that concerns the environment remains underdeveloped in all of the Estonian churches. There is a growing need for the churches to offer a Christian perspective on the care of the natural world, not only so that Christians themselves will take this ministry to heart, but so that the concern can be heard in the public arena as well. At the moment other religious communities, such as New Age and new pagan groups, tend to speak louder on this matter.

Discipling the Nations

Most of the time during the past twenty years, Estonian Christians have been on the receiving end of Western mission aid. But over the past couple years, in particular, the tide has been turning and the Methodist church, along with other churches, is learning to give and serve those whose needs are even bigger. There are approximately ten Finno-Ugric indigenous people groups inside Russia, totaling more than three million people, whose languages are related to Estonian and who are struggling to preserve their culture and language. Those nations who have largely adopted Orthodoxy have also tended to "Russianize," losing more of their cultural and linguistic uniqueness. Four of the Finno-Ugric groups in Russia have only superficial connections with Orthodox Christianity, and the traditional pre-Christian religion remains the dominant spiritual factor in people's lives. Currently there are only a few indigenous evangelical Christians in the Finno-Ugric groups and they need encouragement. Estonian Christians, being also part of a small nation, are in a good position relative to them, especially because of the shared history under Soviet rule and the very real feeling of being related nations, essentially family.

With this in mind, since the year 2000, the Baltic Methodist Theological Seminary staff and students have participated in mission trips to the Finno-Ugric people. They have been working together with local Christians in reaching out to their people and showing that God can communicate in their language and has not forgotten them. This is crucial, for they often think Christianity is the Russian religion and to become a Christian necessitates giving up their language and identity. Yet, as seen throughout the Bible, God is concerned about all the nations and the celebration of the rich diversity of this world culminates in the new creation when people of every tribe and language and people and nation will bring their wealth and praises into the city of God (Rev 7:9; 21:24).[17] The Seminary students and graduates who caught this mission vision come from different denominations and through them many churches have become involved. In order to make this work more effective, a Missions Work Group was formed under the Estonian Evangelical Alliance. In co-operation with the Seminary, the Evangelical Alliance has launched a Finno-Ugric Christian training program to prepare indigenous, culture-sensitive leaders for these small ethnic groups.

The United Methodist Church of Estonia demonstrates how a small church can be strong if it focuses its life on Christ and his mission. Ministering in a post-Christian, postmodern society does not mean that the church has to lower its standards in order to be accessible. Faithfulness to Christ's mission is the key. When the ministry of making disciples flows out of an understanding of the great purposes of God as revealed in scripture, genuine community emerges and lives are forever changed.

17. See Wright, *Mission of God*, 393–420.

13

Making Disciples in a Eurasian Parish

Lena Kim

Critical Challenges

AFTER THE DISINTEGRATION OF THE SOVIET UNION IN 1991, PEOPLE IN Eurasia were very receptive to the gospel, as well as all other things new. With the restoration of the freedom of speech, conscience, and religious beliefs came a flood of ideologies and religious traditions to fill the vacuum left in the wake of the Soviet collapse. Innumerable missionaries and evangelic teams arrived from other parts of the world at that time to take advantage of this new-found liberty. They preached freely in the streets and later paved the way for the first Protestant churches of the new era in Eurasian history. This period of receptivity to the good news, at least in Russia, was short lived. At a recent United Methodist conference, Bishop Hans Växby noted that modern post-Soviet countries that were liberated from the communist ideology quickly began to turn to the idol of materialism or capitalism, and this process has been moving very quickly.

During the past fifteen years, in the territories of the Commonwealth of Independent States (CIS), the regional organization of former Soviet Republics formed during the breakup of the Soviet Union, there has been an increasing tendency for leaders to leave the Protestant churches for the world. Others convert to the Russian Orthodox Church or simply continue to practice their faith in the privacy of their homes, not attending formal Christian assemblies, but defining themselves as Christian nonetheless. This development reflects the disappointment that many people felt towards the church and the church's leaders when the initial wave of enthusiasm began to fade. Russian Protestant leaders, in particular, feel exhausted, depressed, and some admit that they made many mistakes and feel disappointed by the present condition of the churches. This situation was especially critical between 2003 and 2005.

Examining the condition of the United Methodist Church in Eurasia, in particular, during the opening years of the new millennium, leads to the same basic conclusions. It reflects the same tendencies toward malaise and stagnation. These years have been characterized by an obvious fading of spirit in most of the communities and a lack of trustful and loving relationships among members of some churches. At such a time, when insecurities mount, it is easy for Christian leaders to default to styles of leadership that are authoritarian and fail to empower the whole people of God. To change this way of thinking requires a high level of effort and intentionality. Similarly, some of the problems present within the United Methodist Church today are related to what some have called "fast evangelization." The number of United Methodist groups increased rapidly during the first decade following the Soviet collapse—the last decade of the twentieth century. The church needed leaders desperately and some active and devout members of congregations were appointed to positions of church leadership without having the necessary pastoral gifts. Now these churches are suffering and succumbing to decline or stagnation.

In some territories of Eurasia, United Methodists also face the difficult situation of living among some unfriendly and hostile Russian Orthodox Christians. United Methodist Christians, like Gentiles in an alien land, confronted the same issues that characterized some of the earliest forms of Christianity. David Bosch describes such a parallel situation: "As Matthew looks at the members of his own community—living at a frontier, experiencing difficulty in defining their own identity on the borderline between increasingly hostile Jews and as yet alien Gentiles—he reminds them of a rather bewildered band of simple folk on the slopes of a mountain in Galilee, just across the border from Syria where they are now living, and he wishes his community to know that mission never takes place in self-confidence but in the knowledge of our own weakness, at a point of crisis where danger and opportunity come together."[1]

1. Bosch, *Transforming Mission*, 76.

In the contemporary Eurasian context, in the face of these challenges, Christian disciples need to find their voice again in order to proclaim the good news to people where they live. At the point of crisis in which they find themselves, where danger and opportunity meet, they need to find a way to work fruitfully for the sake of Christ and his mission. But hope springs eternal, and there are wonderful signs of hope in this context today.

Scriptural Images

One of the scripture texts most pertinent to the Eurasian context today is the narrative of 2 Kgs 22:1—23:3. This portion of the Hebrew Scriptures recounts the story of King Josiah of Judah and the reforms that he enacted during his reign. Hilkiah served as High Priest at this time and found a copy of the Book of the Law when King Josiah commanded the refurbishment of the Holy Temple. His rediscovery of the Word and his preaching led to the renewal of Judah and a return to the worship of Jahweh, the God of Israel.

In spite of the celebration of one thousand years of Christianity in the USSR in 1988, most people who live in post-Soviet countries seem never to have been evangelized. This can be explained, in part, by the fact that so many of the people throughout that period remained illiterate. The most recent translation of the Bible into modern Russian occurred in 1876. Before that year, the Bible was only available in Church Slavonic. Only the most highly educated, in other words, were able to read the Bible. Moreover, the Russian Bible Society was not reconstituted until 1991. While literacy has improved, many remain biblically illiterate. If, in fact, faith comes from reading and hearing the message contained in the Word (Rom 10:17), then this challenge can only be overcome by a rediscovery of the Word. So, evangelists today have a huge task before them in Eurasia—to bring the Word of God to the modern person; to encourage persons to open and read the Word that they might encounter the truth in a personal way.

This is why the story of Josiah and Hilkiah relates so directly to the present situation. New "temples" are under construction throughout Eurasia today. But, just as in the time of Josiah, the overwhelming majority of people do not know the Bible. The people of ancient Israel encountered the truth when King Josiah read the text directly to them.

Holy Scripture can touch the hearts and minds of the people today in an equally dramatic way.

> The king went up to the house of the Lord, and with him went all the people of Judah, all the inhabitants of Jerusalem, the priests, the prophets, and all the people, both small and great; he read in their hearing all the words of the book of the covenant that had been found in the house of the Lord. The king stood by the pillar and made a covenant before the Lord, to follow the Lord, keeping his commandments, his decrees, and his statutes, with all his heart and all his soul, to perform the words of this covenant that were written in this book. All the people joined in the covenant. (2 Kgs 23:2b–3)

Evangelistic Practice and Christian Vitality

Eurasian Christians must find a new way of bringing the gospel to the people today because the old way of evangelization is no longer acceptable or effective. The overwhelming majority of people in the society are either thoroughly secular or deeply superstitious. Understanding the history of Russia—her cultural roots and background—is absolutely essential to finding an effective means of communicating the gospel today. The idea of the "death of God" was already present in the minds of the Russian people in the nineteenth century. Dostoyevsky in his novels, as well as many other great Russian philosophers, writers, and thinkers, described this painful crisis, predicting many events that would happen within Russia (Eurasia) in the twentieth century.

During much of the twentieth century, for almost seventy years in the former Soviet Union, the doctrine of atheism reigned on every level. In the 1990s, when the USSR collapsed, the vast majority of people espoused no faith at all. Almost all territories of the former USSR (Russia, Belorussia, Ukraine, Uzbekistan, Kazakhstan, Kirgizstan, Tajikistan, Turkmenistan, Georgia, Moldova, Armenia) were atheistic states, fundamentally secular in their view of the world. For as many as five generations, most of the people never heard about God as a living being or reality. Many felt certain that God did not exist. It seemed that the only place where God or ideas about God remained was in Russian culture: in museums where Russian icons were on exhibit, in conservatories where Russian people might hear beautiful oratories dedicated to

God, and in the works of great Russian composers and authors of past centuries.

There were Christians in Eurasia, of course, throughout the years of atheism. These believers could be found in the Russian Orthodox, Russian Baptist, Roman Catholic, and Lutheran Churches, and among other underground Protestant traditions. But the percentage of Christians at that time and now—according to statistical observation—has not changed much. Now it fluctuates from four to five percent, where one to two percent are Christians who do not belong to Russian Orthodox Church. The overwhelming majority of Russian-speaking people (142 million in 2009) still remain atheistic, despite the fact that as many as 70 percent of Russians say that they are Orthodox believers. The roots of this "nominal Christianity"—more culture than faith—run deep. Traditions of the Russian Orthodox Church and the cultural heritage associated with it, as well as the increasing political influence of the established church, exert a strong influence on all Eurasian people.

Those who seek a new evangelization must pay close attention to these factors. It may be the case that other Christian traditions will always be a minority living in a monolithic Orthodox culture. While the Russian Orthodox Church continues to reform its structure and mission, the minority traditions of the faith in Eurasia can do much good for the majority of nominal believers, many of whom are, in point of fact, unbelievers. Two areas of mission stand out: social ministry (orphan houses, hospitals, prisons, food pantries and services, drug and alcohol rehabilitation programs for the addicted and their families, homes for the elderly) and educational programs (for the churched and unchurched alike).

Almost all of the United Methodist churches in Eurasia are involved in these missional practices of the church. Despite recent attempts to block the church's involvement in some social ministries, the work continues and brings greater recognition to and appreciation for authentic Christian discipleship.

In an attempt to discern a missional vision for Christ's continuing work in Eurasia, all the Annual Conferences in 2009 focused their energy and prayer around one central question: How do we find our own vision and place in society where we live and serve in spite of all the struggles and difficulties that we face? On August 27, 2009, the Central Conference of the Eurasian United Methodist Church formulated a mission statement for the churches in Eurasia to direct their ministry, witness, and service over the next six years. By 2015 they hope to see the United Methodist Church of Eurasia "dynamically growing, recognized in the society, and helping people to become committed Christians."[2] The Conference agreed to direct its material and human resources towards five particular areas of concern: quality of ministry; education; self-sufficiency; mission, evangelism, growth; and social service. On October 14–15, 2009, Bishop Hans Växby convened a "Eurasia UMC Roundtable" to further explore these themes with Asian, North American, and other European colleagues. He presented the Eurasia United Methodist "Roadmap," describing the five elements of the plan as "signposts" into the future. In addition to the "Roadmap," they looked, in particular, at five related areas of church life: worship attendance, financial self-sufficiency, lay leadership, Christian service, and achievement of annual ministry goals.

The year 2009 marks the 120th anniversary of the Methodist tradition in Eurasia. In spite of its suffering through much of the twentieth century, the Methodist tradition has maintained a continuous presence, even if only through a handful of congregations in former Soviet-Baltic territories. The next generation of Methodists is finding its way now into new avenues of witness and service. When the young people leave their home towns and move to other locations to further their education, they carry their faith with them, try to find a Methodist congregation in their new surroundings, and participate fully in the life of the church. They have developed a strong identity within this family. Their witness brings growth to the church. The theological seminary for Eurasian Methodists, located in Moscow, celebrates its 15th anniversary in 2010 and continues to flourish despite difficulties and financial constraints. Almost three-fourths of the present pastors received their theological training at this seminary. About 10 percent of the churches are near to self-sufficiency. In all these things, signs of new life abound and a new vitality is present in the life of the churches as a result of a new vision of making disciples and practicing the faith.

---

2. See "Eurasia UMC Roundtable."

Global Contributions

Ivan Aleksandrovich Il'in (1883–1954), in his book, *Crisis of Atheism*, describes a situation very familiar to the Eurasian Christian of the last century:

> The persecution of the faith in the Soviet Union was not an episodic act, but a central and most necessary link in the system of a bolshevist worldview for those who dreamed of conquering the entire world. But the clash was inevitable between believer and nonbeliever, Christian and atheist. A mad fanatic-atheist grabbed the collar of a languid, semi-enlightened, and semi-believing Christian—without an idea, without a will, without courage, without character, and only half-sincere—to put him on his knees and force him to renounce God, to humiliate him, to enslave him, or take his earthly life.[3]

This statement evokes deep emotion, and most particularly the feelings of grief and depression. But the communist regime collapsed after only seventy years, and without any bloodshed. That period proved to be both a curse and a blessing to the Christian community. The blood of the martyrs became seed for a new and hopefully even more vibrant faith.

Alexander Men, the famous Russian Orthodox priest who was killed at the beginning of *perestroika*, said that the period of atheism in the Soviet Union put an end to hypocritical belief. During this period of persecution, the church was forced to clarify its identity and to rediscover the authenticity of genuine faith. This was just as true for Methodists as it was for any other faithful community throughout that period. A boundary was drawn, de facto, between sincere faith and nominal affiliation. Those who really believed in and served Christ emerged in that time of danger and bore witness to a living faith. The new, post-Soviet era in which God calls the church to faithful witness anew presents a different context. What does it mean to be a faithful disciple when nobody is coerced either to believe or to abandon belief, and when all people enjoy a measure of religious liberty for the first time in decades? In this new era, God is bringing about a genuine return to Christian faith throughout Eurasia, and all must pray that God will sustain this move-

---

3. Il'in, *Crisis of Atheism*, 479.

ment of the Spirit, in many ways, founded upon the sweat, blood, and tears of the previous generations.

The difficulties and challenges of this present time, therefore, are not even comparable to the suffering of the witnesses and martyrs of the bygone age. Despite the realities of an atheistic state, God managed to salvage morality and human courage, which no anti-Christian or anti-religious oppression were able to break. If God never turned away from Eurasia, even when it openly turned away from him, when the principalities and powers rejected God, destroyed God's temples, killed God's servants, and incarcerated God's people—if God offered his love and mercy and forgiveness in those days of militant atheism, how much more hope should we have now, and through this hope, more love and power and faith and strength. In a world characterized in many quarters by oppression and injustice, this is a message of hope that the Christians of Eurasia offer to all who suffer and die for the sake of Christ.

14

Enabling People to Believe and Live
Mission and Evangelism in the German-Speaking Context

Achim Härtner (Translated by Paul W. Chilcote)

Mission and Evangelism Reconsidered

IN 1996 THE GENERAL CONFERENCE OF THE UNITED METHODIST Church declared that evangelism was its priority and stressed the role of the local congregation in this missional practice. The recent Episcopal addresses of German bishops Walter Klaiber, "Salt of the Earth—Light of the World" ["Salz der Erde—Licht der Welt," 2005], and Rosemarie Wenner, "Imbue Faith with Life" ["Den Glauben ins Leben tragen," 2008], express the same sentiments for the *Evangelisch-methodistische Kirche (EmK)*.[1] In 1999, speaking to the Synod of the *Evangelische Kirche* (Lutheran Church) of Germany in Leipzig, noted theologian Eberhard Jüngel raised awareness of mission and evangelism to a new level: "If the church had a heart, a living, beating heart, its pulse would be largely regulated by mission and evangelism, and any deficiencies in the church's missionary activity would immediately lead to serious cardio-vascular disturbances. If we are concerned for a church life with a healthily functioning circulatory system, we are bound to be concerned with mission and evangelism."[2]

---

1. *Evangelisch-methodistische Kirche* is the legal name for The United Methodist Church in Germany.
2. Jüngel, "To Tell the World," 203–16.

In order to understand the importance of this missional vision for the German-speaking Methodist Churches of Germany, Switzerland, and Austria, one must understand the broader context within which they practice the Christian faith. The following statement summarizes the twin characteristics that currently obtain. First, Methodists represent a minority position in a post-Christian culture. The prevailing majority of the population belongs nominally either to a Protestant state-related church or the Roman Catholic Church. The Methodist Churches, like all "free churches" in the German-speaking world, stand independent of the state. Altogether, these traditions represent less than 1 percent of the total population. Second, in an increasingly secularized society, large numbers of people dissociate themselves entirely from both the institution of the church and Christian systems of belief. The dominant cultures in these nations reflect post-Christian attitudes as well as an evolving postmodern worldview. This means that their own countries have become "mission fields" again in which the rediscovery of evangelism and mission are increasingly critical.

Critical Challenges

The context of the German-speaking churches presents two particular challenges to the ministry of making disciples.[3]

The Effects of an Information Age

In Central Europe, once considered the seedbed of "Western culture," individuality and autonomy stand out as critical values. It could be argued that, taken to their logical extreme, however, these values have led to a disintegration of the social order. According to the philosopher Paul Feyerabend, a particular slogan dominates just about every aspect of life, namely, "Anything goes!" The worldwide financial crisis is only one example of how in a "risk society" (Ulrich Beck), the unbridled pursuit of personal or individual advancement can bring whole systems to the brink of collapse in unpredictable ways. It would seem that today, an army of experts from a diversity of disciplines and perspectives would

---

3. See Härtner and Eschmann, *Predigen Lernen*, 52–59.

not be able to agree on "whatever holds the world together in its inmost folds" (Johann W. von Goethe).

We also live at a time in which change seems to come faster and faster. Philosopher Hermann Lübbe speaks of the "shrinking of the present." The pace of life, in other words, has accelerated to such an extent that it is nearly impossible to process the massive storms that so quickly confront us in life. We are flooded with information by books, newspapers, radio, television, and the internet. The sheer amount of information exceeds the capacity of human beings to assimilate it all. "As more information bombards the individual," as theologian Ingo Reuter asserts, "the rush of information turns into a meaningless ambient white noise."[4]

The way in which people process their lives and the way in which their character is shaped changes. Given the way in which economic interests tend to dominate in the flow of information, with their questions about efficiency and usability, religious (spiritual) concerns are often denigrated. In a culture with this orientation to information, there is little room for the dimensions of sense, creativity, or poetry, and these are increasingly filtered out. These effects of the information age challenge a church in its serious intent to present the gospel to people at the deepest level of their lives, in their obvious or hidden quests for meaning and purpose in life.

Changing Norms and Values

Disintegration of tradition also marks the German-speaking world. Values and norms which have offered stability in the past have lost validity. In a postmodern context, the "grand narratives," as philosopher Jean-François Lyotard describes them, disintegrate. Individuals determine what is significant to them on the basis of their independent judgments. At the same time, cultural currents destroy the traditional foundations from which one could have obtained clues with regard to meaning and purpose. Theologian Albrecht Grözinger describes this ambivalent situation appropriately: "Autonomous individuals drift in a sea devoid of stories but are so much in need of stories at the same time."[5] It has become more and more difficult for people to form a se-

4. Reuter, *Predigt verstehen*, 20.
5. Grözinger, "Geschichtenlos inmitten von Geschichten," 484.

cure identity and to find reliable reference points in their lives. So the postmodern person is left to develop a patchwork identity, a self-image composed from different possible life patterns and models. On the positive side, this means that people have a greater capacity for self-determination as long as they have suitable money, diligence, and perseverance. One should not be rash to deprecate these creative possibilities, but the disadvantage should be obvious: It is an arduous task to be constantly constructing the self on the basis of one's own ingenuity.

This postmodern phenomenon impacts religion and Christian belief directly. The meta-narratives that have defined religious institutions and communities are no longer plausible in the eyes of many. The postmodern person develops his or her spirituality on the basis of particular, individual choices, formed into a unique, eclectic patchwork with little coherence or consistency. A Swiss study reveals that someone "who goes to church regularly on Sunday morning, will read a book in the afternoon about Sufi music, dance, and religious practices or listen to a radio broadcast about early Irish Celtic mythology."[6] In such a situation, evangelism necessarily entails defining the Christian life clearly in hopes of bringing disciples of Christ into conversation with those who seek an authentic spiritual life. Moreover, Christians must prioritize the life-enriching vision of Christian theology and practice because the God who created life loves it and wants every person to experience abundant life (John 10:10b).[7]

Scriptural Images

Sent by Christ

Mission and evangelism originate, not from any human impulse, but from Christ who instructs his disciples and commissions them to "Go . . . and make disciples of all nations" (Matt 28:19). The imperative "to make disciples" is linked to the participles related to "going," "baptizing," and "teaching," with Jesus' reminder that "all authority in heaven and on earth has been given to me" (28:18) and "I am with you always" (28:20). Jesus' words provide a profound assurance to those who strive to be faithful witnesses and a necessary safeguard against pride related

---

6. Dubach and Campiche, *Jede/r ein Sonderfall. Religion*, 306.
7. See Zulehner, *Helft den Menschen leben*.

to their victories and accomplishments, for evangelists are involved in Christ's work and not their own. Christ sends laborers into the harvest to engage in the *missio Dei*, to participate in God's ongoing work of making disciples, not their own mission.

Comprehensive Evangelism: The Proclamation and Incarnation of the Gospel

Four New Testament concepts mark the divine mandate to communicate the gospel:

- Witness (*marturia*)—testimony to God's mercy and love in sermon and conversation
- Service (*diakonia*)—loving service to others in the world; the "philanthropy of God" (Titus 3:4)
- Community (*koinonia*)—fellowship with other Christians in union with Christ
- Worship (*leiturgia*)—public and private praise of God.

In the dynamic interaction of these elements, evangelism involves the proclamation and incarnation of the gospel in such a way that God's saving action in Jesus Christ can be realized in people's lives. The goal of evangelism is "that men and women very personally recognize and accept that which God has done as salvation and as a new foundation of their lives and live from it."[8] None of this happens in isolation. As Paul makes clear in 1 Thess 2:8: "So deeply do we care for you that we are determined to share with you not only the gospel of God but also our own selves." The announcement of the good news of God's love in Jesus Christ (proclamation) is connected intimately with the demonstration of that love through action (incarnation). The "body language of the body of Christ," as William Abraham declares, must be consistent with the message proclaimed.

---

8. Klaiber, *Call and Response*, 26.

"Do not be grieved, for the joy of the Lord is your strength"
(Nehemiah 8:10)

In the biblical witness, joy is the central sign of God's reign. Luke reports that the early Christians shared meals together and "ate their food with glad and generous hearts, praising God and having the goodwill of all the people" (Acts 2:46–47). It is important to remember that those who were earlier separated by culture and language were united in joy at Pentecost. The joy of the Lord and the acceptance of the other belong together; both characterize the evangelistic mission of God's reign. Scripture describes the joy of the Lord, not as something superficial or transient, but as a deep blessing, the strength of which is proven in the challenges of life.

Even if the Lukan representation of early Christianity is idealized, it begs the question: How does the spirit of the church today compare with that of the community depicted in Acts? A general malaise seems have fallen over small, struggling churches that are constrained by financial pressures and divided by disputing factions. The Orthodox theologian Alexander Schmemann observes: "It is only as joy that the Church was victorious in the world, and it lost the world when it lost that joy, and ceased to be a credible witness to it. . . . To enter into that joy," and to be "a witness to it in the world, is the very calling of the Church."[9] The idea that Christians need to be infected over and over again with joy is nothing new. Paul exclaims: "Rejoice in the Lord always; again I will say, Rejoice" (Phil 4:4). The hymns of Charles Wesley exude this infectious joy and provide a unique means to both celebrate it and share it with others.

Evangelistic Practice

The Congregation as a Space of Healing for the Weary

Given the challenges of a postmodern world, the most helpful strategy for evangelism is to be found in an emphasis on the positive, life-giving aspects of the gospel, not in a retreat into Christian fundamentalism or moralistic critique. In this age of information and consumerism, effective evangelistic practice focuses on quality rather than quantity, on

---

9. Schmemann, *For the Life of the World*, 24–25.

depth and growth of spirit rather than an increasing number of programs. The Christian community can create a space for the healing of the weary, particularly for those beaten down and loaded down by the demands of life today. Jesus says, "Come to me, all you that are weary and are carrying heavy burdens, and I will give you rest" (Matt 11:28). Evangelistic work today begins in this space. For those experiencing "weariness of the self" (Alain Ehrenberg) due to the hectic nature of everyday life, there is a pressing need to slow down the tempo of life, to provide time for the mind, soul and body to recover, and to move from the superficial into the profound. The church can offer hospitality and space for creativity, poetry, and recovery, enabling the weary to redefine their world on the basis of God's vision and way.[10]

The Congregation as a Space of Immersion in Story

Worship provides guidance and dependable signposts for people in their journey through life. Given the changing dynamic of a post-Christian culture, Albrecht Grözinger advises preachers that they can count less and less on traditional, well-formed arguments to bring people to and keep them in church. They must preach at a very elementary level, starting at the beginning. The sermon must be immediately understandable, without any prior knowledge, working towards the desired affirmation from "square one," and self-authenticating. Grözinger describes this as "initial preaching."[11] Preachers are most successful in this approach to preaching, evangelism, and the introduction of basic Christian beliefs, he believes, when they use narratives, because storytelling is a fundamental means of human communication. Good stories are self-authenticating. They do not impose anything on the hearers and yet manage to capture their attention. Narrative enables the hearer to enter into God's own story—to become part of the biblical narrative—to discover his or her own relationship with God and place in the world. The message of God's unmerited love, mercy, and grace stands in relief against the excessive demands that people put upon themselves, and enables them to accept their brokenness and vulnerability. The proclamation of God's love and the dignity of all persons, in the face of hopeless human efforts

---

10. Cf. Thompson, *Soul Feast* and Heath, *Mystic Way of Evangelism*.
11. Grözinger, *Predigen aus Leidenschaft*, 61–78.

at self-justification, liberate people and enable them to discover their true humanity and that of others.

The Congregation as a Space of Growth in Grace

People shaped by vast social and cultural changes today demand concrete examples and clear criteria that enable them to understand the relevance and significance of the Christian life. The proclamation and practice of the biblical message in faith communities both inspires and forms a particular way of life in the world. An approach that is attentive to the practical aspects of discipleship permits the development of various paradigms of formation without having to offer ready solutions. The biblical witness proclaimed and lived in the community of faith is dynamic and, most particularly in the experience of corporate worship, reveals various paths of Christian discipleship that offer true life. This life-shaping event or space makes growth in grace, or sanctification, possible. While it is God who acts principally in this process of restoration through the Spirit—in the same way that God's prior grace justifies the sinner—the whole person, body, mind, and soul is fully engaged. Moreover, sanctification has a personal and a communal dimension. Wilfried Härle has observed that, while life in Christ connects disciples more intimately with God, at the same time, the Holy Spirit is at work to connect them more intimately with one another.[12] Whenever the proclamation of the good news awakens belief, it also motivates the believer to translate the love he or she has experienced into concrete action. This active love extends, not only to the loveable, but to all people, everywhere. In a society in which individuals are increasingly alienated from themselves and others, this thought is of particular significance. The biblical narrative encourages the people of God to cross cultural and social borders as an essential aspect of their discipleship in Christ.

Christian Vitality

These practices related to making disciples can be realized in principle in any community that discovers the evangelistic mandate of Jesus Christ and is willing to change. There are many examples of places

---

12. Härle, *Dogmatik*, 375.

in which dedicated Christians are attempting and experiencing these very things. Some of these developments related to mission and evangelism can be seen in remarkable ways in international communities. In Germany, Switzerland, and Austria there are a growing number of multi-national congregations in which expatriates meet together, either in common-language or cross-cultural communities. For displaced immigrants, newly established churches with worship conducted in their own language and style, function like "homes away from home," a piece of the native country they have lost and have not found in their new context. The protocol of the European Council of Methodist Churches (2008) notes: "Several people mentioned that 'immigrants are a gift and a blessing from God to the churches.'"[13] Only those who open their hearts and lives to these communities, however, can receive the treasures and blessings that they have to offer.

Peace Church United Methodist in Munich offers a winsome model in this regard. This vibrant community recently celebrated its twenty-fifth anniversary. From humble beginnings in 1984, with only thirteen members, more than a hundred worshipers now gather from all over the world, Sunday by Sunday, in this English-language congregation. Originally designed as a ministry with the families of American soldiers who were stationed in Munich, Peace Church now functions as a spiritual home for people from more than twenty-five countries, some of whom have sought asylum from dangerous situations in their various homelands. As the current pastor, Christine Erb-Kanzleiter, observes:

> The richness of Peace Church is its people: people as diverse as the different countries of this earth can be. So again we need to be reminded that we belong together, that we are God's worldwide family, no matter how different we are and how different our lives and looks are. We are loved by God, welcomed by God, cared for by God. And God calls us to love, to welcome, and to care, too. . . . We are asked to show to the world what God can do with the lives of people who have the love, the passion and the courage to be the body of Christ. At Peace Church everybody is constantly challenged and challenging others to overcome boundaries, differences, fears and inhibitions.[14]

---

13. European Council of Methodist Churches, "Minutes," 6.
14. Erb-Kanzleiter. "Peace Church News."

Certainly, it is desirable that German-language congregations open their doors to people of all cultures, languages, and nations and foster an atmosphere in which they can celebrate diversity-in-unity and radiate the good news of God's love to all people.

Global Contributions

The social situation in the German-speaking context is far more complicated, admittedly, than an essay as brief as this one can demonstrate fully. A post-Christian, secular society confronts the church with huge challenges related to mission and evangelism. At the same time, the context facilitates the rediscovery of a positive, biblical vision that can be incarnated in new and exciting ways. Certainly, a renewed vision of mission must be oriented around the *missio Dei*—God's own work and way—and not simply the desire for growth in the church. Moreover, mission and evangelism must be understood increasingly as an ecumenical task. All efforts of the church to be faithful in this work are founded upon the certainty that God "desires everyone to be saved and to come to the knowledge of the truth" (1 Tim 2:4). God give us willingness and courage as "the people called Methodists" to create space to do God's will and to serve in such a way that people discover what it means to believe and to live.

15

Making Disciples in Britain

Graham Horsley

Challenges

The biggest single challenge facing the church in Britain today is to discover confidence in its ability to proclaim the good news of Jesus Christ in a way that will persuade men, women, and children to become disciples of Jesus Christ within the fellowship of the church. This challenge is greatest for the historic denominations struggling to come to terms with the steady and apparently inexorable decline in churchgoing in Britain. Describing the challenge is straightforward, understanding why the church and individual Christians lack confidence and what can be done to rectify the situation is more difficult.

Simply painting a picture of uniform decline would be misleading. The overall statistics hide a complicated situation—it is also true that in the past decade there has been a veritable explosion of new forms of church which defy easy explanation. There has also been a growing awareness in the historic denominations that beneath their radar has been a huge growth in ethnic minority congregations—especially black led congregations whose members are of African or African-Caribbean extraction.

It is important to think carefully about the sort of confidence the church is seeking to discover. Rapid changes in British society mean that the church must learn how it can work effectively at the margins of society when it had been used to setting the moral and political agenda, influencing the whole approach to education and values, and had an automatic right to being consulted about almost everything. Confidence can no longer be found in terms of the church's status in society, but what is really needed is a confidence in God's grace: "My grace is sufficient for you, for power is made perfect in weakness" (2 Cor 12:9). This does not come easily to a church which has been used to thinking and working in a Christendom context. Some Christians are still hoping to return to Christendom (shout louder, work and pray harder!), others are left feeling lost and powerless in a strange world (private religion—my faith works for me but I'll keep quiet about it outside church), yet others revel in a return to a way of working that is closer to the New Testament than we have seen for 1,500 years (Christ at the margins, working incarnationally).

In an unpublished lecture at the Mission 21 Conference, held in Bath in November 2009, Dr. Martyn Atkins, General Secretary of the Methodist Church in Britain, recently illustrated the impact that these changes and challenges have had on our approach to evangelism by describing the changing way that evangelists offer a challenge to those outside the church in the following progression:

1. "You will" (the coercion of a context where not to be Christian is distinctly disadvantageous)

2. "Will you" (the classic invitation to a powerful, influential faith)

3. "Please will you" (the beginning of recognition of an increasing sense of marginalization—the beginning of grudging recognition that the world is not as it was, that it is a pluralist world)

4. "Will you pretty please" (desperation beginning to kick in, in order to get people to comply we will sugar the pill, make the seats more comfortable—take them out if you like! The arrival of seeker-friendliness, a certain kind of mission-shapedness, indigenization.)

5. "Why won't you" (the real attempt to try to see things from the perspective of the other. What is it about us that causes so few people to want to join us? So how can we reach secular people—post-Christianity and church-leaving is analyzed, and different degrees of response made)

6. "Why wouldn't you (want to)" (the embodying of an incarnational faith in such authentic ways that it becomes its own advocate.

"Beauty of life causes strangers to join our ranks – we do not talk about great things; we live them" [Minucius Felix]. After all, free samples are always more welcome than sales pitches.)

7. "You wouldn't want to" (the intriguing claim to such a serious, life changing challenge, that it cannot be reasonably assumed that anyone would opt for it! But such a serious version of discipleship is rarely lacking in takers, and such is necessary for some of the youth tribes about today. Quite simply, nothing but a huge challenge will work.)

The first three approaches are unhelpful because they belong to an age that is gone. The fourth teeters on the edge of pandering to a consumer mentality which is unfruitful, in the end, because it has a reductionist approach to the good news of Jesus. The good news becomes what people will respond to and the secular world is in charge of the agenda rather than God. The fifth to seventh approaches are where the church in Britain is trying to invest its resources and creativity. They all take seriously the context of those outside the church and seek to work incarnationally. They are all appropriate for some but not all of the people outside the church.

These massive societal changes have impacted the church through various external and internal factors.

External Factors

The external factors fit into two general categories:

1. General changes in society which, although they have no overt religious content, have serious ramifications in the way that the church fulfils its mission.

These are almost too numerous to list! British society has seen tremendous changes since the Second World War: changing patterns of family life; vastly increased mobility; women in paid employment; divorce and fragmented families; increased choice, specialization, and availability of leisure activities; Sunday working and shopping; longer working hours—all of these changes have placed considerable pressure on people's availability to attend church activities.[1]

---

1. Cray, *Mission Shaped Church*, 1–6.

Britain has also become much more of a consumer society. People know exactly what they want and are no longer willing to be satisfied with a "one size fits all" approach to life. Rather than putting up with a diverse church on the grounds that it is trying to meet the spiritual needs of a whole community, they tend to walk away because it does not meet their specific needs. Another feature of consumerism is that there has been a change from consuming possessions to consuming experiences.[2] Those churches that place a high value on religious experience (Pentecostal, charismatic, and sacramental traditions, in particular) have tended to do better than those with a more cerebral approach to worship.

The last and perhaps most important change in society is the seismic shift from Christendom to post-Christendom already alluded to above.[3]

2. Changes in the way that Christianity is viewed which have a negative impact on the church and its mission.

British Christians find it difficult to come to terms with the fact that many people outside the church regard themselves as more spiritual than churchgoers. Churchgoers are "religious," which is bad, whereas these Christian detractors are "spiritual," which is good. A recent survey of attitudes towards church and churchgoers found that people outside the church have a very negative perception of church. Churchgoers are old, old-fashioned, narrow-minded, judgmental, hypocritical, and unable to cope with doubt.[4] Interestingly, this perception is not changed by the fact that the only Christians they have met are loving, generous people. Forty percent of the population of Britain has neither Christian heritage nor meaningful contact with the church—their only perception comes from a culture and a media which is either suspicious of or hostile to Christianity.

---

2. Pine and Gilmore, *The Experience Economy* is a secular marketing book which explains this very clearly.

3. See Murray, *Post-Christendom*.

4. See Spencer, *Beyond the Fringe*.

Internal Changes

At the same time that these external changes have been taking place, there have also been huge changes inside the church. For a long period in the second-half of the twentieth century, the Methodist Church in Britain was dominated by a liberal theology which placed a high value on social action and the struggle for justice, but a low value on evangelism. The net result of that emphasis is that a Methodist Christian in Britain is twice as likely as an average Christian to be involved in social action, but half as likely to be involved in evangelism.[5] There has also been a crisis of confidence as Methodists are no longer sure that the faith that has nurtured them will nurture their friends—this has produced a reluctance to invite friends to church. The church has also struggled to find an effective way to make disciples, but exciting rediscoveries in the life of the church today are helping many to become disciple-makers in community.

Scripture Images

In British Methodism, perhaps the most relevant Bible picture of evangelism in our recent history has been the parable of the "losts"—the lost sheep (Luke 15:1–7), the lost coin (Luke 15:8–10), and the lost son (Luke 15:11–31). We have regarded ourselves (with some justification) as a Christian country, calling back to faith those who have wandered. This is still an appropriate methodology for some of the population, but it is a declining and aging part of the population. Sometimes it has felt as though the church is doing its best to have the party in the hope that the lights and the festivities will draw the prodigal home, rather than seeking for or waiting for his return. It has become increasingly apparent that holding evangelistic events on church premises in the hope that lapsed Christians will attend is having less and less effect (there are exceptions to this trend; "Back to Church Sunday" equips and encourages Christians to invite their friends to church on a particular Sunday in September. In 2009, this event led to 3,700 people returning to 262 churches. Previous experience suggests that only 15 percent of them will still be attending in nine months time.).

---

5. See Escott and Gelder, *Church Life Profile 2001*.

In our post-Christendom context, we need to re-engage with Bible passages that speak of mission on the margins in alien cultures. The story of Cornelius (Acts 10:1–48) challenges us to do mission without the familiar trappings of church. The sending out of the twelve and the seventy-two (Luke 9:1–6; 10:1–20) remind us of the importance of entering into different cultures on their terms rather than ours and of identifying the "person of peace" who will take the good news of Jesus into a new culture in a way that those of us who are outside the culture never can. The Jerusalem Council (Acts 15:1–29) challenges us to incorporate new Christians without weighing them down with outmoded and non-essential church practices. The "mixed economy" church where the traditional and the contemporary work hand in hand is beautifully illustrated in Gal 2:6–10 where Peter's role as apostle to the Jews complements that of Paul, the apostle to the Gentiles. The Methodist Church in Britain is currently seeking to identify a number of "apostles to the Gentiles" who have the ability to communicate the good news of Jesus in a post-Christian culture by emphasizing the importance of evangelism and contextual mission ability as well as the more traditional pastoral and teaching roles of Christian leaders.

Missional and Evangelistic Practice

Fresh Expressions

The most significant change in the landscape of denominational Christianity has been the enormous growth of "fresh expressions" of church. These are often defined thus: "A fresh expression is a form of church for our changing culture established primarily for the benefit of people who are not yet members of any church. It will come into being through principles of listening, service, incarnational mission and making disciples. It will have the potential to become a mature expression of church shaped by the gospel and the enduring marks of the Church and for its cultural context."[6]

Early in the new millennium it became apparent that something new was beginning in the "church planting" area. There was a sudden

---

6. Croft, *Mission Shaped Questions*, 9. This definition first appeared on the Fresh Expressions web-site (www.freshexpressions.org.uk) but has now been widely adopted.

upsurge of activity and a large diversification in the sort of churches being planted as pioneers began to wrestle with the challenge of forming culturally appropriate churches. In 2005 The Fresh Expressions mission agency began as a partnership venture between the Church of England and the Methodist Church. By 2009, several hundred new churches had been launched, 15,000 people had been introduced to the vision of Fresh Expressions and 2,000 had undergone a one year training course (Mission Shaped Ministry) in forty venues around the United Kingdom. There are growing numbers of stories of people from right outside the church finding faith and being discipled as followers of Jesus. Many of these Fresh Expressions are happening outside our normal statistical gathering mechanisms, so we are trying hard to research what evangelistic impact this new movement is having. Early indications are that it is significant.

Relational Evangelism

From the mid 1990s onwards, there has been a large growth in extended courses which work in a relational way and encourage people to think about faith. The best known of these is Alpha, but there are many others. Many of them have taken on the "Alpha" format—beginning with a meal, then a presentation of Christian basics followed by a time of discussion. All of these courses take seriously the fact that most people in Britain have so little Christian knowledge that they need a series of six to twelve evenings in order to have any meaningful encounter with Christian faith. As they go through the course, their experience is shaped as much by their belonging to a Christian group as it is by an understanding of Christian doctrine.

Different Spiritualities

Another significant development has been the willingness of the church to engage with non-Christian spirituality. This mostly means the spirituality of people who have some sort of Christian heritage (though often lost in the mists of time) rather than allegiance to other historic faiths.[7] There has been a considerable change over the last three or four

---

7. The Methodist church has produced a work book on sharing faiths with people of other faiths. Horsley, *May I call you Friend*.

decades in Britain. Not very long ago, every spiritual experience would have been described in Christian terms and often (though not always) recognized as the Holy Spirit at work. From the 1960s onwards, a whole new vocabulary came into existence to describe spiritual things. This vocabulary is drawn from an eclectic mixture of sources, religious and secular—Eastern religions, paganism, pop and drug culture. Initially this non-Christian approach to spirituality was received with great suspicion and hostility by Christians. As "new age" and "body, mind, and spirit" fairs proliferated, the first response of Christians was to stand outside with placards protesting against their heresies. In recent years, the Christians are more likely to be found inside running a stall offering Christian healing or Ignatian meditation. This change recognizes that what people are describing may well be the work of the Holy Spirit in their lives and we need to create a culture of openness and dialogue rather than one of condemnation. Of course it is true that not all spiritual experiences are healthy and we must exercise discernment. This discernment is offered in the spirit of Acts 17:22–23. We must explain who the "unknown God" encountered by people actually is.

Proclamation

The Methodist Church in Britain has an amazing record in social engagement in all sorts of ways. A hostile media does not always notice the Christian motivation behind the social action, but individual Christians and churches have enormous credibility in their communities because they have demonstrated the love of Christ in practical ways which the whole community recognizes as beneficial. However, if we are good at loving people until they ask why, we are less good at explaining the source of our love. A traditional Methodist approach to preaching in an apologetic way now seems like a "modern" anachronism in a postmodern world. What must we do? Abandon preaching as irrelevant? An old-fashioned preacher might offer three ways that preaching can be reclaimed for a twenty-first century world:

1. Recover the art of story-telling.
2. Invent new parables rather than explaining old ones.
3. Be provocative rather than didactic. Ask questions of the audience rather than telling them what to believe.

All three of these approaches have strong biblical precedent and will resonate well with postmodern culture. They also resonate well with a Methodist theological emphasis on prevenient grace—the preacher assumes that the listener has experienced the presence of God in their lives and is helping them to reflect upon that experience and respond to it. An approach to preaching that assumes the preacher knows the answers and that his or her hearer is ignorant of spiritual things will either be ignored or be received with hostility.

Discipleship

Whole-life, world-changing discipleship has recently become a major theme in British Methodism. This is, as yet, a fledgling initiative, but it is taking more seriously than the church has for some time the importance of equipping Christians to live well in their families, their careers, and their communities. It is hoped that this initiative will enable the church to rediscover in new ways some of the historic values of Methodism—particularly small group accountability and discipleship, social holiness and passionate evangelism. The connectional initiative is drawing together a number of things taking place at grass-roots level, which is a hopeful sign.

Britain and the World Parish

Some sociologists of religion have argued that the path of secularization that has taken root in Europe is unique and will not be replicated in the rest of the world.[8] If this is true, it places Europe in a context that makes it difficult to share mission initiatives with the global church. Within Europe, British Methodism and the other conferences in European Methodism are working more closely together to discern ways forward in the face of very similar problems.

However, in many ways, Britain is a microcosm of the whole world parish because of the massive impact of immigration on our culture. There are now large numbers of ethnic congregations from Africa and Asia in Britain, often receiving hospitality in the form of shared buildings from long established British Methodists. At the moment, they

---

8. See Davie, *Europe*.

are growing strongly as ethnic congregations, but have generally not succeeded in crossing over into Western culture and maintaining their growth. There are increasing signs that the leaders of many of these vibrant churches are moving beyond puzzlement as to why the indigenous British are so lukewarm about their faith (as they would see it) and are trying to engage with and understand the British context.

16

Making Disciples in Eastern Europe

Pavel Procházka

Critical Challenges

CONTEXT DEFINES THE CRITICAL CHALLENGES TO DISCIPLE-MAKING. In 2004 the Slovak Republic joined the European Union and since that time this membership has shaped Slovak society significantly in many respects. The prevailing European ethos rapidly influenced traditional Slovak values. Roman Catholicism has dominated Slovakia for generations, and this situation did not change during the long period of the communist regime from 1948-1989. Neither political pressure and intimidation nor state persecution dissuaded Slovaks from practicing their faith in traditional ways.

After the first decade of democracy in Slovakia, demographers analyzed the census of 2001. According to this survey the majority claimed to belong to the Roman Catholic Church (68.9 percent), another 6.9 percent to the Evangelical Lutheran Church, 4.1 percent to the Greek Catholic Church, and 2 percent to the Reformed Christian Church. Of the remaining Christian denominations, none had more than 10,000 members. These figures seem to be changing dramatically, however, as current intense human and cultural interchange within the European Union brings increasing diversity. This diversification of both ethnic and social elements creates new challenges related to disciple-making as well. For the small member churches in the Slovak Republic, including the Slovak United Methodist Church, the cultivation of partnerships will be critical to the relevance and vitality of their mission and ministry.[1]

Central to disciple-making are the ways in which the followers of Jesus and the churches they represent transmit God's grace through *kerygma* (preaching), *koinonia* (community), and *diakonia* (service). These elements which constitute the process of making disciples relate directly to people and their identity. What are the roots of traditional Slovak identity? The term "identity," in its broadest sense, connotes the similarity, sameness, oneness, or unity experienced within a given group of people. It also entails historical experience and memory, the continuation of tradition and the integration of community based on a common language. Identity provides concord, harmony, understanding, and peace. The same concepts and values undergird Christian discipleship as well, because it is equally concerned with the creation and experience of identity. The churches' ability to make disciples will be determined, in large measure, by the effort of the faithful to understand and appreciate the ways in which any given group of people co-operate and experience community in their own context, and by the way they maintain relationships on a personal level. As national identity represents a specific or particular aspect of human existence—a collective form of self-identification and self-interpretation—those who seek to cultivate disciples of Christ must engage in a perennial dialogue with these forces. This is all the more true in situations where solidarity and togetherness have played an important role in circumstances of oppression or danger.

A double tension characterizes the way in which the national identity is shaped in a European context involving ethnic diversity and integration: 1) a tension immediately surfaces around the issues of "localism" and "globalism" and 2) a tension emerges between the values or claims of self-rule and international cooperation. With regard to the first issue, a large state is not able to solve the problems of regional differentiation through typical bureaucratic channels. On the other hand, a state that is too small cannot reach unilateral solutions related to the international economic and ecological problems that increasingly characterize life. More typical for the Slovak context, with regard to the second issue, the rights of self-determination and self-governance clash with the need to

---

1. Procházka, "Slovak Small Membership Churches," 143–53.

both create and inhabit increasingly diverse space. Cultures collide and a way forward for all is often elusive.

National self-esteem in Slovakia is strongly connected to the nation's history and culture.[2] It is not strongly connected with values such as social justice, equality of opportunity, social benefits systems, or functional democracy. Churches face all of these challenges in their various missional and evangelistic endeavors.

Recent research among Methodist pastors in two countries of similar heritage, the Slovak Republic and the Czech Republic, supports these conclusions related to identity, culture, and change. Respondents to a questionnaire related to disciple-making in their context expressed a conviction that the key challenges they faced were related to identity issues. In the opinion of the participants, a number of related elements reflect this concern:

- The personal dimension of disciple-making—the identity of the one who brings the gospel shapes the process;
- The ecclesial dimension—the church must demonstrate its genuine and responsible concern for others, rather than engage in "kingdom building;"
- The particularity dimension—evangelists must reach out to people where they really are if there is any hope of their gaining new converts. Concern for the maintenance of identity often prevents the majority of people from entering a "new church" building or joining a "new church" activity;
- The contextual dimension—disciple-making is presently effective when the gospel is indigenized appropriately, rather than forcing converts to accommodate to a predetermined "acceptable way;"
- The needs dimension—for disciple-making to be effective it must reflect the needs and concerns of the people, rather than the needs of the church.

These reflections come from people who are involved in disciple-making on a daily basis. They understand this task to be a complex process, requiring a depth of understanding related to these issues, an appreciation for the background that has shaped the identity of the

---

2 Slovak Academy of Science, "Národná identita a hodnoty společnosti."

people, and a Christian community that is flexible enough to be able to cope with those challenges.

Scriptural Images

Just several years ago, Dana Hanesová conducted a detailed study of Bible teaching in the European Union.[3] She analyzed school curricula for Bible teaching in all the countries of the European Union as well as prospective scholarly literature on Bible teaching in those countries. Her interest, in part, revolved around the question about what approaches to biblical instruction were being developed to cope with the challenges of the changing social context of the Union. One of her discoveries relates to the distinction between simply teaching the Bible as a text like any other and teaching the Bible as a faith-engendering process. She concluded that the way in which the Bible is taught—the way in which students engage biblical images and stories—can facilitate a shift from mere teaching to disciple-making, provided that:

1. an active participation of the students is encouraged;
2. a heuristic approach and detailed understanding is made accessible;
3. discussion is welcomed;
4. critical thinking can be applied while allowing self-reflection;
5. contextual learning engages the local cultural context;
6. the pedagogy points to the goal of Bible teaching—to *personal transformation;* and
7. *active dialog characterizes the whole process.*

Many scriptural images and stories resonate closely with the Slovak and Czech contexts as the participants in a survey conducted by Pavel Procházka reveals. Some of the most pertinent biblical narratives to which they alluded include:

Stories in which Jesus fulfilled people's needs:

1. Matt 4:23–25: Jesus heals the sick;
2. Matt 8:14–17: Jesus heals many;

---

3. Hanesová, *Nabozenska vychova*, 41.

3. Matt 14:13–21: Jesus feeds the five thousand;
4. Matt 20:29–34: Two blind men receive their sight;
5. Mark 4:35–41: Jesus calms the storm;
6. Luke 17:11–19: Jesus heals ten lepers;
7. Luke 18:35–43: Jesus heals the blind beggar;
8. John 2:1–11: Jesus changes water to wine;
9. John 5:1–15: The healing at the pool.

Stories in which Jesus describes his followers and their actions:

1. Matthew 5:13–16: Jesus calls disciples to be salt and light;
2. Mark 12:28–34: The Greatest Commandment;
3. Luke 8:16–18: Jesus describes his followers as a lamp on a stand;
4. John 12:1–11: The anointing of Jesus at Bethany.

Stories in which Jesus proclaims the message of the kingdom:

1. Matt 19:16–30: The rich young man;
2. Matt 20:20–28: A mother's request;
3. Matt 23:1–39: The seven woes;
4. Mark 9:33–37: Who is the greatest?
5. John 4:1–26: Jesus talks with a Samaritan woman.

Stories in which Jesus addresses the demands of discipleship and relation to God:

1. Matt 6:24: No one can serve two masters;
2. Luke 7:41–42: Two men owed money;
3. Luke 17:7–10: The Lord and a servant;
4. Luke 18:1–5: The parable of the persistent widow.

These various Gospel texts correspond to the concerns raised by the analysis of Procházka. These narratives, in particular, relate well to an East European context and the process by which disciples are formed through both evangelism and Bible teaching in the paradigmatic way that she described.

Evangelistic Practices

Perhaps no other evangelistic practice continues to be as important in the life of the church as preaching. This *kerygmatic* action entails at least two important dimensions in which the Holy Spirit is at work: the transcendent dimension of God's offer of grace in Jesus Christ and the immanent dimension of the human response to God's redemptive work through Jesus Christ. In a Slovak setting, preaching is not only an act of the church that involves the proclamation of God's love and grace; it is an act that engages people wherever they are, rooted in the particular socio-religious context that has given shape to their identity in the past. The *kerygma*—the proclamation of the Word of God—not only holds within itself the ability to change the quality of a person's life, but enables the recipient to forge a new identity, even overcoming the stereotypes and lesser identities by which he or she has been known.

A group of researchers from Slovak universities, under the auspices of the University of Matej Bel in Banska Bystrica, recently undertook research on the practice of preaching in churches. The initial findings related to this study were published recently in a book entitled *Homileticka cinnost cirkvi a kvalita sucasneho zivota [Homiletical Activities of the Churches and the Quality of Life]*.[4] This study sheds light on the way in which evangelistic practice is understood in the Slovak churches and how it can be adapted to respond more effectively in this context. The researchers tackle the problem of preaching in relation to subjective life-satisfaction (perspectives, feelings, beliefs, and desires). On the basis of their analysis of responses from a large sample of participants in the study, they determined that preaching helps people most in the following areas:

- finding meaning in life;
- realizing and implementing love, acceptance, and togetherness; and
- helping one another.

On the other hand, participants perceived preaching as deficient when it focused on:

---

4. Masarik, *Homileticka cinnost cirkvi*.

1. self-actualization;
2. positive acceptance of sexuality;
3. the meaning of family support;
4. a sense of leisure in the use of one's free time; and
5. the meaning of hobbies.[5]

This research actually helps demonstrate that evangelistic practice and disciple-making in the Slovak context conforms to very traditional patterns in terms of preaching ministry, while giving little attention to contemporary changes in the lifestyle and self-identified needs of the people.

The issue of identity surfaces once again in these considerations, but in a slightly different context. Slovak evangelical theologian, P. Hanes, addresses the crucial issue: "A theology of evangelization must clarify the problem of the identity of the messenger, his relationship to God, and the addressee of the message (2 Cor 1:22; 5:5; Eph 1:14). Maybe the most important issue today is the position of the messenger (preacher or evangelist); how does he or she dare to speak in the name of God? Is it possible to claim what the apostle said about himself and his co-workers? We are therefore Christ's ambassadors, as though God were making his appeal through us. We implore you on Christ's behalf: Be reconciled to God (2 Cor 5:20, NIV)."[6]

Nothing is more important than the identity of the messenger—his or her authenticity and integrity. The practice of evangelism, or disciple-making, requires dedicated men and women. Paul Tillich was right when, pointing to the witness of Paul (2 Cor 5:17), he said all that matters is the "new being"—the new creation. Given the increasingly pluralistic character of Slovak society today, Christians must speak and act in a distinctive way that captures the hearts and minds of the people, rather than simply representing one voice among many others. People respond with enthusiasm to the message of the gospel when it comes to them through the ministry of exceptional people who demonstrate their personal involvement, dedication, and commitment in clear and dynamic ways.

---

5. Ibid., 27–28.
6. Hanes, "Theology of Evangelization," 107.

Christian Vitality

Signs of new life and vitality abound in the life of the church as a result of the vision and practice described above. A survey of developments over the past ten years bears this out. The United Methodist Church in Slovakia understands its mission in the context of the universal mission of disciples in the whole world—in every nation. The Methodist "connectional" self-understanding has been instrumental in shaping and implementing the evangelistic and disciple-making mission in Slovakia. In spite of the fact that there are only a few local churches in Slovakia with only several hundred active believers and limited resources, the church has accomplished much due to personal and material sharing in a global community. The vision of a world church that is concerned about every community, no matter how small or marginalized, changes one's perspective regarding the existence and further development of the church. As a consequence of this decade of ministry and mission, Methodism has gained in legitimacy in Slovakia, and other people are beginning to appreciate its impact on society. All of this can be seen in two areas in particular.

Education

For a long time there has been strong cooperation among Slovak small membership churches in the area of university-level training for church pastors, mission workers, and teachers. The Baptist Union, Evangelical Free Church, Assemblies of God, and the United Methodist Church founded the Department of Evangelical Theology and Mission (DETM) in 1993 under the auspices of the School of Education, University of Matej Bel in Banska Bystrica. This department exists for the purpose of cooperatively meeting the needs of the evangelical churches in Slovakia and other countries. Education through the DETM covers three main areas: the development of cognition, ministry skills, and Christian character and professionalism. This program gave the churches in Slovakia, as well as in several other European countries, trained men and women of faith who are now instrumental in disciple-making processes in their respective settings. Out of the twenty-seven persons in the ministry of the United Methodist Church, Slovak District, there are twelve graduates of DETM, including the District Superintendent.

Another educational opportunity is the Advanced Pastor Training Project. Everyone in ministry is required to complete fifty credit hours of continuing education each year through the reading and review of theological literature, by participating in theological conferences, or by receiving credit through post-graduate education. During the previous two years of this project, many of the clergy have been able to successfully complete actual courses of study in theological disciplines, and the church has benefited greatly as a consequence.

Educational opportunities, moreover, are not limited to clergy. There is a two-stage lay program for all people in the churches. The first stage of this program offers a Slovak version of the *Disciple Bible Study* material, fully adapted to the Slovak context. The fundamental method of this intensive program of biblical study has been retained, but both textual and video materials have been either interpreted or revised with the use of indigenous people. The second stage of the program seeks to implement the learning in the day-to-day activities of the disciples.

New Church Planting

The second distinctive feature of the church's work over the past ten years has to do with an aggressive program of new church planting. Since the church now has a critical mass of well-educated, informed disciples of Jesus, there has been a strong desire to start new churches. Despite the fact that the United Methodist Church has very limited financial resources, there have been a number of people who have taken up this evangelistic appeal with enthusiasm. Long-standing support from the Connecting Congregations Program of the World Methodist Council's World Evangelism division, as well as connection with the In Mission Together Program of the General Board of Global Ministries, fanned the flame of evangelistic passion in their hearts of the people. Since the political changes of 1989, new churches have been organized in Bratislava-Petrzalka, Trnava, Piestany, Michalovce, and Slavkovce, and new mission centers have been opened. All of these developments involved both clergy and lay people, men and women.

These signs of new life and vitality in the life of the church led the district conference to articulate and adopt a missional plan for the church in 2004 that will direct the work through 2014. Some of its objectives have already been achieved. It envisioned further personnel development (ten ordained elders), the organization of Provisional

Annual Conference, the installation of a Slovak District Superintendent (accomplished in 2007), the attainment of financial self-sufficiency, the organization of at least ten new parish churches (eight have been established to date), and the acceptance of at least one thousand new people into membership as disciples of Jesus Christ.

Global Contributions

Does the Slovak church really have anything to contribute to the world parish on the basis of lessons learned about disciple-making? This question was actually asked in the Procházka survey distributed to pastors in the Czech and Slovak Republics. Many respondents gave no answer; others were skeptical. A general feeling was that Methodists in this part of Eastern Europe ought to listen more closely to others and implement their findings since the Methodist presence and experience in Slovakia is not as rich as that of many others.

From among the few who suggested anything to share with the rest of the world, however, there came several suggestions:

- Our disciple-making process may be an encouraging phenomenon for others who also wrestle with the Great Commission under stifling conditions. There is no other way than to rely on God's support when we go to people with empty hands, with no power, a short history, and cultural hostility from the majority. Jesus is fulfilling our daily needs in evangelism and discipleship.

- The disciple-making process in our context compels all involved seriously to accept the biblical principle of genuine commitment as a disciple of Jesus Christ. Disciples of Jesus in this setting are here for others. That requires their time, their reliance on the gifts of the Holy Spirit, and all their energy.

- Becoming disciples of Jesus means assuming a minority identity. This is not easy and may even have the effect of lowering one's social status eventually. Discipleship, in other words, is costly.

- Evangelism and disciple-making draw people of all backgrounds—of diverse ethnic cultures and traditions—together. This is a gift. Slovaks, Czechs, Hungarians, Russians, Romanians, foreigners living in Slovakia—all have to cope with society's traditional or current issues of hostility and distrust, because in Jesus we are all brothers and sisters, children of one glorious family.

Further Reading on European Contexts

Atkins, Martyn. *Resourcing Renewal: Shaping Churches for the Emerging Future.* London: Inspire, 2007.
Ballard, Paul, editor. *The Church at the Centre of the City.* Peterborough: Epworth, 2008.
Michael I. Bochenski. *Theology from Three Worlds: Liberation and Evangelism for the New Europe.* Macon, GA: Smyth & Helwys, 1997.
Cavanaugh, William T. *Theopolitical Imagination: Discovering the Eucharist as a Political Act in an Age of Global Consumerism.* London: T. & T. Clark, 2002.
Clark, David B. *Breaking the Mould of Christendom: Kingdom Community, Diaconal Church and the Liberation of the Laity.* Peterborough: Epworth, 2005.
Conference of European Churches. *Mission of the Churches in a Secularised Europe: Mission and Secularisation.* 2 vols. Geneva: CEC, 1989.
Cracknell, Kenneth. *In Good and Generous Faith.* Peterborough: Epworth, 2005.
Croft, Steven. *Growing New Christians: Developing Evangelism and Nurture in the Local Church.* London: Marshall Pickering, 1993.
———. *Transforming Communities: Re-Imagining the Church in the 21st Century.* Maryknoll, NY: Orbis, 2002.
Croft, Steven, et al. *Evangelism in a Spiritual Age: Communicating Faith in a Changing Culture.* London: Church House, 2005.
Eschmann, Holger, et al. *Freikirche Landeskirche. Historische Alternative—Gemeinsame Zukunft?* NeukirchenVluyn, Germany: Neukirchener, 2008.
Fletcher, R. A. *The Conversion of Europe.* New York: HarperCollins, 1997.
Hollinghurst, Steve. *Mission Shaped Evangelism: The Gospel in Contemporary Culture.* London: Canterbury, 2010.
Kim, Kirsteen. *Joining in with the Spirit: Connecting World Church and Local Mission.* Peterborough: Epworth, 2010.
Linn, Gerhard, editor. *Hear What the Spirit Says to the Churches: Towards Missionary Congregations in Europe.* Geneva: WCC, 1994.
Malaska, Hilkka. *The Challenge of Evangelical Missions in Europe: A Scandanavian Case Study.* Pasadena, CA: William Carey Library, 1970.
Murray, Stuart. *Changing Mission: Learning from the Newer Churches.* London: Churches Together in Britain and Ireland, 2008.
Nelstrop, Louise, and Martyn Percy. *Evaluating Fresh Expressions: Explorations in Emerging Church.* London: Canterbury, 2008.
Pilli, Einike. *Terviklik elukestva õppe kontseptsioon Eesti protestantlike koguduste kontekstis.* Tartu: Tartu Ülikooli Kirjastus, 2005.
Pillinger, Pete, and Andrew Roberts, editors. *Changing Church for a Changing World: Fresh Ways of Being Church in the Methodist Context.* London: Trustees for Methodist Church Purposes, 2007.

Samuel, Viney, and Albrecht Hauser, editors. *Proclaiming Christ in Christ's Way: Studies in Integral Evangelism*. Oxford: Regnum, 1989.

Wanner, Catherine, *Communities of the Converted: Ukrainians and Global Evangelism*. Ithaca: Cornell University Press, 2007.

Weinrich, Michael, et al. *Contextuality in Reformed Europe: The Mission of the Church in the Transformation of European Culture*. Amsterdam: Rodopi, 2004.

Werth, Martin. *Theologie der Evangelisation*. Neukirchen-Vluyn: Neukirchener, 2004.

Williams, Rowan. *Mission-Shaped Church: Church Planting and Fresh Expressions of Church in a Changing Context*. London: Church House, 2007.

PART FOUR

Latin America & Caribbean
Tacking into the Wind

Introduction to Part 4

THE WIND OF THE SPIRIT IS BLOWING ACROSS LATIN AMERICA AND the Caribbean. The rapid rise of Pentecostal and charismatic churches among the poor and now the middle class is one of the startling missiological facts of the twentieth century. With such strong winds, it is sometimes necessary to tack into the wind in order to take full advantage of its power. Despite these developments, Protestant traditions remain a minority, and a tiny minority, in some Latin American nations, and the social challenges they face are formidable. The Spirit calls the community of Jesus to make disciples in a context characterized by a monumental division between "haves" and "have-nots," to reach out with loving concern to people who are eke out an existence in desperate poor, and to declare the gospel of liberation in the face of injustice.

George Mulrain writes from the perspective of a native from the twin-island Republic of Trinidad & Tobago, who has served in Haiti and Jamaica, and now oversees the work of Methodism throughout the Carribean and the Americas. He describes the complexity of life in these Island nations, demonstrating how the history of the region brought Americans, Europeans, Africans, and Asians together into a kaleidoscopic mix of language, custom, and religion. Of particular interest are his discussions of biblical "sea images" that resonate with the life of the Caribbean people and shape their understanding of disciple-making. How does one connect gospel and culture in this context? What does it mean to be fully Christian and fully Carribean?

Costa Rica presents distinct challenges constitutive of this South American setting. The diagnosis and prescription offered by Nidia Fonseca necessarily revolve around the issue of abject poverty. The diagnosis: the masses (but particularly women and children) live in extreme poverty with little hope. The prescription: the church must develop a holistic model of disciple formation that restores life and dignity to all. Conversion in this context (a lesson of equal value to all who seek to follow Christ) involves a "turning from oneself in order to be totally open to God and others." It is a complex process rooted in God's call to mission. Only those whose lives have been realigned to the rule of God in life and who seek to be conformed to the image of Christ have the capacity to invite those excluded from society into the house of God.

What happens when the forces of time remove "method" from Methodism? This is the question with which Raúl García de Ochoa struggles in his examination of disciple-making in Mexico. In response to the four primary challenges of a centripetal community of faith—sharing the faith, preserving the fruit, training and teaching new believers, and sending disciples to evangelize and disciple others—Bishop García issues a clarion call to rediscover the meaning of discipline. He draws analogies from the military images of scripture to articulate a vision of churches composed of small group dynamos that have rediscovered the meaning of method.

17

Caribbean Perspectives on Mission/Evangelism

George Mulrain

Critical Challenges

A Multicultural Context

THE CARIBBEAN CONTEXT IS MULTICULTURAL, BUILT UPON A BASE of indigenous Amerindian tribes, including Caribs and Arawaks. Historical records indicate that during the fifteenth century invasion of the Spanish, Europeans used the Caribbean as a battleground in fighting one another to capture island territories and to secure the attendant wealth of sugar plantations. The Amerindian settlers were subdued as the Europeans effectively established their supremacy. This scenario set the stage for the present multicultural context. In the Caribbean of today, although most of the islands are politically independent units, there are still those that belong to England, France, and the Netherlands. Four European languages—Spanish, English, French, and Dutch—are spoken, as well as locally developed languages that bear names such as *créole*, *patois*, and *papiamento*.

When the Europeans had established themselves as the virtual owners of Caribbean islands, the Indians provided cheap labor on the plantations. They were later joined by blacks whom the Europeans had captured from the west coast of Africa and brought as slaves into the region. Early in the nineteenth century (1807) this trade in human cargo ceased. However, in the British colonies, the institution of slavery dragged on for three decades before coming to an end (1834). Emancipation resulted in a serious labor problem. As a corrective, workers from other parts of the world, including the Indian sub-continent, were issued an invitation and accepted to come as indentured laborers who incidentally contributed another interesting facet to the culture of the Caribbean.

A Multi-Faith Context

Today's Caribbean context is as multi-faith as it is multicultural. Very little is known of early Amerindian religious beliefs and practices, but Dale Bisnauth's book on the region's history provides instruction in this regard.[1] The Europeans introduced Christianity, though it must be admitted that the conversion of Amerindians took place on pain of death. When the slaves arrived they brought their unique African religious expressions. The Indians from the sub-continent came with Hinduism and Islam. Some of the religious traditions and practices that are now current, including those that bear a Christian label, can best be described as syncretistic because they have combined aspects of European Christianity with the religions of Africa and Asia.

This multi-faith context highlights an important point that must always be borne in mind by those involved in mission and evangelism. Whatever the method being employed, it must emphasize conviction, not coercion. It is paramount today not to return to those dark chapters in the region's history when the good news, instead of being lovingly presented, was thrust at the edge of a sword. One lesson the Caribbean has learned is how to be respectful towards men and women of other faiths. Respect and sensitivity are two key qualities that any Christian would do well to cultivate. Refrain from referring to persons of other faiths as heathens or pagans. Avoid being patronizing. Do not make the mistake of referring to them as anonymous Christians. Stay clear of any suggestion or description of them that would be an affront or an insult to their dignity and intelligence.

It is only natural that in presenting the gospel to others, an evangelist or missioner will refer to his or her own cultural orientation. In the history of the Caribbean, however, what was only natural became a dilemma. In elevating their own culture, missionaries almost always condemned the "inferior" culture of their hosts. Those who were drawn to the Christian faith, therefore, were forced to wrestle with the question

1. See Bisnauth, *History of Religions in the Caribbean*.

as to whether they should reject their own culture, in part or completely, in order to wholeheartedly embrace the culture of the missionary that was so bound up with their faith. In particular, those who sought to propagate the faith insisted that the culture of the descendants of African slaves was inherently evil. They viewed their drumming and dancing as "demonic"; hence, not to be incorporated into Christian worship. Similarly, the descendants of Indian indentured workers who became Christians were prohibited from employing their musical genre in worship.

These attitudes were so deeply engrained that there is still the lingering reluctance on the part of Caribbean Christians to use indigenous cultural forms in the liturgy. Progress, however, is being made. It is acknowledged that becoming a disciple of Christ does not necessarily mean that one has to reject one's culture. Hymns and songs coming out of European and North American contexts are acceptable in offering praises to God, but so too are the hymns and songs of faith that originated in Africa and Asia and those that are couched in the local calypso and reggae idioms. Christians not only attach value to the use of organs, but other musical instruments, including the steel orchestra—a twentieth century invention that had its birth in Trinidad & Tobago and then spread across the region—facilitate worship as well. The present challenge facing the region is the same one encountered during the 1970s in particular, namely, how to be fully Christian and fully Caribbean. Applying this on the broader global scene, the question is, how one can be fully Christian while identifying fully with one's own geographical, national, and cultural contexts?

Scriptural Images

The Call to Discipleship

Because the islands in the region under scrutiny are washed by the blue waters of the Caribbean Sea, biblical stories such as those that tell of Jesus at the seaside are likely to have a familiar ring. Caribbean hearers feel a sense of identity with the adventures of the fishermen who accompanied Jesus as well as with the overall message contained in the Gospels. One such narrative at the very beginning of Mark's Gospel relates directly to discipleship: "As Jesus passed along the Sea of Galilee, he saw Simon and his brother Andrew casting a net into the sea—for they were fishermen. And Jesus said to them, 'Follow me and I will make you fish for people.' And immediately they left their nets and followed him. As he went a little farther, he saw James son of Zebedee and his brother John, who were in their boat mending the nets. Immediately he called them; and they left their father Zebedee in the boat with the hired men, and followed him" (Mark 1:16–20). Caribbean Christians relate to the setting and the vision of discipleship depicted in this scene.

The Value of All Human Beings

One of the most powerful images from the Hebrew Scriptures that resonates with the Caribbean context comes from the Genesis account of creation (1:26–27). This narrative acknowledges that all persons have been created in the image and likeness of God, irrespective of culture or faith commitment. It provides the foundation upon which to base all evangelistic or missionary activities. This affirmation speaks volumes in the Caribbean. It states categorically that *all* persons are of worth in the sight of God, directly contradicting the suggestion in the region's historical past that the indigenous inhabitants and those who came afterwards were inferior to Europeans. The New Testament reference to the human bodies as the temple of the Holy Spirit affirms the same principle and is equally appealing (1 Cor 6:19). This good news (gospel) counteracts the historical contention that persons of color did not have souls or anything suggestive of a divine presence in their lives. Moreover, in a region facing the serious problem of violent crime—in which some think nothing of taking the lives of others—this concept of the human being reminds everyone of the value of human life and the righteous judgment that falls upon those who devalue it. It teaches a fundamental respect for life, and this has direct relevance for disciple-making.

The Significance of Cross-Cultural Encounter

Stories that describe a meeting of cultures communicate effectively in the Caribbean context. At Jacob's well Jesus meets a Samaritan woman and the transformation that takes place through that encounter leads to her evangelistic witness in her community (John 4:7–29). "Then the woman left her water jar and went back to the city. She said to the people, 'Come and see a man who told me everything I have ever done'" (John 4:28–29)! A Syrophoenician woman demonstrates the depth of her faith when told that it was not right to take the children's crumbs and give them to dogs, a slur upon her culture and her people (Mark 7:24–30). Jesus makes a special point to honor her faith and show his disciples that his kingdom is for every person. These cross-cultural encounters—many of them with women—reveal Jesus' respect for all people at all times and all places, even people of other faiths and traditions. Given the multi-faith context of the Caribbean, it is of particular interest to note the scriptural warning against a "superiority complex" implicit in these narratives. Christ challenges all who follow him to faithfulness in this regard and to a spirit of uncompromising hospitality and respect for all, otherwise "the kingdom of God will be taken away from you and given to a people that produces the fruits of the kingdom" (Matt 21:43).

The Power of the Gospel

It ought also to be noted that the Caribbean, heavily influenced by Africa, espouses a cosmology that acknowledges "other worldly" dimensions in life. In addition to the reality of the physical world, most people believe in a world of spirits as well. Those passages of scripture, therefore, that emphasize a wrestling, not simply against flesh and blood, but against principalities and powers, tend to have special meaning in the communication of the good news to the people of the Caribbean (see Eph 6:12). Victory over these malevolent powers is an important facet of the gospel message. Mark demonstrates Jesus' authority in this regard right at the outset of his Gospel: "They were all amazed, and they kept on asking one another, 'What is this? A new teaching—with authority! He commands even the unclean spirits, and they obey him.' At once his fame began to spread throughout the surrounding region of Galilee. . . . That evening, at sunset, they brought to him all who were sick or possessed with demons. And the whole city was gathered around the door. And he cured many who were sick with various diseases, and cast out many demons; and he would not permit the demons to speak, because they knew him" (Mark 1:27–28, 32–34). This demonstration of gospel power connects with people of the Caribbean.

Evangelistic Practice

In the actual practice of mission and evangelism, the people of the Caribbean know that nothing is wrong with being eclectic in the methods employed. It is essential that one develops an openness so as to learn from others and to apply new practices to good effect wherever appropriate and necessary. Methods of evangelism, therefore, vary. In this region as elsewhere, when people share the gospel on a person-to-person basis, positive results almost always occur. Indeed, most people attach credibility to personal and practical expressions of care. By getting alongside persons and hearing their stories, one becomes better acquainted with their felt needs and is in a position to work meaningfully towards alleviating their situation. Personal evangelism will undoubtedly remain the core missional practice of the church. But the church also provides care to people on a broader, community level, living out its missional character in areas that might traditionally be regarded as the domain of the government. These activities lead to the making of disciples nonetheless.

The Methodist Church in Haiti provides a case in point to illustrate how the gospel is lived out through the humanitarian activities that are an essential part of the church's mission. Historically the church has communicated the good news, not only through preaching or the verbal proclamation of the message of Jesus Christ, but through education, health care, and community development. This approach reinforces an important lesson concerning the way in which the Holy Spirit does the work of evangelism and disciple-making. It is not necessary to insist that people who receive the benefits of the church's missionary activity become members. In the final analysis, people will align themselves wholeheartedly to the Christian community and commit their lives to Christ if they are convicted inwardly by the Holy Spirit.

The experience of the Haitians in this regard has also taught the church that, in its commitment to mission and evangelism, it must address the whole person. During the period of his earthly ministry, Jesus demonstrated an interest not only in spiritual matters but in practical, physical, down-to earth concerns. When addressing the crowds and perceiving their interest in hearing his message of good news, he was attentive to their primary needs and supplemented his presentation by offering them physical food (see John 6:1–15). People appreciated this then and they appreciate it now. The social outworking of the gospel demonstrates the genuine nature of God's love and care. Involvement in social service can be a costly enterprise that governments seem more equipped to undertake, and the church often finds itself constrained to seek outside assistance. In the Caribbean region, in which various subcultures and faiths coexist, Christians work together with organizations that are no overtly Christian in order to improve life for everyone in the community. The compromise required in the process is that such "partners" share aims and objectives that are similar to those embraced by the church. The important thing is that God's rule is more fully realized through all these efforts; these works proclaim the gospel in tangible ways.

Christian Vitality

Today there are signs of new life and vitality within the Caribbean church. This is particularly true among the young. Youth find themselves attracted to congregations where there are significant numbers of young people. In one sense, vibrant worship serves as a magnetic force. In an atmosphere of care, where young people feel loved and appreciated, they remain open and receptive to the message of the gospel. The primary challenge facing congregations with large numbers of young persons is how to maintain their zeal and enthusiasm for the gospel. Creatively thought out programs are crucial. Youth love music, drama, and dance. They remain attached and engaged if the community caters for this passion. How to sustain this interest in persons when they move out of their teens and into young adulthood presents a further challenge. Youth and young adults often declare their concern about issues of justice very openly. If they perceive that the church shares their interest and commitment to justice, it may be that more youth will remain within the fold. Whenever youth are allowed to play a part in the leadership of the church, or in any organization for that matter, they develop a sense of "ownership" and remain engaged and active participants in the larger community.

For evangelism to be effective, it must be started at the earliest age. Whenever the "cradle roll" functions in a healthy way within Caribbean Methodism—when the community takes its baptismal responsibilities seriously—it pays great dividends. If every baby baptized is enlisted and monitored caringly in a pastoral sense, and the parents and the entire community are reminded frequently of their promise and responsibility to raise their children in the knowledge and love of God, then the probability of everyone's continued faithfulness is enhanced. The simple fact is that everyone discovers what it means to be a disciple of Christ when all participate fully in a living community of faith.

The abiding value of children and youth organizations cannot be overestimated! These help to inject discipline in the lives of young boys and girls. They provide a shaping force in terms of character formation and the development of values that are consistent with the reign of God. On the basis of the testimony of those who have been involved in these organizations, they have helped youth develop a moral and ethical framework for life. If the church does not hold the young people lovingly in its embrace, there are criminal elements that will certainly be happy to do so, gangs that are not necessarily there to teach them to walk along the straight and narrow path. Such groups, in fact, are a growing threat in the Caribbean. Many of the gangs in several of the Caribbean islands are dedicated to molding rough and tough youth who spend their lives breaking the law and being the perpetrators of dastardly acts including rape and murder.

Apart from the exciting signs of renewal and energy visible among the youth, signs of vitality are also evident among Caribbean women. Throughout the world women, in fact, do play a vital role and exert much influence in church and community. Within Caribbean Methodism, women have become increasingly visible in roles of leadership over the years. The majority of Sunday School teachers are women. Women are well represented in the leadership of youth and young adult organizations. There has been a significant rise in the number of women offering themselves as candidates for the Christian ministry. It is of tremendous importance in any missionary or evangelistic enterprise to ensure that women are fully involved. To ignore or underestimate their contribution constitutes a mistake from which the church can never easily recover.

Global Contributions

The lessons that are being learned about disciple-making in the Caribbean context make a contribution to the theory and practice of mission and evangelism in the rest of the world. Perhaps the most important lesson has to do with the necessary connection between "gospel" and "culture." For someone to embrace the good news of Jesus Christ does not necessarily mean that they must deny their culture. All cultures must come under the judgment of the gospel of Christ, but it is important to acknowledge those good aspects of culture that do not contradict the faith and exploit them in appropriate ways. The Christian community may determine that some facets of the culture are incompatible with the way of Jesus, but there is much in culture upon which to build. Discerning together what must be purged and what must be embraced is, in and of itself, an important aspect of disciple-making.

With so many cultures, ethnic groups, and religions in the Caribbean, this region is a microcosm of the larger world. Perhaps the missional challenge here is the challenge everywhere. In light of the differences within the human family, how does one remain true to one's "cultural self" and become a faithful disciple of Christ and the laws of God? As Jesus affirmed on one occasion, we must "Give to the emperor the things that are the emperor's, and to God the things that are God's" (Mark 12:17). Christian discipleship involves the adventure of navigating these difficult waters, even the beautiful, blue Caribbean.

18

The Mission of God and the Mission of the Church in Latin America

Nidia V. Fonseca R. (Translated by Philip Wingeier-Rayo)

Starting Points

LATIN AMERICAN LIBERATION THEOLOGY WAS BORN AT A TIME WHEN the suffering from military dictatorships reached its peak. The people were suffering, not only from the psychological conditions that all dictatorships impose, but also from the material shortages that the majority encounter. The suffering of believers challenges the "bigger" brothers and sisters of the faith—pastors and priests—as the questions of their impotence in relation to their "smaller" brothers and sisters challenges their deepest understanding of the faith and their perspective of God.

It is important to acknowledge this context as a starting point for this reflection. In this regard, eight particular topics or perspectives, first identified by José Míguez Bonino, frame the exploration of the mission of the church in Latin America.[1]

1. *The Perspective of Ethics*: What does it mean, here and now, to be witnesses of the kingdom of God, of the fair and generous government of God? What should I do? The Word of God is to be "done," not merely heard. This posture is what motivates Latin American theologians to revise their theological task and their own Christian praxis.

---

1. See Bonino, *Ama y haz lo que quieras*.

2. *The Perspective of Anthropology*: True existence is when the human being responds freely and joyfully beyond conventional barriers and limitations, beyond merely what the law requires, maybe even beyond what the law allows, in solidarity with the needs of one's neighbor (Luke 9:37).

3. *The Perspective of Faith*: Faith in Christ is a new reality that has burst into our world. It is a new power that we can see at work, a new existence that has been made accessible to us (1 Cor 15:35a). It is a community act, an act of relationship, an act of love. Life in this community of faith transcends humanity and all of creation.

4. *The Perspective of Politics*: Faith is conceived as a political act of God that affects all human reality. "It could be said," claims Guichard, "that political activity is an increasingly more important demand of faithfulness."[2] Faith as a social practice should be conceived according to a specific context and be consistent with one's faith. Theology is political theology when it critiques the status quo through the lens of eschatology, demonstrating God's promises and their realization.

5. *The Perspective of Salvation*: Salvation is a unique and complex process of holistic liberation that includes communion with the human being, God, all of creation and communion among human beings, which implies historical concreteness. In this context revelation is a critical and public dimension of faith in response to the Word of God.

6. *The Perspective of Poverty*: Poverty is the state of being deprived and dispossessed by an exploitative economic system. Gustavo Gutierrez advanced a three-fold definition of poverty which includes "material and cultural poverty, poverty as spiritual infancy and poverty as a commitment of solidarity and protest, and establishing ties between these two levels."[3] According to Julio de Santa Ana, "someone who is poor is dependent, lacking and is

---

2. Guichard, *Iglesia*, 32.
3. As cited in Tamayo-Acosta, *Para comprender la Teología*, 244.

limited in his existence and therefore awaits that his condition will be vindicated in God and justice will be done."[4]

7. *The Perspective of God's Preferential Option for the Poor*: God liberates the oppressed in the Hebrew Scriptures and, in the New Testament, delivers the poor through Jesus. God demonstrates his solidarity with the poor. In God's reign the poor erupt in history as conscientious actors are motivated by the praxis of faith discerned in community, struggle against injustice, and reflect on faith, celebration, and transformation.

8. *The Perspective of Liberation*: The "new creation" begins with the eradication of the oppressive consciousness of revenge from the minds of the oppressed. It is reconciliation in its fullest sense. This concept of liberation into a new order of existence is not only the broadest conception of salvation history, but it connects salvation history—the realization of the "new creation"—with the salvation of history.

These eight themes constitute the theological cosmology out of which we reflect on the mission of God and the mission of the church.

Missio Dei in Latin American Liberation Theologies

For Latin American liberation theology, the church is only part of the mission of God when it listens to the call to be in solidarity with the poor. It presupposes that persons and the community go through a process of conversion and commitment. Conversion—turning from oneself in order to be totally open to God and others—is a complex process rooted in God's call to mission. When oriented intentionally around the poor, this requires a complete revision both of the typical conception of mission and of the church.[5]

The first movement of this reorientation is the development of a larger conception of faith that is connected to the reign of God. This faith is a covenant—an alliance between the people and God—not a covenant with an individual person. According to Victorio Araya, although each individual has faith in a radically autobiographical sense,

---

4. de Santa Ana, *El Desafio de los Pobres a la iglesia*, 108.
5. See Araya, *El Dios de los pobres*.

"this personal faith in God makes sense only when it is lived, not by an autonomous individual, but in the interior of a community."[6] God, first through Abraham, Moses, and the prophets, and then through Jesus, called the people because the kingdom of God was at hand. Leonardo Boff identifies the scriptural locus of this mission-church-reign interface: "Jesus did not go forth to preach the church, but to preach the kingdom of God. 'This is the time of fulfillment. The reign of God is at hand! Reform your lives and believe in the gospel!' (Mark. 1:15) . . . the notion of the kingdom of God embraces all reality, including infrahuman reality, inasmuch as this reality too is to be purified of its evil and inserted into God's absolute lordship."[7]

God's call to mission aligns the covenant community with the kingdom. This orientation of the missional church toward the reign necessitates that disciples of Christ attend to all who cry out of pain (oppressed people and nature). God's reign and the poor, in other words, as Araya has argued, are inextricably intertwined: "The community of Jesus' followers does not exist as end in itself, but for service to the world in the service of the reign of God."[8]

The church already has a paradigm to realize this covenantal, missional vision—the way of Jesus Christ. So, one can say that the mission is profoundly Christological. Jesus' mission, in which we are invited to participate, is both historical and universal, but even transcends the church itself. *Lumen Gentium: The Dogmatic Constitution on the Church,* of the Second Vatican Council of the Roman Catholic Church, states: "Just as Christ carried out the work of redemption in poverty and persecution, so the Church is called to follow the same route that it might communicate the fruits of salvation to men."[9] The church does not create its own mission; rather, God plants his mission and invites the people to realize it, together with him, in the context in which the church finds itself, challenging local churches and their leaders. Engagement in the mission of God demands constant vigilance and intentionality as the church reflects on the mission of God itself, the signs of the times, the roll of the people and the churches in God's project, and the preferential option of God in each historical moment.

6. Ibid., 133.
7. Boff, *Ecclesiogenesis*, 51.
8. Araya, *El Dios de los pobres*, 133.
9. *Lumen Gentium,* Chapter I: The Mystery of the Church.

God reveals this project progressively through history. In the Bible, we see the broad parameters of God's work in creation, redemption, and eschaton. Whenever the people of God are involved in creative and liberating experiences, they feel united with God's project and are better able to discern God's presence or revelation. "That is why," according to José Duque, "it is said that the origins of biblical faith lie in an historical event of liberation, namely the liberating act of the Exodus."[10] The church, therefore, must pay attention to the signs of the times in the historical context in which it is situated. Frequently these signs reveal profound contradictions and expose tensions between polarities within life situations: development/stagnation, wealth/poverty, liberation/oppression, and life/death.

A more fully textured understanding of the category of "the people of God" made possible the birth and development of the "Base Christian Communities," as well as other types of local churches and national organizations. Christians in Latin America quickly recognized that these communities provided concrete spaces where faith—as an act of God—could become concrete, and where faith—as a reciprocal human action—could be nurtured. According to Jon Sobrino, in Base Christian Communities the fundamental structure of the life of Jesus is revived: incarnation in the life of the poor (kenosis); practice of love and fraternity, which should be translated into an efficient praxis of liberation; a spirit of mission which involves taking up the cross, in other words, engaging in conflict, persecution, and death; living like one is resurrected here in history, with hope in the final fulfillment.[11] As Alberto Parra observes: "The most specific characteristic of the very being of the church, its constitution and its mission, is the mystery of and participation in communion which is inseparable from the process of liberation . . . no one can wisely assert that just because the Christian communities surge from below, from the people, that this movement of ecclesial life is not ecclesial."[12]

The Council of Latin American bishops meeting in Puebla in 1979 insisted on connecting mission with the preferential option for the poor and described authentic mission as "establishing a dignified human community or building a just and free society: promoting and

---

10. See Duque, *Modulo Mision de la Iglesia*.
11. See Sobrino, *The True Church and the Poor*.
12. Parra, *De la iglesia*, 21.

defending the human rights of the poor, marginalized, and oppressed. It also means solidarity with the poor, where the word 'solidarity' is free of paternalism."[13] Consistent with this vision, Renoldo Muñoz describes mission as "a sacrament that unites the universe and liberates the oppressed," and argues that mission starts with the "divisions, conflicts, and real oppression, as the church sides with the oppressed and serves as a witness to the liberating God to anticipate together the provisional signs of eschatological reconciliation."[14] According to Antonio Fragoso these conflicts require that the church exercise its function as an educating and evangelizing entity.[15] Only as such can it establish solidarity with a church of the poor and discover the political projection of faith.

Implications for Making Disciples

The church makes disciples in the context of its *kerygma* (proclamation of the death and resurrection of Jesus Christ), *koinonia* (community life in which all are valued), *diakonia* (service as an expression of active love), *leiturgia* (celebration in response to the revelation of God's love in Christ), and *didache* (instruction in the way of Jesus). The body of Christ—the church—is a privileged space in which community and theology encourage one another. As an instrument designed to realize the mission of God, the church has the challenge, first, to make the paradigm of the Son of God incarnate a vicarious model for humanity, and secondly, to rediscover the meaning of scripture in order to discern God's purpose for us today. So these are visible spaces for the redemption and transformation of human beings, where the faithful learn justice, well-being, peace, and liberty.

Unfortunately, today these spaces, for the most part, are dominated by patriarchal ideologies and a capitalist vision. This restricts egalitarian relationships and a coherent practice of the kingdom perspective. This situation demands a clarification of God's message and an understanding of the salvation process as dynamic—an emancipatory process that becomes incarnate in each historical moment. In the Latin American context, one particular question, among others, erupts in the minds of the faithful. What does salvation mean in contexts where the poor

13. Tamayo-Acosta, *Para comprender la Teología*, 41.
14. Muñoz in Ibid., 257.
15. Ibid., 289–91.

are seen as transgressors of the dominant order and where women are abused and children are scandalized? To find an answer to such a difficult question, one must turn to scripture and bring its transformative power to bear on the context of the poor and oppressed. A thorough examination of scripture reveals that one challenge runs through the entirety of narrative, namely, the challenge of inviting those excluded from society into the house of God.[16]

Mission Alongside Extreme Poverty

Thousands of families living in extreme poverty eke out an existence through the crucible of impossible decisions: to eat or dress, rent or squat on vacant land, pay for a child's education or go to the doctor. These families are lonely and alone. They do not have the means to meet their material, emotional, and spiritual needs; they simply struggle to survive. Poverty, however, is not insurmountable because it is structural. It is produced by the dominant social economic order. This situation of poverty generates a unique psychological outlook of self-exclusion, depression, and insecurity that impedes the poor from entering a process of change. Gender also factors into this vicious cycle of poverty. The majority of the churches are comprised of women, who, because of the culture, have the responsibility of caring for their families. Not only are they responsible for childrearing, but they often care for the elderly and are the breadwinners. Making Christian disciples in this context necessarily entails dealing with the structures of poverty.

Mission in the context of structural poverty requires:

- Strengthening each member of the community with the goal of achieving holistic transformation in their lives, in their families, and in the faith community
- Understanding that conversion is not only a religious matter, but a life project coherent with the faith that professes and depends on group cohesion (family and faith community)
- Transforming the anti-life process in our personal, family, and community life into a testimony to God
- Committing each person to seek coherent alternatives through group unity and alliance with other groups.

---

16. See Russell, *La iglesia como comunidad inclusiva*.

Experts on the psychotherapy of the oppressed (particularly Alfredo Moffat of Argentina) assert that in the context of misery (economic, ethical, and cultural crises) the initiative to change usually starts from those with social advantages. The majority of the members of local ecclesial communities are poor women who require pastoral accompaniment through warm human relationships that incarnate justice, equality, and tenderness and provide the necessary impetus to transformation. Liturgical aspects of the discipling process related to such women enhance their self esteem and ritual home within which to resituate their lives. It is particularly important for them

- to attend to the liturgical spaces and celebrations as spaces to create ties
- to have mutual visitation times (community and the leadership team) to reach agreements and maintain coherence between what we say and what we do and uproot magical faith
- to plan concrete worship times to share and celebrate life, to testify to our commitment to share and experience faith, as well as to practice and build personal and group skills.

A Holistic Model of Disciple Formation

Humans are comprised of biological, psychological, social, and spiritual dimensions. These interdependent factors within a socio-cultural context mold the human being and the communities of which they are a part. Each functions in a unique way for form identity, and each is critical in the formation of a disciple of Christ.

From the biological perspective, this means that physical health, self-care, care of one another in community is a learned behavior that can be practiced within the family and the faith community.

From the psychological perspective, this means that the community and the family can offer personal models of emotional development where one's self-understanding is in balance with one's relationship to the world and vice-versa.

From the sociological perspective, this means that one can perceive and experiment with one's sense of self and how this is acknowledged by the other as both usual and unique. In other words, sameness does not exist without otherness.

From the spiritual perspective, this means that personal understanding and a collective understanding of the meaning of life and the world—as well as the deconstruction and reconstruction of these meanings—can be facilitated through the spiritual practices and traditions of the community.

Finally, this interdependent perspective presupposes that a balanced life-style is one in which all of these elements relate and in which all persons are interdependent, but not dependent, co-dependent, or indifferent to the needs of one another. In the Christian community, a healthy and faithful life requires interdependent relationships of mutual support.

I believe that these two critical issues of mission alongside the poor and holistic discipleship that touches every dimension of our humanity must be held together. In order to accomplish this, first, a contextual re-reading of the Bible is paramount in an effort to discover the centrality and significance of the kingdom of God. Second, the community of faith must find ways to provide hospitality for all God's children—space to transform the self-exclusion of impoverished persons through communitarian pastoral care and to understand that the church is only one of the avenues to carry out God's mission. Third, more than anything else, making disciples is about companionship; so it is crucial to respond to the following questions and discern in community the most appropriate historical and contextual answers: Whom does one accompany? Why does one accompany them? On what does one accompany them? How does one accompany them?

"The time is fulfilled, and the kingdom of God has come near; repent, and believe in the good news" (Mark 1:15).

19

Disciple-Making Systems and Models for Mexico

Raúl García de Ochoa

Critical Challenges

FOR MANY YEARS THE MEMBERS OF THE METHODIST CHURCH OF Mexico have generally understood the need to share their faith with others, but evangelism and discipleship have not been strong areas of concentration until recently. After 135 years of working in this country, the Methodist Church of Mexico only has about 30,000 members in full communion. In 1935 Baez and Grubb summarized the situation for the Mexican Methodist Church, which applies even to this day: "The members of the Mexican Churches as a whole are conservative in doctrinal outlook; they exhibit little enterprise; they seem unable to realize the possibilities of spiritual work outside the Church; and rely too exclusively on the efforts of their minister.[1]

Local church program activities are usually attended exclusively by church people. Most of the activities happen inside the church itself. In addition to the number of supporters that they have, Methodists enjoy favor with the government due to the institutional work that was begun by missionaries, the high social values that they promote, the relationship of true respect that the church maintains with regards to the government, and the good internal organization they sustain.

Mexican Methodism, as much as possible, needs to curtail national, conference, and district level activities and devote more attention to the work of evangelism and discipleship—practices that are always

1. Camargo and Grubb, *Religion in the Republic of Mexico*, 101.

best done at the local level. It is essential that local churches implement specific systems or models of evangelism and discipleship that are well-grounded biblically and culturally relevant in order to reach those who are without Christ, bringing them to the point of being disciples who make disciples. Some of the most important challenges that the Methodist Church of Mexico faces in the process of making disciples involve sharing the faith, preserving the fruit, training and teaching new believers, and sending people to evangelize and disciple others.

Choosing a Model of How to Share the Faith

Each church should investigate, choose, and teach their members at least one way to share their faith. A simple model is better than no model at all. Frequently pastors exhort their congregations to speak with others about the Lord and make disciples, but there is little teaching or clear and specific training about how to tell others the message of salvation. In respect to this, every member of the congregation requires training both in theory and in practice.

Choosing a Model to Preserve the Fruit

Every local church should research, choose, and teach at least one way to continue feeding persons who have come to know Christ in such a way that the spiritual fruit they have harvested will endure. Those who have come to faith in Christ need to be integrated fully into the life of the local church. On many occasions Christians share the gospel with someone else one time, but little or no effort is directed to the development of a relationship, and no time is set aside to provide follow up and attention to the persons who have shown interest in the good news of Christ.

Choosing a Model to Train and Teach New Believers about Their Life in Christ

In Matt 28:20, Jesus mentioned the importance of teaching in the discipleship process: "*teaching* them to obey everything that I have commanded you." The content of this instruction is "all that I have commanded you" and the goal is obedience to the new law of love that Jesus has enjoined. This part of the process implies development of adequate materials, strategies for small groups and cell groups, training of teachers and leaders for these groups, and improvement of Sunday School programs on the basis of proven effectiveness in each local church setting. True disciple-making re-forms people through their engagement with the Word of God and their integration into a new style of life—the way of Jesus.

Choosing a Model of Sending People to Evangelize and Disciple Others

The community or institution best positioned to educate, organize, train, and send is the local church. When the local church studies and analyzes the most effective ways to evangelize and disciple others within their own context, according to their own cultural practices, this cultivates a body of knowledge and a base of understanding for training that empowers individuals, providing them confidence to function as witnesses for Christ.

Each local church needs to establish the ways and means by which their members can be sent to do this work. Whenever mission and evangelism—the missional practices related to disciple-making—are simply left to the discretion of the individual, very little concrete action happens. Likewise, whenever the church talks about sending, pastors must not only give lip service to this aspect of the church's life, preaching and teaching its importance firmly and effectively, but they must embody this concern in their own action, modeling the way and encouraging others through their example.

District, conference, and national levels of the church need to function as facilitating agents for the work of evangelism and discipleship. These structures within the church can contribute to the success of the work of making disciples if they accomplish their mandate to propose and promote programs, produce materials, train personnel, sustain writers and teachers, and orient seminary programs toward the work of evangelism and discipleship. Methodist educational, health, and social service institutions, should continue projecting Christian values among the people they serve. Nevertheless, these institutions can contribute greatly by offering their clients an experience of faith in Jesus Christ and opportunities to grow in the grace and knowledge of him.

Institutions within the structure of the church can easily support the work of the local churches in the communities where they serve and get support from the local churches as well.

It is urgent that Methodists discover a systematic, though not mechanical, program of evangelism and discipleship today. Each phase of the process of discipleship is vital. Each member should understand the various aspects of this process, why they are important, and how they can participate most effectively in them. Within our own heritage as Methodists, we have resources upon which to draw, particularly the small group structure of earliest Methodism, replicated today in classes, cell groups, and Wesley groups—a network of small groups that can function as a context for the larger disciple-making process.

Biblical Images

One biblical image that can be very useful in the church today in relation to evangelization and discipleship, despite its militaristic orientation, is that of the army arrayed for battle. In the Song of Songs, Solomon proclaims: "You are beautiful, my darling, as Tirzah, lovely as Jerusalem, *majestic as troops with banners*" (6:4 NIV, my emphasis). One can easily understand the rejection of every form of violence by the church, especially in those cases where an army attacks a nation without sufficient cause, and this has contributed, in part, to the reticence of the church to use military images, such as *majestic as troops with banners*, in its discussion of the church's work. But the New Testament does compare the church to soldiers and armies (2 Tim 2:3–4; Jas 5:4; Rev 19:19). Elton Trueblood wrote with regards to this image: "The effective Christian pattern is always a base and a field. The base—whether it be in a private house or in a church building—is the center to which the soldiers of Christ repair, periodically, for new strength. The field is the world, and this is where Christians are supposed to operate."[2]

To achieve success in battle or in any other venture in life, discipline must be maintained. When the members of the army are distracted, when they do not understand the weapons they have, when they do not have adequate training, or when they get over fed or intoxicated, everything devolves to chaos and they are too easily defeated. Order also is crucial for the success in battle. The way that the army lines up to

2. Trueblood, *Company of the Committed*, 74.

be sent to fight and the timing of their actions can define the final result of a war. In the same way, the church needs to put its army in order. Who will make the first contact? Will they use relational evangelism or another method to make contact? Who will do the follow up? Will it be the same person or team of persons? How long will the follow up phase last? What happens next?

If compared to the various roles of soldiers in an army, the members of the church need to know what their jobs are and when and how to do them. It is essential to teach, train, and send out the members of the church with the objective of making disciples of Jesus. God calls every disciple to be involved in the some aspect of the process of making new disciples of Jesus. As Howard Snyder has observed, "We shouldn't think . . . that only the gift of evangelism is evangelistic! All the spiritual gifts contribute to evangelism in one form or another."[3]

The Practice of Evangelism and Discipleship in Context

Thinking about evangelism and the cultivation of disciples in this highly intentional, disciplined way means that nothing should be left to chance or conceived as a contingency plan. Every member of every congregation needs to be trained in one or more of the methods of evangelism or ways of sharing the faith. Such a variety of methods of sharing the faith have been practiced to good effect, beginning with personal testimony. If trained properly, Christian disciples will be able to discern which method best suits their unique situation. This is not unlike giving weapons to soldiers and teaching them how to use them.

Also, it is necessary to analyze the rhythm of life for the majority of the people, particularly in the cities, in order to plan adequately for evangelistic activities. Although anyone can at any time share the faith, there ought to be times specifically dedicated to this end and the members of the congregation must be invited to get involved. Evangelistic activities can be planned on a weekly basis: going house to house, visiting the hospital, inviting persons in the neighborhood to come to a house where the message of God's good news is shared, sharing the gospel through a clown presentation in the park, identifying people with specific needs and responding to them in appropriate ways. The primary objective is for people to encounter the message of God's love

3. Snyder, *La Comunidad del Rey*, 151.

in Jesus Christ and to have the opportunity to respond to it. This part of the process proves to be difficult for many, for ironically, Methodists today are not very disciplined in this area and are not accustomed to conforming their lives and practices to principles and mandates.

When people show interest in hearing the message of Jesus, there ought to be a specific plan of follow up, subsequent visitation, and relationship building. Disciples must tend the fruit they have cultivated. As soon as possible, those who have responded to the gospel should be invited to and incorporated into cell groups or Bible studies so that they can receive guidance in the living of their new faith in Christ in relation to their family and circle of friends. Teaching the Word of God enables them to grow and to develop a strong faith in hopes that they might reach maturity and be able to become disciple-makers themselves. This happens primarily within the context of a small group of believers. Such groups, like the early Methodist bands and classes, gather weekly and the leader provides instruction and pastoral care for those who are seeking Christ. At the same time, the disciple-in-training begins to relate to the local church, although in many cases it may take some time to make this connection. When the time and preparation of the disciples-in-training are adequate, they need to be introduced to the experience of sharing their faith. Later on, they may be given the opportunity to get together a group of new converts and form another nucleus of believers. This is the moment when the process comes full circle and the disciples-in-training become the ones who make disciples—at this point, purposeful multiplication occurs.

The development of systems and processes is essential. The teaching and training of the congregation with regard to these systems and the process also are important. When the system begins to bear fruit, this brings the highest sense of achievement to the local church. The most pressing need for Methodists today is the development of appropriate models, systems, and processes that bring others to Christ for the purpose of changing them from disciples to disciple-makers.

Signs of Vitality

In the year 2000, a local church pastor in the city of Reynosa, proposed a plan to his bishop and district superintendent that involved starting a new congregation with a core group of leaders from his own church.

They would form the new congregation on the basis of a cell group model. A group of about eighty to a hundred persons committed to this new work, and about one hundred fifty sustained the original congregation. The new congregation began to meet in a rented space and organized a network of small groups. They started training their people in the "Evangelism Explosion" system and began contacting their neighbors, sharing the good news and their vision with them. They also established ways of providing follow up for new believers using small groups to assimilate them into the fellowship. The cell groups continued to be their primary method of giving attention to new disciples. They also developed an intentional process of leadership development for their small groups. Today five hundred people attend their Sunday services and the majority of them are new converts, many of whom continue to participate in cell groups.

The group that retained the use of the church facilities also sought to develop an intentional system to reach others and to follow up with the teaching and training of new believers. They have been very creative in the ways they have shared their faith and also have put in place a structure of small groups. They implemented a school of discipleship that helps them to teach and train the new believers. Due to the growth they have experienced, they had to construct a larger sanctuary. Today, they average between six and seven hundred in their Sunday program. In 2006 the General Conference of the Methodist Church of Mexico decided to promote the work of the church through cell groups.

While many churches today are exploring the use of small group programs and are experiencing growth, there is still a great need for substantive teaching about models and systems of disciple formation, especially those that inculcate a spirit of reaching out, preserving the fruit, forming and training disciples, and sending the followers of Jesus out into the world to share their faith.

Global Contribution

The experience of the churches cited from the city of Reynosa demonstrates the fact that Methodists around the world need to rediscover the relevance and importance of systems and methods related to disciple-making. Nothing is more important than an effective system for reaching out and then forming new disciples of Christ. Ironically, there is great need and urgency to "methodize" Methodism. Many assume that the Methodist churches are perfectly structured in every way to carry out this mission effectively in the world. The fact of the matter is, however, that Methodists today needs to reclaim their original purpose, outward dynamic, and structural organization to achieve the mission given by Jesus.

The churches of Reynosa have implemented a system to reach out to those that do not know Jesus in their own context. Also, they have established specific forms of educating and instructing new disciples in their new life of faith. Moreover, these churches have looked for and found specific models (including times) to send members of the church out into their communities to share their faith, which has resulted in more people giving their lives to Jesus. All of these steps are essential in the organization of the local churches of worldwide Methodism to focus their attention and direct their efforts in their fundamental task of sharing the faith and making disciples.

History indicates that early Christians, as well as early Methodists, gathered in small groups in their homes as the fundamental base of dynamic relationships. At a time when John Wesley was consolidating the network of Methodist Societies that he had established, in his journal account of August 25, 1763 he expressed his worry with regard to the organization of Christians for the work of making disciples: "I was more convinced than ever, that the preaching like an Apostle, without joining together those that are awakened, and training them up in the ways of God, is only begetting children for the murderer. How much preaching has there been for these twenty years all over Pembrokeshire! But no regular societies, no discipline, no order or connection; and the consequence is, that nine in ten of the once-awakened are now faster asleep than ever."[4]

It is time to reclaim our heritage of being a worldwide movement organized to win souls and make disciples!

---

4. Wesley, *Works* (Jackson), 3:144.

Further Reading on Latin American Contexts

Arias, Mortimer. *Announcing the Reign of God: Evangelization and the Subversive Memory of Jesus.* Philadelphia: Fortress, 1984.
Boff, Leonardo. *Desde el lugar del pobre.* Bogotá: Paulinas, 1996.
———. *New Evangelization: Good News to the Poor.* Maryknoll, NY: Orbis, 1991.
Cardoza-Orlandi, Carlos. *Mission: An Essential Guide.* Nashville: Abingdon, 2002.
Castro, Emilio, editor. *Pastores del pueblo de Dios en América Latina.* Buenos Aires: Matropress, 1974.
Costas, Orlando. *Christ Outside the Gate: Mission Beyond Christendom.* Eugene, OR: Wipf & Stock, 2005.
———. *Liberating News: A Theology of Contextual Evangelization.* Grand Rapids: Eerdmans, 1989.
Deck, Allan Figueroa. *The Second Wave: Hispanic Ministry and the Evangelization of Cultures.* New York: Paulist, 1989.
Deiros, Pablo A. *Los evangélicos y el poder político en América Latina.* Michigan: Nueva Creación, 1986.
Fernandez, Eleazar. *Toward a Theology of Struggle.* Maryknoll, NY: Orbis, 1994.
Gutiérrez, Tomas, editor. *Protestantismo y política en América Latina y El Caribe.* Lima: CEHILA, 1996.
Kirkpatrick, Dow, editor. *Faith Born in the Struggle for Life: A Re-reading of Protestant Faith in Latin America Today.* Grand Rapids: Eerdmans, 1988.
Míguez Bonino, José. *Doing Theology in a Revolutionary Situation.* Philadelphia: Fortress, 1975.
———. *Faces of Latin American Protestantism: 1993 Carnahan Lectures.* Grand Rapids: Eerdmans, 1997.
Míguez Bonino, Miguel. *Rostros del protestantismo latinoamericano.* Buenos Aires: Nueva Creación, 1995.
Padilla, C. René. *Mission Between the Times: Essays on the Kingdom.* Grand Rapids: Eerdmans, 1985.
Parra, Alberto. *De la iglesia ministerio a la iglesia de los pobres.* Bogotá: Pontificia Universidad Javeriana, 1984.
Pimentel, Jonathán. *Modelos de Dios en las teologías latinoamericanas.* San José: UNA-EBILA, 2008.
Pope-Levison, Priscilla. *Evangelization from a Liberation Perspective.* New York: Peter Lang, 1991.
Santa Ana, Julio. *El desafío de los pobres a la iglesia.* San José: EDUCA, 1977.
Sigmund, Paul E., editor. *Religious Freedom and Evangelization in Latin America: The Challenge of Religious Pluralism.* Maryknoll, NY: Orbis, 1999.
Tamayo-Acosta, Juan José. *Nuevo paradigma teológico.* Madrid: Trotta, 2003.

Tamayo-Acosta, Juan José. *Para comprender la Teología de la liberación*. Estella: Verbo divino, 2000.
Tamez, Elsa, and S. Trinidad. *Capitalismo: violencia y anti-vida*. La Tomo I. San José: Educa, 1978.
Yamamori, Tetsunao, and C. René Padilla, editors. *The Local Church, Agent of Transformation: An Ecclesiology for Integral Mission*. Trans. Brian Cordingly. Buenos Aires: Ediciones Kairós, 2004.

PART FIVE

North America
Exploring a New Ocean

Introduction to Part 5

NORTH AMERICAN CHRISTIANS SWIM TODAY (MOSTLY AS INDIVIduals) in an uncharted ocean. The seismic shifts and rumblings in the deep of the cultures that comprise this continent have left many stunned. The radical changes that now characterize life have disoriented churched Christians and dislodged them from previous positions of power and influence in their communities. Most consider Canada to be one of the most secular societies in the world. In the United States, the Christian community itself defies easy description or explanation. Despite the fact that increasing numbers of people distance themselves from organized religion, let alone Christianity, and that formerly "mainline denominations" reel from the staggering losses of the late twentieth century, the vast majority of people still believe in God and remain open to conversation about God in their lives. A string of "isms"—postmodernism, pluralism, secularism, materialism, consumerism—dominate the discourse concerning North American culture. Most everyone agrees that Christendom collapsed. In the midst of this confusion and consternation, the four contributors to this section all point in one way or another to an ancient-future paradigm as the community of faith charts a new course into an uncertain future.

In the face of urbanization, increasing pluralism, and the irrelevance of the Christian faith, Dan Sheffield, Director of Global and Intercultural Ministries for The Free Methodist Church in Canada, advocates the recovery of an "apprentice model" of making disciples. Christians must find a way to step outside traditional roles as "placeholders" in society and seek to embody the reality that has claimed their lives. They must live out in community what it means to be formed in a new way and shaped by a brand new set of assumptions and expectations about life and their relationship to a living God.

According to Elaine Heath, five critical challenges confront the church today. Buildings delude us into thinking that an "attractional model" still works. Budgets siphon off limited resources for institutional maintenance. Those in positions of power find it difficult to assimilate emerging bivocational leadership models. The boxes of church, academy, and mission and the boundaries that maintain comfort and safety inhibit movement, innovation, and permeability in the church. While these vestiges of Christendom ultimately lead to the death of a missional vision for the church, those who are courageous enough to open holes in the roof of the church discover the joy of discipleship in the spirit of Jesus.

Kim Reisman believes that knowing "the story" leads the Christian community, inevitably, to remember its first love. People today remain open to the gospel, but the church must rediscover the practices of a "grace-full disciple-making" that is authentic and embodies the integrity of the gospel of Christ, both its personal and social dimensions. "Whenever the church has been most vital, most prophetic, and most effective in disciple-making," she maintains, "it has been the church in the margins. It has also been a church grounded in contemplative ways, listening to and cooperating with the Holy Spirit."

According to Bryan Stone, the major challenge for those in the United States is the reality of "empire." He employs a number of metaphors to describe the nature of Christian discipleship that stands over against the imperial view. Rather than "making" disciples, it might be more accurate and fitting to describe this process as "birthing." The process itself is akin to a Spirit-led journey in which a company of pilgrims make their way toward the goal of God's reign. Over against the Christendom model that was shaped by the imperial way—in which those in power permeated all aspects of life and sought to extend their control as far as possible—the emerging church will be "a Spirit-empowered and Christ-shaped performance of an alternative social imagination in which first are last and last first."

20

Making Disciples in the Canadian Context

Dan Sheffield

Critical Challenges

When I met a recent Free Methodist immigrant to Canada from the Democratic Republic of Congo, I was chastised for how "Christian" Canada is such a "godless" place! If Canada was ever "Christian," it was probably during the mid to late nineteenth century. However, was Canada *more* Christian then than now? In terms of those who professed Christian belief, yes. More than a decade ago, however, Canadian professor John Stackhouse Jr. said, "But in terms of justice for women and minorities, in terms of civil rights for all, in terms of community support for the poor and disadvantaged, there are many respects in which Canada keeps better to biblical guidelines *today*. Because of this, we cannot look back to some golden age of a Christian Canada as our model."[1]

In 2006, 22 percent of Canadians aged fifteen and over reported that they had "no religion." That is, in regard to religious affiliation, they responded they were either agnostic, atheist, humanist, or had no religion. Stats Canada suggests that this represents a 6.5 percent increase over 2001 figures. But that's not all. Attendance at religious services has declined even among those with a religious affiliation. In 2006, only 27 percent of people aged fifteen and over—who had some kind of religious affiliation—reported they attended religious services on a weekly basis, compared with 34 percent in 1985. On the other hand, the per-

---

1. Stackhouse, "Whose Dominion?"

centage of those with a religious affiliation never attending a religious service increased from 24 percent to 41 percent in the same period. That is, more than one-third of those who claim a faith background don't attend services.[2]

This little overview serves to suggest the increasing irrelevance of existing forms of faith participation in Canadian society. I would like to suggest three critical challenges to making disciples of Jesus in our present Canadian context.

Irrelevance of the Christian Faith

First, the *seeming irrelevance of the Christian faith* to the average Canadian, and in particular, the place of organized or institutional Christianity, presents a formidable challenge. While people value "spirituality" increasingly in society as a whole, they consider Christian spirituality to be anathema. For many this antipathy is largely unfounded because they have very little real experience of any Christian community. Stereotypes and caricatures of Christians (as conservative, right-wing fundamentalists) abound in the public media and in the public education system and serve as the scapegoat for any kind of meaningful engagement with Christian faith. The average Canadian could not care less about the role of the church in their neighborhood, let alone in their personal lives.[3] So what is it about our making of Jesus-followers that must change?

Increasing Pluralism

Secondly, *the increasing pluralism of Canadian society* challenges disciple-making practices as well. In 1901 Canada had people from twenty-five different ethnic origins; today that figure is more than two hundred. In 2006, one Canadian resident out of five was not born in Canada (19.8 percent). In the previous five years, that foreign-born population grew by 13.6 percent, compared with Canadian-born population growth of 3.3 percent. The Canadian society of the future will be substantially different than its present complexion. This will also include diverse values,

---

2. Clark and Schellenberg, "Who's Religious?" 2–8.
3. Coggins, "The State of the Canadian Church."

religious beliefs, social practices, and personal lifestyle choices.[4] So what is it about our making of Jesus-followers that must change?

The Urban Context

Thirdly, Christian discipleship must address *the challenge of the urban context* with its social alienation, physical disconnection, life paced to maximize innumerable consumer options, and the overwhelming power of consumer debt. Urban planning models disconnect workers from their homes, increasing the reliance on countless weekly hours of commuter transportation. Social and cultural differences increase interpersonal anxiety and caution. So many outside-the-home social and consumer opportunities exist for adults, families, children, and youth that many families lack the ability to develop the cohesion and stability that is so central to the development of healthy identities. So what is it about our making of Jesus-followers that must change?

Scriptural Images

Several scriptural images inform the way faithful Christians and communities can respond to these challenges in the Canadian context. First, Matt 28 provides a mandate related to the way in which God calls the church to "make disciples;" second, the regular "house parties" in the Gospels' stories of Jesus' ministry provide a model for disciple-making; and third, the church as a stumbling block in the neighborhood provides a key to the transformative nature of goodness in the world (cf. 1 Pet 2:4–25).

These images point to the need to recover an *apprenticeship model in disciple-making*. For a long time in the Western church, Christian leaders have assumed the classroom-based, curriculum-oriented, teacher-student model of discipleship. The apprentice-learner (*mathetes*) of the Gospels differs from the student-learner in the methodology used to pass on knowledge and skills. The student-learner studies texts and ideas, acquiring knowledge, in a school or other semi-formal learning environment. Apprenticeship involves personal, hands-on, communal, and experiential formation.

---

4. Chui, *Canada's Ethnocultural Mosaic*.

Apprentice learning requires observation, imitation, trial and error, learning from mistakes, formation of habits and skills, reflection on why things happened as they did and what could be done differently next time, and so on. A master seeks to progressively alter his or her disciples' habits of perception and standards of judgment. Further, apprentice learning cannot be done by a solitary individual; it requires collaboration and a sharing of practices.

The apprentice model calls God's people into community, requiring the investment of time, energy, and gifts in a collaborative effort. Christian believers who actively engage in fellowship and community together, in the pursuit of knowing God, and being conformed to the image of Christ by means of spiritual disciplines, suggest to their neighbors that Christian faith is not just a "take it or leave it" form of institutional spirituality.

These scriptural images also *give more attention to the household-based, neighborhood-oriented model of Jesus' ministry* in the Gospels. Jesus most frustrating ministry experiences were in the so-called sacred spaces of the religious institutions of his day, the synagogues and the Temple. His most rewarding ministry experiences were in households like that of the centurion in Capernaum and the Jewish homes of Peter, Matthew, Zaccheus, Mary and Martha. He had profitable ministry experiences at local watering holes (the Samaritan woman), community gathering spots (the fish market by the wharf in Capernaum), and nearby hillside parks (the Sermon the Mount, feeding the 5,000). Similarly, the Methodist movement was birthed outside the organized religious settings in eighteenth century England. Class meetings were based in homes, society meetings and agape meals were held in community halls. Wesley and other lay leaders frequented the community gathering spots to preach. They expected seekers and new believers to attend a weekly class meeting in their own neighborhood. In this way friends and neighbors could hold a believer accountable for the way he treated his wife and children or conducted himself with local business people.

Rediscovering this mode of discipleship will draw disconnected, distorted people back into relationship and community, shaped by the life and ministry of Jesus. Sociological analysis would seem to mandate that the church adapt its evangelistic and disciple-making methods to engage with urban social realities—interest-based networks, work-related connections, technology-driven communities. Maybe so. But is it not also essential for the community of faith to recover face-to-face, family-oriented, small fellowships that serve as incarnational salt and light in particular neighborhoods?

The gospel images demonstrate how *small incarnational fellowships can function as Jesus-centered stumbling blocks for neighbors.* The writer of 1 Peter describes Jesus as "a stone that makes them stumble, and a rock that makes them fall" (2:8). They stumble because they disobey the message—something they were destined to do given their ignorance and sin. He suggests that believers are living stones that are being built into a spiritual house on the chosen and precious cornerstone which is God's Son (2:4–5). God calls this chosen people, this royal priesthood, this holy nation, God's own people (2:9)—the Body of Christ—to mediate the presence of God wherever they are, in their neighborhoods, in their families, and among their friends and neighbors. Many will "stumble over" God's faithful people, because they don't know what to do with a community of people actually living as Jesus intended. Confronted with the authenticity of the gospel lived out in the day-to-day lives of Jesus' disciples, those who are without hope immediately see the relevance of the faith. Those who are without faith can no longer decry an institution, because they are confronted with a neighbor who is simply living a blessed and honorable life among them. They cannot find fault; they may even see those good deeds "and glorify God" (2:12).

As neighbors encounter the Other (God) within in these incarnational communities (as they stumble over God's people!), the Holy Spirit is able to open eyes and begin the process of personal transformation.[5] This very personal connection to the presence of Jesus (through these small household-oriented fellowships) also challenges those whose lives are defined by other religious systems to consider the reality of Christian truth as it is lived out in their midst. No longer a distorted, abstract concept, the Christian faith takes on concrete shape in that unusual group of friends who gather to sing and pray and care for their neighborhood. Those people just next door!

Evangelism and Disciple-Making in Practice

If God calls the community of faith to "make Jesus-followers" who carry on God's continuing mission in the world by proclaiming the good news

---

5. Sheffield, "Encountering the Other."

and by seeking shalom (John 20:21), then how does all this happen in practice? In a society in which so many do not even give a hearing to Christian proclamation, it is imperative that Christian congregations step outside their traditional roles as spiritual "place-holders" in their communities. Christians must become more attentive to the work that God is already doing in the lives of people in their neighborhoods—the drawing, desiring, convicting activity of the Holy Spirit. Critical questions emerge: Are we close enough to people that we are able to sense God at work in their lives? How is God preparing them for awakening and grace-filled responses to Jesus' good news?

This approach assumes a post-Christendom reality. The fact of the matter is that most people do not know the biblical framework; they do not know the Jesus story. Jesus is just a respected spiritual leader, listed along with Buddha, Confucius, Krishna, Mohammed, Mother Theresa, Gandhi, and Martin Luther King Jr. Given this frame of reference, unbelievers will only ask questions when they begin to note an embodied reality which they cannot explain. In the context of such genuine questions—through relational engagement—an opportunity presents itself to place the Jesus story before them as a truth to consider. Persuasion, conviction, and conversion are all the domain of the Holy Spirit's activity. The role of the evangelist is to build a relationship to the point that the neighbor is prepared to hear the name of "Jesus" without gagging or turning away in disgust.

If God, by the Holy Spirit, draws that person into a transforming relationship, then the process of disciple-making requires the formation of a new worldview, entails a new primary socialization, with a brand new set of assumptions and expectations about one's place in this world, in relation to the living God. It requires a discovery of the character of God as revealed in the Christian scriptures, an introduction to the spiritual disciplines of the Christian tradition that aid growth and transformation, an understanding of the nature of Christian worship and the significance of Christian community.

Permit a personal reflection. I wonder sometimes, however, if our present congregations, long-rooted in the notion of a "churched" Christendom, have the capacity to reorient around a missional vision of this nature—an orientation that is more about the mission than about the church? Our congregations should create within us the capacity to engage with our neighbors and neighborhoods; if they don't, they have become an entity unto themselves. Recently my wife and I had an opportunity to experiment with some of these ideas during the Christmas season. A young couple with two toddlers whom we had been discipling, were struggling with how to participate in a Christmas Eve activity that didn't involve taking their children to church right at bedtime (the time for traditional Christmas Eve services in many Christian churches). Relatively new believers, this couple had a limited view of how to make this evening meaningful for themselves or their children. The woman's mother, who had not attended church in forty years, was also going to be part of the evening.

Then a Chinese immigrant family with whom we have been relating for almost eight years asked if they could spend Christmas Eve with us. Growing up in communist-era China they had very little spiritual formation of any kind, although Buddhism was part of their parent's heritage. For them the Christmas story was a garbled mix of evergreen trees, Santa Claus, Rudolph, a baby in a straw basinet, and lots of candles. We met in the home of the young family so the kids could be at ease and drop off to sleep when necessary, and Grandma wouldn't feel out of place. Our Chinese friends came to join in with their teenage son (a friend of our son). Their son played violin along with guitars while we sang secular Christmas songs and traditional Christian carols. We discussed the historical connections and disconnections between the different Christmas traditions – for the sake of our Chinese friends, the toddler children, and the newly-believing parents. We used an ancient candle-lighting liturgy with scripture and responsive readings. Our Chinese friends read the from the Gospel of John in Mandarin. We sang more carols, lit candles, prayed, and ate together before going back to our own homes.

When I think of evangelism and disciple-making in our present Canadian context, I'm imagining more experiences like this: being intentional about mission, listening for the subtle direction of the Holy Spirit, letting the scriptures speak for themselves, functioning in community, and not worrying about "how we've always done it."

Christian Vitality

A couple Canadian congregations of Methodist lineage are working diligently to connect in a meaningful way with their neighbors, to embody the good news of Jesus, and to make disciples in collaborative communities of practice—the Freeway and the Story.

The Freeway is a new congregation of The Salvation Army, in Hamilton, Ontario. They are rooted in a particular neighborhood, but their visible expression—their building, at least—is a coffee shop. The leaders were able to sell the old Salvation Army building in the city center and purchase a building that suited their incarnational purpose more fully. On any given day you can walk into their "spacious" space and find people holed up in a corner reading, others engaging in animated conversations, a physically disabled person in a wheelchair just staring off into space, and you're likely to see a developmentally handicapped person wiping tables. They serve fair-trade coffee, and the place is mostly operated by volunteers.

They advertize themselves as "a holistic Christian community—a community of people who are committed to making the Kingdom of God tangible in our neighborhood. We believe that people should be able to touch it, taste it, see it, sense it. We seek to be part of the rhythms of our city, to be good neighbors, good friends and good servants."[6]

Leaders and members live in the neighborhood. Their building doesn't have any parking—so people have to walk. They are immersed in the culture of their neighborhood. They engage with other social service providers in connecting with the marginalized, forming deep relationships with local residents through their daily engagement. Many in the group have reoriented their lives around this community. They understand their church community as a catalyst for transforming their everyday actions and priorities. Discipleship is rooted in their daily engagement and dialogue with one another and their community. On Thursdays they gather in homes for "neighborhood networks" for "a meal, open space discussion, and simply sharing our lives with one another."

Walking through the door to their Sunday night worship gatherings you'll instantly notice the aroma of great coffee, soft lighting, candles, leather couches, nice rugs, café style tables and chairs, laptop computers, televisions, and projections showing words and images. By combining ancient Christian and freshly created rituals, liturgy, music, and visuals the congregation experiments with finding new connections between worship and everyday life.

6. The Freeway, "Church?"

The Story in Sarnia, Ontario, is a congregation in the Free Methodist family. Several years ago they began to imagine a new way of thinking about Christian community, mission, and discipleship. When talking about the name for their church they say: "We've all got our own tale, but at the same time we've come to realize that we're also a part of something bigger – an overarching story where we are the real life characters. For us, this leg of the trip is being written in the city of Sarnia where as individuals in collective community, we look to tell the Grand Narrative of Jesus, day by day and moment by moment, simply by the way we live our lives. Jesus himself put it this way: 'Love God, love others.' This is our story, and we're stickin' to it."[7]

The Story's building is a "store-front" located on a downtown street that, just a couple years ago, was full of boarded-up retail spaces. As one of the investors in this neighborhood, they have come to be regarded as a community stakeholder. Their space includes a video production studio and a large room used by a local ballet and dance teacher, besides the open kitchen and living room atmosphere of their worship environment.

In the summer, they are just as likely to have worship gatherings in various homes in the area with a meal following as they are to meet in their downtown venue. Web-based content enables participants to interact with resources both collectively and in their own homes. Open hospitality is a feature of their community life, evidenced by neighborhood-based BBQs and frequent meals together in homes. Congregational camping trips are a normal part of their ongoing "storytelling" (disciple-making).

These congregations are signs of new life and vitality, as Christians in the Methodist tradition are seeking to engage in the marketplace again, at a time when the "masses" are not coming to the churches, just as in Wesley's day. They are re-contextualizing their disciple-making and mission practices, attentive to the needs of their particular contexts and rooted in the biblical witness of God's vision of shalom.

Global Contributions

The lessons of disciple-making in the contemporary Canadian context call for a recovery of the Wesleyan notion of continual reform and re-

---

7. The Story, "Handles."

newal. Just as Wesley assimilated and reshaped the multiple influences of his spiritual journey to develop a model (or "method") of engagement with his unique context, so the Jesus-follower today must be attentive to the voice of the Spirit in the particularities of his or her time and place. This involves connecting ancient, orthodox truths with an understanding of contemporary society and its impulses, being rooted in the Christian scriptures, and engaging this witness with real people in real neighborhoods. To continue to prop up models and practices that are no longer connecting with those who still need to meet Jesus, just doesn't seem right. The experiments that are surfacing in this postmodern, post-Christian society will continue to thrive and serve as "possibilities" for renewal in much the same manner that the English religious "societies" and the Moravian bands of Wesley's day led him to re-cast and synthesize mission and disciple-making practices for the working-class masses of his time and place.

21

Making Disciples in a Post-Christendom USA

Elaine A. Heath

As I write this chapter I am sitting in my living room, gazing out the window where a few neighbors are raking leaves. We are a study in diversity. Though Garland, Texas is predominantly Hispanic, some of our neighbors were born in India, some in Africa, and others describe themselves as fifth generation Texans. The cars on our streets run the gamut from Lexus to rust bucket. We are black, white, brown, straight, gay, old, young, educated, and illiterate. Economically our block is mostly middle class, but this pocket is surrounded by what real estate agents call "a changing neighborhood," code for "if you want your property values to go up in the years ahead don't buy here." A few streets over, many of our neighbors live below the poverty line.

Garland is part of the Dallas-Fort Worth metroplex, a teeming microcosm of a globalized, increasingly diverse United States. Here in our city we share all the challenges, opportunities, and questions that are facing the nation as a whole. Residents in our community struggle with problems of immigration, inadequate healthcare, and economic crises. Home foreclosures in my neighborhood are at an all time high. Families throughout our city pray for their children who are soldiers fighting in the Middle East. Next door to them other families pray for their loved ones at risk in the same regions—their parents, siblings, and friends whose homes and businesses are now bombed out ruins. My neighbors and I are engulfed in a culture of rapid change, uncertainty, and plurality of every kind.

So it is that when I survey the ecclesiastical landscape of my own city, I see the same challenges that face congregations from coast to coast as the church in the United States struggles to make sense of its context. We live in the midst of massive cultural shifts brought about by globalization, rapidly changing communication and information technology, consumerism, the increasing gap between the rich and the poor with a shrinking middle class, and unprecedented threats to the entire biosphere due to war, pollution, disease, poverty, and disasters related to global climate change. Linked to these tectonic shifts is the fact that Christendom—the marriage of the church with secular power—is all but over. We are in a post-denominational, post-Christendom United States. Even in Dallas, the buckle of the "Bible Belt," the church is irrevocably moving to the margins of society. There we will no longer enjoy the privileges of Christendom, but we will have the opportunity to become a prophetic people once again. From the margins we will experience new opportunities and challenges in making disciples.

Five Critical Challenges

The biggest challenge to the church in the United States today is to recover its missional identity so that congregations understand and embrace their disciple-making vocation. Missional identity and practice are grounded in a two-fold stance of contemplation and action. Disciple-making requires that we become deep listeners, both to the culture around us and to the Holy Spirit. We cannot make disciples if we do not know the culture, cannot speak the language of our neighbors, and will not discern what the Spirit is saying to the church. In order to retrieve a missional identity and become a church of contemplation and action, we will have to engage five critical challenges.

Buildings

The first challenge is to overcome the deeply ingrained belief that the church is a building where Christians gather for religious programs and activities. Related to this erroneous belief is the conviction, especially among mainline Christians, that a congregation is not fully established until it owns a building identified as "the church." The belief that a church is a big building with pews, programs, and professional clergy who carry out the ministry has led to an "attractional" model of ministry in which evangelism is understood to be a process of attracting "unchurched" people to come to the building called "church." There they will hear sermons and music that will attract them to Christ. Once they are "churched" (regular attendees at the building) they will financially support the programs, clergy, and building called church.

There are many theological problems with the building-centered attractional model, beyond its ineffectiveness in taking the gospel to "Jerusalem, Judea, Samaria, and the uttermost parts of the earth." The most basic problem is that the Bible teaches that the church is organic, the Body of Christ, the people of God who are created, called, gifted, and sent out in partnership with God in God's mission to the world. From Genesis to Revelation the message is clear: the ecclesia is a God-gathered people, not a building, and our identity is rooted in God's redemptive, healing mission. Churching people does not necessarily make disciples of them. Sometimes churching inoculates them against real discipleship, with its costly demands and rigorous expectations.

The word "mission" means "sent out." The disciple-making church of tomorrow will return to the biblical understanding of church as the people of God in mission to the world. There will be a de-emphasis on owning and maintaining expensive buildings, and a new emphasis on Christians mobilizing for worship and service in smaller, often multi-purpose spaces such as homes, office buildings, community centers and the like. The use of borrowed space for worship will increasingly be seen as a responsible, God-honoring practice. The former practice of building massive edifices to house worship for thousands of church attendees will come to be seen as theologically misinformed. Instead there will be a turn to a "tabernacle" theology in which God's people are on the move in mission, thus in need of flexible, fluid ministry space. Thus the very space in which worship and teaching take place, will reflect missional ecclesiology, the church's self understanding as God's people sent out into the world with the good news.

Budget

Part of what will drive the move to smaller and more flexible meeting space for the missional, disciple-making church will be a more rigorous practice of stewardship. That is, as missional Christians look at their ministry budget, they will increasingly find ways to minimize the amount of money spent on themselves and their own comfort, in order to maximize their financial resources for mission. They will embrace a kenotic, self-emptying identity that will help to heal the spiritual wounds inflicted on the world by power-hungry, mammon-intoxicated Christendom. By meeting in homes or other borrowed space for worship, or by sharing a building between two or more congregations, disciple-making churches will free significant financial resources with which to provide ministry among their suffering neighbors. This will be seen as a mature choice. Some congregations will choose to convert their large, urban church buildings into mission centers with seven day a week ministries to hurting people.

The stewardship of money will be taught and practiced within a context of stewardship of God's creation, including a deep commitment to heal the environmental wounds that are a consequence of rampant consumerism. The missional, disciple-making church will practice a modest, sustainable lifestyle in relation to its life as a congregation and individual practices of Christian stewardship. The disciple-making church will take seriously its responsibility to shape environmental healing with theological discourse, and with a praxis of sustainability. Whereas in the twentieth century evangelism was overwhelmingly separated from social justice ministry, in the missional church of the future these two will reunite so that the good news of salvation is proclaimed holistically. Disciple-making will therefore include both spiritual formation and justice formation, and these will have a central place in the church budget.

Bivocationality

In keeping with missional ecclesiology, a kenotic stance, and more holistic practices of stewardship, the disciple-making church of the future will show preference for emerging leadership models that are more adaptable to the development of networks of small faith communities. In short this will mean that churches will move away from the dominant model of pastors earning a living by leading congregations that can pay them a fulltime salary with benefits, toward teams of bi-vocational pastors leading networks of small communities.

In mainline disciple-making churches there will be an intentional retrieval of leadership practices from the apostolic, first century church, as well as from early Methodism, and the underground church in twentieth century China, all of which bear wisdom for our rapidly changing cultural contexts. These leadership models will enable the church to deploy itself to a wide array of neighborhoods, particularly among those who are economically, and in other ways, disadvantaged. These models will make more sense in equipping a missional church that is arrayed as networks of small, praying, active communities in which members participate in mission.

Bi-vocationality will increasingly be seen as a preferred missiological strategy for leadership rather than as a temporary situation until a church becomes "successful" with its own building, a fulltime pastor who does most of the ministry for the church, and so on. Because of this shift toward bi-vocationality, new models of theological education will emerge in order to equip Christians for bi-vocational leadership. Theological seminaries will be challenged to adapt to the new leadership needs of the church, including a move toward more web-based classes, non-degree programs for comprehensive theological education for lay people, and the adaptation of curriculum in traditional masters degree programs so that students are better equipped for missional leadership in emerging contexts.

Boxes

The flexibility and creativity that will be necessary for these new leadership models and new forms of theological education to emerge, will generate increasing pressure within what are currently rigid systems of ecclesiastical polity and theological education in mainline denominations. Indeed that pressure is already at work, evident in the growing number of churches who can only afford a part-time bi-vocational pastor. Beyond economic factors, though, today more and more evangelical pastors in the United States gain their theological formation not from traditional seminaries, but from alternative means, including "teaching churches" that have become regional training centers for ministry.

In the last century the bureaucratization of all mainline denominations resulted in clearly marked boxes for church, academy, and mission. These boxes are now becoming permeable, a trend that will only increase for those denominations that determine to cultivate missional churches. Thus the missional, disciple-making church will increasingly be marked by hybridity in the mutual work between church, academy, and mission. Larger mainline churches that remain viable will do so in part because they become much more focused on leadership development for God's mission rather than for institutional survival. This will be done in tandem with seminaries. Similarly, theological seminaries that survive and thrive will do so because they are much more in partnership with healthy, missional churches as an integral part of their program. The use of decentralized, contextualized learning environments outside of the seminary will be critically important to the vital seminary. In summary, the boxes that currently stifle the emerging work of the Holy Spirit in terms of church polity and theological education, will give way to hybridity for disciple-making churches of the future. So will ossified systems of ordination. The Holy Spirit will not be bound.

Boundaries

During times of great cultural change, as Phyllis Tickle notes in *The Great Emergence*, what is always at stake and what is always challenged as the new work of God to emerges, is the location of ecclesiastical authority. Ordination is a traditional bestowal of positional authority for persons who are called to pastoral leadership that includes ministries of word and sacrament. Over the past five hundred years ordination in mainline denominations gradually came to require advanced theological degrees and was predicated upon the expectation of ministry as a profession and a career. Ministry was to be under the supervision and much of it carried out by professional clergy. It was and still is a system with rigid hierarchies of power where congregants formed the base of the pyramid. Boundaries were clear. The clergy were a gated community presiding at the front of the building called church. This pyramidal structure will not remain in its current shape as cultural emergence continues, with its flattening and decentralization of authority. As a result, the meaning of ordination and what "counts" as a gift and call toward ordination, will undergo change. The gated community is losing its fence.

While ordination isn't going away, and will continue to have a necessary place in the church, in disciple-making churches of the future, ordained clergy will function much less as ministry professionals and much more as equippers of the saints. Ordained ministry will be seen in a more biblical light as equipping, leading, and facilitating the priesthood of the believers. A growing permeability of boundaries will be experienced in what "counts" as ministry, both for ordained and non-ordained Christians. This shift will be deeply connected to the trend toward bi-vocationality, toward networks of smaller, missional congregations, and in the increase of disciple-making and justice oriented ministries led by non-ordained persons.

A Lesson from the Five Friends (Mark 2:1–12)

The story is told in Mark 2:1–12, about five friends with a stretcher who could not get through a crowd to Jesus. The friend on the stretcher was paralyzed, an infirmity that was both spiritual and physical. As the four who were mobile looked at the hindrances to their healing mission, they devised an extraordinary plan. They would open a hole in the roof above the room where Jesus was teaching. They would lower their friend down into the center, right in front of Jesus. In this way they would remove the obstacles and make it easy for their friend to encounter the Great Physician. The friends followed through with the daring plan and the outcome was a new disciple who was healed of his affliction and forgiven of his sin.

These friends represent disciple-making Christians whom the Holy Spirit is calling to open a hole in the roof of the church. They demonstrate the kind of resourcefulness, persistence, and deep faith of missional Christians of the future who will understand, engage, and overcome the five obstacles to disciple-making in a post-Christendom American church. Such Christians will be risk-takers, innovators, and intercessors. They will be people of contemplation and action, a new cadre of apostles sent out by the Holy Spirit with the good news of Jesus' love.

The opening in the roof of a post-Christendom church is already at hand, evident in a host of grassroots renewal movements within and beyond the mainline church. Significant among these are the new monasticism and the emergent conversation. Both of these movements involve missional Christians moving the church out of the church building and into the secular world, especially the abandoned places of empire. The retrieval of contemplative practices and a rule of life, coupled with a commitment to inhabit the neighborhood and love and serve the neighbors who also live there, are common to emerging and new monastic communities. In other words, a renewal of a sense of geographic parish is afoot. Both of these movements take seriously the massive cultural shifts in the United States, and are grounded in missional ecclesiologies. The new monasticism in particular is well suited to engage the mainline church and to work alongside and within it, to help the church reclaim its missional vocation.

Other signs of life are evident in some of the large congregations that are becoming mission training centers for clergy and laity, as well as their move toward decentralization and forming networks of smaller, missional communities that reach out in disciple-making ministries of various kinds. Ginghamsburg Church in Dayton, Ohio is a good example of a large United Methodist congregation that is pioneering the way forward for other large churches to follow. In Ginghamsburg and other churches like it, the thrust toward disciple-making is not about creating larger church membership rosters or shoring up a foundering institution. Instead, disciple-making is about participation in the kingdom of God. Membership is a commitment to missionary life.

The World is Our Parish

When I began this chapter I noted the ways in which my city is a microcosm of the United States as a whole, with all the challenges of a rapidly changing, globalized culture. In discussing the challenges and opportunities of the church in the United States that increasingly finds itself moving toward the margins of society, I mentioned the importance of the first century church, early Methodism, and underground church of twentieth century China. Two of these sources of wisdom come from Christianity outside of the United States. The third, early Methodism, came to North America as a missionary movement from England. The fastest growth in Christian disciple-making today is outside of the United States, primarily in the southern and eastern hemispheres. It is clear that the post-Christendom church in the United States must look beyond our borders to learn how to be missional once again.

At the same time, in God's global parish, it is important for the rapidly growing church in nations that are moving through their own industrialization and modernization, to learn from the story of the church in the United States. The alignment of church with secular powers—Christendom—ultimately leads to the death of missional ecclesiology.

Thus the temptation to wed secular power to ecclesiastical goals must be resisted at all costs. Whenever the church has been most vital, most prophetic, and most effective in disciple-making, it has been the church in the margins. It has also been a church grounded in contemplative ways, listening to and cooperating with the Holy Spirit.

As the church in the United States regains missional vitality, the gifts it will offer back to global Christianity will be incarnational, inherited wisdom from more than two thousand years of faithful witness from saints from "every tribe and nation." Out of this shared, lived heritage, God's church will continue to make disciples in a global parish.

22

Graceful Articulation

Kimberly D. Reisman

A Critical Challenge . . . Knowing the Story

WHEN I WAS IN THE EARLY STAGES OF MY DOCTORAL STUDIES IN EVANgelism, I attended a local art exhibit of a friend. Many people from the community were there including a gentleman I knew from a secular community organization of which we are both a part. As each of us introduced our spouses, he mentioned to his wife that I was a United Methodist minister currently working on my doctorate, but he was not sure of the area of study. I explained that I was studying the theology of evangelism. At the mention of the word "evangelism," the couple—almost in perfect unison—recoiled from me with shocked expressions. Realizing the obvious negativity of their reaction, they quickly recovered their composure and the gentleman sought to relieve the awkwardness of the moment by saying that he was surprised I was studying evangelism as he perceived me to be a very open-minded and compassionate person. The conversation that followed was one which I can only hope improved this gentleman's understanding of evangelism and emphasized that its practice does not preclude being open-minded or compassionate.

The image of evangelism requires restoration. If it has not been thoroughly tarnished by negative images of narrow-mindedness and a lack of compassion, the concept of evangelism continues to be confused and misunderstood in the minds of many people. Apart from disapproving views of evangelism as intolerant or undergirded by an attitude of superiority, there is uncertainty as to what exactly constitutes evangelism. Is it simply proclaiming the good news? Is it embodying "social holiness" as a witness to the world?[1] What is the goal? Is it conversion? Is it initiation into the kingdom of God?[2]

It is beyond the scope of this chapter to thoroughly resolve all the questions regarding the nature of evangelism, but I believe there are certain distinctives that are important to highlight, particularly in the cultural context in which mainline Protestants in the United States find themselves today. It appears that whatever else evangelism may entail, it involves, at some level, the making of disciples. If this is an acceptable starting point, it is apparent that appropriate teaching is a crucial element. In order to *become* a disciple of Jesus Christ, and continue as a faithful disciple, one must know what it *means* to be a disciple. On the surface this may seem self-evident. One of the most critical challenges facing the church in the United States, however, is a lack of understanding concerning the basic tenets of the faith. This translates into an inability to gracefully articulate that faith to the wider culture, whether through authentic corporate and individual embodiment or corporate and individual faith-sharing. Thus, in order to *make* disciples, Christ-followers must understand what it means to *be* a disciple.

This is not to say that making or being disciples is simply about mentally ticking off assent to a particular list of theological propositions. On the one hand, it *is* about right belief; there are things that are within and outside the boundaries of Christian thought and understanding, and grappling with those things is foundational for a life of faith. Yet on the other hand, it is also about *believing in the right way*.[3] In 2008, for example, Christian groups in the United Kingdom placed ads on buses in London with quotations from scripture. However, if nonbelievers were interested in investigating the sponsoring group by visiting their website, they were informed that they would "spend all eternity in torment in hell."[4] Atheists, not surprisingly, countered with their own bus ads and a back and forth battle began. Lest this be thought an English phenomenon, a similar scenario unfolded in Des Moines, Iowa. Certainly Christian faith involves an understanding of

---

1. See Stone, *Evangelism after Christendom*, 16.
2. See Abraham, *Logic of Evangelism*, 95.
3. See Rollins, *How (not) to Speak of God*.
4. Beckford, "Atheist bus."

God's judgment; yet, it is arguable whether proclaiming a message of eternal torment is the most grace-filled or loving way to live out such an understanding. Peter Rollins is right when he asserts that, at its heart, rather than being reducible to mere affirmations of religious dogma, Christian faith is about being "caught up in and engulfed by that which utterly transcends."[5] Thus, becoming a disciple of Jesus Christ is not just about right belief; it is about believing in the right way—believing "in a loving, sacrificial and Christ-like manner."[6]

While holding on to the importance of believing in the right way, one of the greatest challenges in making disciples remains that of articulating the faith in ways that are meaningful and relevant to those currently outside the church. This is important on many levels—preaching, the worship and sacramental life of the community of faith, the church's embodiment of the gospel message in the context of the wider world. Yet, undergirding all of these is the need for individuals to have a robust understanding of what it means to be a disciple. By this I am not talking about the detailed theological knowledge Christ-followers might obtain from seminary. I simply mean an understanding of the basics of faith, a clear sense of why it is that they are Christian themselves and the confidence with which to share their experience of faith with another person. Again, I am not talking about presenting a theological treatise on what and why another should believe. I am pointing to the practice of sharing one's personal experience of faith in an informed and natural way and explaining how it brings meaning.

Remembering Our First Love

The message to the church at Ephesus in John's Revelation is significant in this context: "I know all the things you do. I have seen your hard work and your patient endurance.... But I have this complaint against you. You don't love me or each other as you did at first" (Rev 2:2, 4 NLT)! First love is a powerful thing. Many people can vividly remember the first time they set eyes on the person who would become their spouse or their first date or first kiss. First love can take one's breath away. The strongest marriages are those in which the partners remain in touch with the power of that first love, building on it and deepening it through

---

5. Rollins, *How (not) to Speak of God*, 1.
6. Ibid., 3.

time. What holds true with the emotional holds true with the spiritual as well; anyone who has experienced the enthusiasm and passion of a new believer can attest to that. New believers are hard to contain! The strongest believers are those who remain in touch with the power of their first love, building on it and deepening it through time.

In my work in evangelism I have the opportunity to worship in many different contexts—traditional, contemporary, emergent; both the variety and the similarity are remarkable. Worship is meaningful at many levels: the praise, sacrifice, supplication and intercession offered to God, the shared sacrament. An additional crucial but often overlooked aspect is the consistent opportunity worship affords to announce the story of faith—through music, prayer, the proclaimed word. For believers, hearing the story is an opportunity to remember their spiritual first love, to reinforce and deepen faith, to appropriate it to daily life. For the nonreligious visitor, hearing the story is an opportunity for the Holy Spirit to work preveniently toward faith and a spiritual first love experience, or to generate that experience for the first time.

Over the years I have noticed an aspect of worship that cuts across all the issues of style that tend to absorb the energies of congregations. This relates to the ability to tell the story and thus experience and/or re-experience spiritual first love. In worship, it often appears as though believers have either forgotten the story or at least do not seem to remember it with any sense of passion. For example, there is a vast body of hymns that ignited the faith and passion of generations of people— moved them toward a first love spiritual experience. Yet the same people whose faith was launched on those hymns sing them now as if they were dirges. It is difficult for anyone to believe that grace is amazing or that there really is victory in Jesus, when hymns describing those things are sung with a decided lack of energy, power, or even a modicum of interest, let alone enthusiasm. Contemporary worship does not avoid the danger simply because it avoids traditional hymns. Praise songs and choruses often do not tell the story in the first place even if sung with enthusiasm and can regularly become private love songs rather than communal proclamations of praise. Similar difficulties affect the liturgical life of the community, with many rituals performed by rote with either no real understanding of why worship proceeds as it does or no visible interest in the meaning behind the actions.

When God instructed Moses in how to lead an Israel freshly liberated from slavery in Egypt, remembrance played a key role:

> Watch out! Be very careful never to forget what you have seen the Lord do for you. Do not let these things escape from your mind as long as you live! And be sure to pass them on to your children and grandchildren.... Commit yourselves wholeheartedly to these commands I am giving you today. Repeat them again and again to your children. Talk about them when you are at home and when you are away on a journey, when you are lying down and when you are getting up again. Tie them to your hands as a reminder, and wear them on your forehead. Write them on the doorposts of your house and on your gates. (Deut 4:9, 6:6–9 NLT)

This word is for Christ-followers as much as for Jews. Individual Christ-followers and communities of Christians can only be faithful disciples and make new disciples when they know the story of faith, keep it ever before them, and become comfortable enough with it to articulate it gracefully to others. When Christ-followers worship with a real sense of their spiritual first love, others are able to discern their passion immediately. When Christians speak with the genuineness and authenticity that accompanies a deep connection to their spiritual first love, they are able to converse, dialogue, and share with others in ways that are open, respectful, attractive, and meaningful.

Grace-Full Disciple-Making

Currently, among many in the church in the United States, there is a sense that cultural forces are aligned against Christians. As a result of this perspective, Christians often feel they must be on the defensive in relation to the rest of society. Such a defensive posture, however, is not conducive to graceful disciple-making. Despite what could appear to be a gloomy situation, secular theorists recognize that the countless predictions of the impending rejection of religion that have been made throughout the history of the United States have been and continue to be proven mistaken.[7] Despite the clamor created by the antagonistic writing of authors such as Sam Harris, most non-religious people are not raging that "God is dead."

---

7. Nichols, "The 'New' No Religionists," 12–14.

According to the U.S. Religious Landscape Survey conducted in 2007 by the Pew Forum on Religion and Public Life, while 16.1 percent of respondents did identify themselves as unaffiliated with any religion, 70 percent of those believe in God and 40 percent said that God was very important in their lives.[8] These figures address only those who identify themselves as not affiliated with any religion. To put these statistics in perspective, there are more people who claim to be unaffiliated with any religion in the United States than all the Episcopalians, United Methodists, and Lutherans combined.[9] Breaking the statistics down by specific age groups reveals that 37 percent of all adults age eighteen to forty-one are outsiders to Christianity; 40 percent of all sixteen to twenty-nine year olds are outsiders; 27 percent of Baby Boomers (42–60 year olds) and 23 percent of adults over sixty-one years also all stand outside the church.[10] Despite this negative appraisal, the remarkable fact is that *70 percent of unaffiliated people reported openness to conversations about faith and spirituality.* Books like *I Sold My Soul on eBay: Viewing Faith Through an Atheist's Eyes*, emphasize this openness and the opportunity it provides.[11] In this kind of environment, the need to regain a sense of one's spiritual first love and to develop a robust understanding of what it means to be a disciple is crucial.

The desire for spiritual conversation offers a wide door for the practice of effective evangelism, but this door can only be entered with confidence and grace. Projecting an attitude of confrontation or superiority, or fixating on "success" or "effectiveness," can distort the gospel. Disciples are not made through marketing strategies or public relations campaigns. On the contrary, Christ-followers enter this wide door with a confidence in and a deep assurance of the love of God for *all* creation— not in a confrontational posture but with a grace that respects the place in which the other stands, wherever it may be. In an environment where those outside the church are open to spiritual conversations, disciple-making must involve a direct but loving engagement with nonreligious people. They live in the same communities, work in the same buildings, attend the same schools, and shop in the same places as Christians. In

---

8 Pew Forum, "U.S. Religious Landscape Survey." Cf. Shah, "Born Again in the U.S.A."

9. Nichols, "The 'New' No Religionists," 13.

10. Kinnaman, and Lyons, *Unchristian*, 18.

11. See Mehta, *I Sold My Soul on eBay*.

order for such conversations to take place, however, Christ-followers must be willing to extend themselves in ways where relationships of trust can develop. Genuine evangelism is about respect and friendship. It requires abandoning stereotypes and making oneself vulnerable to another. It is about honest sharing and patient care.

Extending oneself in a genuine and authentic way that respects the perspective of the other is not always easy. Despite an environment of spiritual openness on the part of nonreligious people, the reputation of Christians as a whole is currently far from ideal. In contrast to a decade ago, when Christians were viewed, by and large, in a positive light, Christians now are more known for what they oppose than for what they support.[12] In his book *Unchristian: What a New Generation Really Thinks about Christianity . . . and Why It Matters*, David Kinnaman provides a challenging and somewhat disconcerting assessment of the perceptions of those outside the church, asserting that outsiders view Christians as hypocritical, too focused on getting converts, antihomosexual, sheltered, too political, and judgmental.[13] Thus, while people may be spiritually open, they are also quite likely to be resistant to Christians. As Christians, we naturally consider these views to be misconceptions about the faith; however, they may have been formed on the basis of outsiders' own lived experience which makes these perceptions, in a very meaningful sense, reality. This fact, in and of itself, simply elevates the need for grace in any effort of disciple-making, accentuating the importance of respect, authenticity, and compassionate love.

In the process of disciple-making, it does little good to create trendy marketing strategies or grand mission statements. Ezekiel provides an important reminder: "When I reveal my holiness through you before their very eyes, says the Sovereign Lord, then the nations will know that I am the Lord" (Ezek 36:23 NLT). This word is as important for Christians in the twenty-first century as it was for ancient Israel. To have integrity, Christ-followers, both individually and collectively, must recognize that *the world is watching*. Thus, "all that we say or do [must be] a public witness to God's peaceable reign and an embodied offer of new creation in Christ, whether that is our treatment of children, our management of money, our habits of prayer, our care of the ecosphere,

---

12. Kinnaman and Lyons, *Unchristian*, 24–26.
13. Ibid., 29–30.

our forgiveness of enemies, or the way we imagine and use time."[14] To be made a disciple of Jesus Christ is to be made a witness to the rest of the world. When Christ-followers take this seriously, they recognize that the difficulties of disciple-making are at their core issues of substance, not of image. It is quite possible, and I might suggest probable, that the negative opinion of Christians that outsiders hold has less to do with misunderstanding on the part of the outsiders, and more to do with a meager conception of and inadequate living out of the faith by Christians themselves. Collectively, Christ followers do not need to brush up their image by "rethinking church" and other such initiatives, as much as they need to *attend to the significant task of their own spiritual formation*—regaining a sense of being "*for* Jesus rather than *against* outsiders;"[15] developing a robust understanding of what it means to be a disciple of Jesus, following the God who is not only concerned with the redemption of human beings but with the restoration of all creation.

Gabe Lyons notes the difficulty in making disciples when existing disciples are not in touch with their first love or lack an adequate understanding of Christian faith: "When we no longer know what it means (much less care) to be salt and light *among* those in our culture and to be an influence for good, we forfeit our role as agents of Christ's kingdom."[16] The task of making disciples is a crucial one; but it is a task that cannot be undertaken without a robust understanding of what it means to actually *be* a disciple. It must be undertaken with a passion that stems from a deep connection with one's spiritual first love and a humble sense of God's profound love for *all* creation. When it is undergirded by both right belief and believing in the right way, it becomes a dynamic process of engaging others in grace-filled, loving ways that not only proclaim the good news but embody it as well.

Grace-Filled Ripples

Grace-filled disciple-making flowing from right belief and believing rightly is an approach that is not limited by culture, but one which generates grace-filled ripples across boundaries as individuals commit themselves to the process of genuine and authentic relationship build-

14. Stone, *Evangelism after Christendom*, 27.
15. Kinnaman and Lyons, *Unchristian*, 217.
16. Ibid., 224.

ing. In all cultures, becoming Christ-like in the way in which one holds one's beliefs is a powerful witness. In all cultures, a confident faith embodied in love and compassion compels those who stand on the outside. As Jesus attended to whole persons, so Christ-followers attend to whole persons as they seek to be and make disciples of Jesus—relating to all others with respect and compassion, beginning conversations, sharing, caring, trusting and being trusted, listening, learning and growing in their relationships with outsiders. In this way environments are created in which the Holy Spirit can move and work, transforming and renewing not only those who have yet to experience God's grace for themselves, but those who are already engulfed by that which utterly transcends.

23

Discipleship and Empire

Bryan Stone

THE ANCIENT APOLOGIST TERTULLIAN ONCE SAID THAT PEOPLE ARE made, not born, Christians. His point was that discipleship is a matter of intentional formation over time rather than a matter of birthright or mere membership in a group. Moreover, because discipleship frequently (if not always) takes place also in the context of *rival* formations, we know that by at least the third century the initial process of becoming a Christian could take up to three years.

In the context of the United States, at the heart of a complex, global empire, is there any reason to believe that the process of being formed into disciples should be any quicker or easier today than it was in the third century? Ours is a context in which we are daily offered "makeovers" of body, face, wardrobe, house, career, marriage, and personality. In fact, given the relentless and pervasive technologies of transformation and conversion directed toward the formation of our desires and behaviors, the path of discipleship could even be compared to an intensive and protracted process of detoxification.

Because the process of becoming a disciple is so intense and intentional, and notwithstanding Tertullian's important point, the language of "birthing" may be more helpful than the language of "making" when it comes to thinking about discipleship. The word "make" can imply an exercise in autonomous production that is remote, external, and objectifying so that Jesus' command to disciple the nations (Matt 28:19) resembles something more like our making a cake or assembling a piece of furniture. But persons are not simply "made" disciples by others nor do we become disciples by following a manual that provides "ten easy steps." If the process of discipleship is intense, protracted, and counter-cultural, that is in no small part because it requires a relationship between disciples and disciplers that is intimate, internal, and even imitative, since what is expected in the disciple must to a great degree already be present in the discipler. One of the greatest challenges for discipling new Christians in the U.S. context is that there must exist in the first place a faithful community of disciples—a church—that possesses the habits, practices, virtues, and disciplines that enable it to birth other disciples.

Pilgrimage and Empire

One way the church might think of itself in this regard is as a company of pilgrims on a Spirit-led journey where discipleship is the ongoing practice of learning the art of pilgrimage and of remaining faithful to the One who is "the Way" on which we journey. But that pilgrimage is made difficult, if not impossible, when we presume ourselves already to have arrived or, as is so often the case with the church in the United States, when we so make ourselves at home in our culture and so identify ourselves with imperial structures of power that we forget the journey altogether.

Another possibility is that we take up that journey, but as tourists rather than pilgrims. For ancient pilgrims, the journey was always as important as the destination, and so the pilgrim would receive "instructions on where to pray, where to spend the night, and so on."[1] Each step along the way was part of a sacred itinerary to be inhabited, even if only as a stop along the way. The tourist, by contrast, is not so much a pilgrim as a consumer, focused on getting to a destination that is little more than a commodity. Pilgrims, however, give themselves over to a "way" designed to transform them, including the transformation that comes from fellowship with a company of pilgrims who are also on that journey.

While a number of features of the U.S. context pose challenges today both to embarking on as well as inviting others onto the path of discipleship as a pilgrimage,[2] one of the most pressing is the reality

---

1. A summarization of Cavanaugh, *Torture and Eucharist*, 183.

2. One might mention, for example, secularization, globalization, urbanization, multiculturalism, and religious pluralism.

of empire. To be sure, most of us who have grown up as citizens of the United States are not accustomed to thinking of ourselves as living in the context of empire. Only recently has empire shown up as part of our vocabulary, and this is due partly to the fact that we have been trained to think of our nation as special, as an exception, perhaps even as part of God's plan in the world—but not primarily as an imperial power.

This is certainly not the first time Christians have found themselves in the context of empire, of course. Whether it was imperial Rome, the Holy Roman Empire, the British Empire, or any number of other empires that preceded that latest in a long line of empires that we today call the United States of America, Christian discipleship has always taken place in the context of empire. But the relationship of discipleship to empire has not always looked the same. It makes a great deal of difference whether disciples are being formed at the fringes and on the underside of empire by a church of saints and martyrs who are marginalized or even persecuted by the empire, or whether disciples are being formed by a church that has assumed the role of chaplain to the empire, succeeding where the empire succeeds and expanding where the empire expands. Martyrdom and chaplaincy, in fact, turn out to be two fairly important and entirely contrasting postures, discourses, and sets of imagination that the church has adopted in relation to empire. And insofar as they represent radically different ways of relating church to empire, they also structure the process of discipleship in dramatically different ways.

Our present imperial context is complex to say the least. Again, we aren't always aware of empire nor do we have much of a vocabulary for its reality in our lives. Though it is centered in the United States, this empire is not easily reducible to a single nation-state, or person, or emperor as its agent, nor is it the product of some grand conspiracy orchestrated by a handful of powerful individuals. It is instead a much more complex, multi-headed, and de-centered Leviathan. Joerg Rieger, in thinking about empires across history, has helpfully defined empire as having to do with "massive concentrations of power that permeate all aspects of life and that cannot be controlled by any one actor alone" but that nonetheless seeks "to extend its control as far as possible; not only geographically, politically, and economically . . . but also intellectually, emotionally, psychologically, spiritually, culturally, and religiously."[3]

3. Rieger, *Christ and Empire*, 2–3.

Because these "conglomerates of power" that we call empire have a stake in controlling virtually every aspect of our lives,[4] the challenge before us as a church is to detect the way Christian existence has come to be shaped by the logic and discourse of empire and yet also to discern why, where, and how Christian discipleship names a path of resistance to being co-opted by empire.

For those of us who grew up on *Star Wars* films where good versus evil was mythologized in terms of resistance against "the empire," the word "empire" automatically has negative connotations. But there have always been Christians who saw expansion of empire in positive terms as God-ordained, as God-blessed, as something beneficial and benevolent, and as bringing peace, education, order, and civilization to the world. But even beyond viewing empire as good for the world, some Christians have viewed empire as good for the church and an aid to discipleship because of the structural support empire gave to Christianity once the two were melded. After all, in the fourth century when the empire became officially Christian, not only did that put a stop to the persecution of Christians (Christians would now do the persecuting), it also made possible the relatively rapid spread of Christianity (or something like it) throughout the far-flung corners of the world via the imperial infrastructure of roads, language, and the *pax Romana*. By having curried imperial favor, by traveling aboard imperial ships to the new world in the service of the empire's colonization of other civilizations, the process of becoming a Christian became easier and quicker (not to mention mandatory) while the path of refusing Christian discipleship would now become the path of courage and conviction. The Church has been paying the price ever since.

Prior to our imperial chaplaincy, the path of discipleship for Christians was visible, costly, and involved counter-cultural economic commitments and a political allegiance to the lordship of Jesus that stood in contrast to the lordship of the emperor. All this would change once the empire was officially Christian so that discipleship had less to do with a distinctive set of behaviors, practices, and social patterns and more to do with one's nominal membership in an institution, intellectual assent to propositions about who Jesus is, or as in our own time, with a private, inward, and dematerialized experience of Jesus as one's

---

4. Ibid., vii.

"personal savior." Jesus can now be lord of my heart, but I can still kill the emperor's enemies if the emperor asks me to.

In so identifying itself with empire through a posture of chaplaincy, the church not only blesses and sings songs about the empire, waving the flag of the empire as its own, while serving and benefiting from the empire's economic conquests. It inevitably begins to imagine the path of discipleship on terms set for it by the empire. Unlearning a form of Christianity that has been deeply shaped by a militaristic, nationalistic, and consumerist culture is not easy, of course, because it means extricating the path of discipleship from the logic, discourse, economics, and violence of empire such that we can once again as a people become the peaceful offer to the world of a strange but genuinely good news.

At least one place to start might be refusing to kill other people simply because the emperor asks us to. The problem, however, is that it is increasingly difficult to know who and where the emperor is or when we are obeying him. Empire has become incredibly sophisticated and, again, multi-headed. It is also true that while it is difficult to resist a pagan empire, to refuse to fight its wars or worship its gods, it is far more difficult to resist an empire that has come to think of itself as Christian.[5] Then too, one of the differences between fourth century empire and the twenty-first century American empire, is that the latter is far less interested in securing and defending a single official religious sponsor or chaplain and more adept at domesticating all religions equally as purveyors and administrators of essentially private experiences. Our empire, rather than persecuting religious heretics or minorities (in most cases), can afford to protect religion as a private good by assigning it to a private space that can be protected from "public" interference, on the one hand, while protecting a pluralistic "public" against the particularities of religion, on the other hand. Ours is a unique context where, on the one hand, presidential candidates have to be people of faith (an atheist could never get elected President of the United States) while, on the other hand, our candidates have to try to convince us that their faith won't actually make any difference to their politics. The church, likewise, is reduced to a privatized arm of the great global machine, and "a vendor of religious goods and services"[6] that poses no threat whatsoever to the pretensions of empire. Indeed, because discipleship is

---

5. Cf. Cavanaugh, *Torture and Eucharist*, 80.
6. Hunsberger, "Sizing Up the Shape of the Church," 338.

conceived of as fundamentally private and individual with at best social implications, the church becomes an afterthought altogether.

This de-formation of Christian witness by a diminishment of the sense in which the church is itself a public ends up de-politicizing discipleship in relationship to empire. For the first Christians, to confess Jesus as Lord was a political act because it meant that the emperor was not Lord.[7] In our time, by contrast, the lordship of Jesus has become an essentially private confession fully compatible with the increasingly hegemonic and far-ranging claims of the empire over our lives. Evangelism, likewise, is then reduced to a set of techniques designed to generate this essentially private confession and so ceases to be the treasonous practice it once was (and continues to be in some world contexts).

In contrast to the posture of chaplaincy that accepts the church's domestication within the space and on the terms that empire has provided us, our primary task is not to find better ways to engage the church more effectively in imperial politics, but rather to *be* a distinctive politics in the context of empire. Too often when Christians do "go public" they do so out of residual Christendom assumptions about the relationship of church to empire so that we come to believe public witness means swinging presidential elections or dominating school boards rather than modeling before the world a new politics of the Spirit that runs counter to prevailing patterns of wealth and poverty, domination and subordination, insider and outsider. In other words, the public witness we do have is too often but a parody of itself, a caricature, and little more than a voting block. A voting block, however, is not a church. And to the extent that this is the most to which our public witness amounts, we will never pose a problem to the aspirations of empire.

Discipleship as a Form of Imperial Resistance

It may be true that no one can escape the empire's influence completely, but it is also true that "empire is never quite able to extend its control absolutely."[8] The good news is that Christian witness has not always been overtaken completely by empire and that from the beginning there have always been Christians who understood the path of discipleship not

7. Rieger, *Christ and Empire*, 23–67.
8. Ibid., 3–4.

as a form of chaplaincy to empire but as a form of obedient response and witness to God. Even today there are signs that the chaplaincy of the church to the American empire is being rejected, especially by economically, ethnically, or racially marginalized communities that have never had any stake in that chaplaincy in the first place. In almost any city in the country, one now finds alternative Christian communities comprised of disciples who have covenanted to live visibly and publicly in ways that run counter to prevailing social patterns and established habits of relating to one's enemies. Within these deviant Christian bodies, social lines are being crossed rather than reinforced, the poor are being valued, strangers are being welcomed; material goods are being shared, and a refusal to celebrate or participate in imperial violence is being cultivated. The witness of these communities is visible, but not always prominent. They do not typically generate large-scale conferences that attract thousands of pastors eager to find out how to grow their churches.

What communities like these demonstrate is that if the church in the United States is to be able to birth disciples in our current imperial context, it will have to find ways to reclaim its public and material witness as the church not merely *in* society, but *as* a new and alternative society, one that understand its primary citizenship as located in the commonwealth of God. One of the features of these counter-imperial communities—whether, for example, that is an outdoor church in Boston that intentionally welcomes persons without adequate housing or whether that is a community of Christians living on the U.S.-Mexican border who practice a variety of forms of hospitality to immigrants (whether documented or not), or whether that is a "new monastic" community in San Francisco that practices a form of common purse as a way of living out their Christian economic commitments—is that they violate the imperial boundaries of public and private and its domestication of religion to a private good. As a result, they make visible the body of Christ in and through their own bodies, both personally and corporately, thereby helping us locate the church. Of course, one might argue that "locating" the church visibly and bodily is not really a problem in the United States. Churches seem to be on every street corner. And after all, we now have Mapquest, Google Maps, Yahoo Maps, and onboard global positioning systems. Do we really need help locating the church?

As most of us know almost instinctively, the church as a community of disciples does not appear in the world simply because there is a sign out front that says "church" or because we happen to encounter tall steeples, bell choirs, and bad coffee. Nor can it be found simply by going to the phone directory and looking under the letter "C." The church is the Spirit-empowered and Christ-shaped performance of an alternative social imagination in which first are last and last first; in which enemies are forgiven rather than being persecuted. It is the embodiment of a new creation in the world, ritualized in baptism, in which all prior social differences, whether given or chosen, no longer become determinative for our relations to one another. Around the table of the Lord, the church is the concrete enactment of a time and space that rivals time and space as defined by empire.

One of the characteristic features of empire throughout history is the way it tends to devalue the particularity of place. Empires expand and maintain their power by the homogenization of place through the imposition of a unified and totalizing "order" that erases difference so that one place is the same as another, all of them being equally dominated by empire. Thus, whether one is in Jerusalem, Antioch, or Nazareth, all is Rome. In the bodies and communities of Christian disciples, however, this universalizing imperial claim to space is contested, and instead, as citizens of heaven, these disciples create a space in the world where the commonwealth of God can appear materially and bodily. If evangelism is an offer to the world of Christ, this the church does by offering a space and a time in which persons can be habituated into Christ's body. But to locate that space and time, the church needs—the church *is*—a communion of disciples who defy the rootlessness and the placelessness of empire.

Admittedly, the church as a community of disciples will look very different today than it did in the second or third centuries. But now as then, a common denominator of the Christian's witness in the context of empire is still that Jesus is Lord and Caesar is not; that, as Paul writes to the Philippians, "Our citizenship is in heaven" (3:20). The reign of God is not real because we make it so. Nor is it made visible and habitable in the world to the extent that oppressive empires are dismantled, terrorists destroyed, and tyrants overthrown. It is made visible when, in the midst of violence, oppression, terrorism, and empire, a people who worship God as their sovereign refuse to find the security and meaning of their lives in their own power and instead forgive others just as they have been forgiven by God. It is made visible and habitable when that people, by placing themselves into the Spirit's hands become dispossessed of every pretense to gaining a foothold in the world for themselves or their cause. Our first and primary responsibility as citizens of the commonwealth of God is to live *as* citizens of the commonwealth of God rather than as citizens of the empire. In doing so, we bear witness to an ultimately more real world in which Christ is risen, and in which the imperial resort to violence is, therefore, no longer an option.

Further Reading in North American Contexts

Arias, Mortimer, and Alan Johnson. *The Great Commission: Biblical Models for Evangelism*. Nashville: Abingdon, 1992.
Bowen, Kurt. *Christians in a Secular World: The Canadian Experience*. Toronto: McGill-Queen's University Press, 2005.
Brueggemann, Walter. *Biblical Perspectives on Evangelism: Living in a Three-Storied Universe*. Nashville: Abingdon, 1993.
Bryan, Stephen D., and Trevor Hudson. *The Way of Transforming Discipleship: Authentic Christian Spirituality*. Nashville: Upper Room, 2005.
Claiborne, Shane. *Irresistible Revolution: Living as an Ordinary Radical*. Grand Rapids: Zondervan, 2006.
Dharmaraj, Glory E., and Jacob S. Dharmaraj. *Mutuality in Mission: A Theological Principle for the 21st Century*. New York: GBGM, 2001.
Guder, Darrell L., editor. *Missional Church: A Vision for the Sending of the Church in North America*. Grand Rapids: Eerdmans, 1998.
Hirsch, Alan. *The Forgotten Ways: Reactivating the Missional Church*. Grand Rapids: Brazos, 2006.
Hjalmarson, Leonard, and Brent Toderash. *Fresh + Re:Fresh: Church Planting and Urban Mission in Canada Post-Christendom*. Eagle, ID: Allelon, 2009
Hunter, George G., III. *The Apostolic Congregation: Church Growth Reconceived for a New Generation*. Nashville: Abingdon, 2009.
Kallenberg, Brad. *Live to Tell: Evangelism for a Postmodern World*. Grand Rapids: Brazos, 2002.
Mead, Loren B. *The Once and Future Church: Reinventing the Congregation for a New Mission Frontier*. Bethesda, MD: Alban Institute, 1991.
Newbigin, Lesslie. *The Gospel in a Pluralist Society*. Grand Rapids: Eerdmans, 1989.
———. *The Open Secret: Sketches for a Missionary Theology*. Rev. ed. Grand Rapids: Eerdmans, 1995.
Pohl, Christine. *Making Room: Recovering Hospitality as a Christian Tradition*. Grand Rapids: Eerdmans, 1999.
Posterski, Donald C. *Reinventing Evangelism: New Strategies for Presenting Christ in Today's World*. Downers Grove: InterVarsity, 1989.
Rawlyk, George. *Aspects of the Canadian Evangelical Experience*. Toronto: McGill-Queen's University Press, 2003.
Sider, Ronald J. *Good News and Good Works: A Theology of the Whole Gospel*. Grand Rapids: Baker, 1993.
Sider, Ronald J., et al. *Churches that Make a Difference: Reaching Your Community with Good News and Good Works*. Grand Rapids: Baker, 2002.
Snyder, Howard A., editor. *Global Good News: Mission in a New Context*. Nashville: Abingdon, 2001.

Sweet, Leonard. *Post-Modern Pilgrims: First Century Passion for the 21st Century World*. Nashville: Broadman & Holman, 2000.

Tickle, Phyllis. *The Great Emergence: How Christianity is Changing and Why*. Grand Rapids: Baker, 2008.

Webber, Robert E. *Ancient-Future Evangelism: Making Your Church a Faith-Forming Community*. Grand Rapids: Baker, 2003.

Wilke, Richard Byrd, and Julia Kitchens Wilke, *Disciple: Becoming Disciples through Bible Study*. 2nd ed. Nashville: Abingdon, 1993.

Wilson-Hartgrove, Jonathan. *New Monasticism: What It Has to Say to Today's Church*. Grand Rapids: Brazos, 2008.

PART SIX

Cross-Continental Witness
Valuing the Confluence of Streams

Introduction to Part 6

SOMETHING SPECIAL HAPPENS TO PEOPLE WHEN THEY HAVE THE OPportunity to step across the boundaries that separate them from other communities and experience the diversity of the human family first hand. These cross-cultural experiences forever change the way they view the world and the nature of Christian discipleship. Crossing into different worlds necessitates the translation of the gospel. One of the miraculous elements of the Christian faith is, in fact, the way in which disciples of Christ embody it, share the fullness of who they are in Christ with others, and facilitate the movement of the gospel into a new milieu, a new culture, a new context. I felt that it was important in this volume on *Making Disciples in a World Parish* to listen to the voices of those who have made these kinds of journeys and who now celebrate their discoveries. Those who have crossed cultural boundaries value the confluence of these streams in their lives.

Sarah Davis is a bishop in the African Methodist Episcopal Church who had the privilege of serving in the Southern African District of her church, comprising Lesotho, Botswana, Mozambique, and Swaziland. Not only does she reflect on personal experiences that demonstrate the need for a holistic vision of disciple-making in which spiritual and physical needs are both embraced, but she shares a poem of her own composition that epitomizes her vision of mission. At its heart, the process of making disciples, from her perspective, involves loving people, praying for God's guidance, listening, and taking people and their environment seriously.

A century ago a Brazilian pastor in London would have been hard to imagine, but today, R. F. Leão-Neto shares ministry in a West London circuit with Africans, Asians, Latin Americans, and, yes, Brits. In a setting as cosmopolitan as his circuit, he calls for a "culture of transformation" and shares the insights of his own liberationist perspective with communities that long to recapture the spirit of deliverance. Finding God in the struggle, rediscovering the liberating message of the Bible, and building transformative communities constitute the central themes of his vision. They point to a holistic understanding of the gospel that unites heart, head, and hands.

Tumani Nyajeka is a Zimbabwean who teaches evangelism in a predominantly African-American seminary community in Atlanta, Georgia. She brings from her homeland a profound admiration for the work and witness of women, and particularly the Rukwadzano (United Methodist Women). She cannot separate her own understanding of disciple-making from the narratives of the women who founded this organization and rooted discipleship in their understanding of baptism. For those courageous women, "being a baptized Christian," as she observes, "means building a joyful community in partnership with God, each other, and all of creation." Finding the strength to abandon fear and to discover unity in the family of Christ, these women-disciples look to Christ the Healer as they embody healing and wholeness for others.

All disciple-making reflects a profoundly auto-biographical element, and Helmut Renders, German theological educator who serves the people of Brazil, shapes his reflections around his own faith journey into the world of South America. The central motif of his pilgrimage revolves around Christ's declaration that we are "no longer aliens" but "members of the household of God." Reminiscing about his pilgrimage with Ghanaian *adofos* back in Germany, Amazonians of the lost Eden, and colleagues in Brazil, he delights in the experience of being discipled by those he was called to disciple.

The experience of the church in Cuba over the course of the past half century bears witness to the validity of Tertullian's claim that "the blood of the martyrs is seed." Phil Wingeier-Rayo, a North American Anglo who served as a missionary in Cuba during some of the difficult years, provides an incisive historical account of the life of the church under Castro. Luke's account of the disciples on the road to Emmaus functions as a paradigm for those who live in despair and would just as soon run away. Small groups and *casas-culto* (house churches) restored hope in the lives of thousands and opened their eyes to see a present and living Lord. Like the revival of faith under the Wesleys, the Spirit-led revival of the church in Cuba offers wonderful insights for the global community of faith.

24

Holistic Mission and Evangelism

Sarah F. Davis

Personal salvation always involves Christian mission and service to the world. By joining heart and hand, we assert that personal religion, evangelical witness, and Christian social action are reciprocal and mutually reinforcing.[1]

MY HUSBAND AND I WERE BLESSED TO LIVE IN MASERU, LESOTHO, AND serve the wonderful people in the Southern African countries of Lesotho, Botswana, Mozambique, and Swaziland for four years. Each country was different from the other in very distinctive ways: the Basothans of Lesotho spoke Sesotho while the Mozambicans spoke Portuguese and fifteen other dialects of their native African language; the Swazis spoke SiSwati, and the Botswanans spoke Setswana. Mozambique was the poorest country of the four we served while Botswana was booming with an infrastructure far surpassing any of the other three countries. While persons in Lesotho and Mozambique had to pay for education at all levels, education in Botswana at all levels was free. Swaziland boasted of their King Mswati III, the last absolute monarch in sub-Saharan Africa, who lives a life of luxury, while many of the people struggle to make a decent living. On the other hand, the Basothans lived in the mountains where there were more rural households and scanty living conditions than in any of the other three countries. Needless to say, sharing the good news of Jesus Christ where we were in Southern Africa required prayerful, relative, creative, and intentional mission and evangelism ministry.

1. *UMC Book of Discipline (2004)*, 45–47.

We were challenged as we endeavored to develop an effective ministry of mission and evangelism in Southern Africa. It became clear to us that we would have to minister with intentionality, patience, and persistence; to embody the freedom to be free with people who did not think as we did or have the same experiences as us; and to trust that there really could be different ways to do what we had always done our way, and that this was alright. Whatever success we were able to achieve in holistically affecting the lives of the people was directly related to our insistence on the need for everyone to be 1) intentional in ministry, 2) patient and persistent in working with persons who did not speak English, and 3) open to new ideas and new ways of viewing situations. If we are to learn anything from our history, we know that we must see people as they are, not as we want them to be. It is important to hear from the people and to listen to what they are saying and not hear what we want to hear. Keeping our agendas and desires in mind, but not ahead of the needs of the people, is a rule worthy of remembering.

Dr. Dennis Dickerson, Historiographer of the African Methodist Episcopal Church, points out that while the AME Church has been involved in formal Christianizing mission outside the United States since 1820, we have not always heard and or listened to those with whom we ministered. According to Dr. Dickerson: "These black missionaries and their innumerable successors in the nineteenth and twentieth centuries . . . arrived in other areas of the Americas and in Africa freighted with cultural assumptions about Christianity and the indigenous peoples whom they encountered. Their 'western' attitudes and actions often inhibited their efforts and compromised the effectiveness of their evangelistic and educational initiatives."[2]

Many times we are so intently focused on the help we know we can give and the good that we can bring, our zeal gets ahead of us and we overlook the needs of the people we have come to serve. We cannot afford to compromise the effectiveness of our ministry of mission and evangelism by falling short in our hearing and listening skills. Our minds cannot be so made up that we fail to look and see or pause long enough to talk with the indigenous people alongside whom we minister. We need to listen in order to hear from them about the places of their greatest need and pain. Those engaged in the ministry of mission and evangelism must minister with intentionality to the whole person.

2. Dickerson, "Worldwide Mission of the AMEC."

We must work carefully, therefore, to insure that passion for adding people to the kingdom of God does not blind us to the tangible needs of the people we have been sent to serve. We find no better model in this than Jesus.

Critical Challenges

In our mission practice, the most pressing challenge was to meet both the spiritual and the physical needs of the people. Two personal accounts of mission/evangelism illustrate this critical issue related to disciple-making.

A Mission in Lesotho

In December 2007, Dr. Cecelia Williams Bryant, Episcopal Supervisor of the Fifth Episcopal District AMEC, came to Lesotho with seventy-eight missioners for the purpose of setting up free satellite clinics and prayer centers and providing workshops for women and training for preachers. People from every denomination and "no" denomination were welcomed to come and receive whatever services they needed. One of the Health Clinics established at the F. C. James AME Center for Service had lines of people outside the building at 6:30 a.m. each morning and the clinic was not opening until 9:00 a.m. These same people were talking about the AME Church and how their needs were met long after the sojourners left Maseru. Some retuned to visit and join our churches. Some gave their lives to Christ through having had their physical needs met first in the free clinics.

Engaging in practices of mission and evangelism in this context taught us that we are called not only to preach good news but also to liberate those held captive to poor health, poverty, abuse, and poverty of spirit. We needed to let go of the stories heard and the stereotypical pictures and images held about people of Africa. Those who came to serve needed to move beyond the presumption that coming south from the north or west privileged them with truth and knowledge. These issues are critical, because such thinking can keep those who really want to make a difference from seeing, hearing, and being able to listen to the "real" people before them. If the church is to be truly missional, it must embrace the theological task of contextualizing the gospel within the life situations of contemporary people in transforming ways.[3] Effective work in mission and evangelism will address what is needed and not simply what we want to do or what we want to give or the number of persons we want to respond to the offer of salvation.

A Mission in Mozambique

On one of my visits to Beira, Mozambique, I found myself overwhelmed by what people had to do merely to survive. I witnessed their ability to "be content" with their situation and this led me to write a narrative poem entitled "I Looked POVERTY in the Face Today." It illustrates the different needs and issues with which those to whom we carried the gospel were struggling. It was clear to us that if they were to hear the good news, they must first experience liberation from the tangible weights of their suffering.

> "I looked POVERTY in the face today"...
> It was a 9-year-old village boy who, when given a peppermint candy, bit it into five pieces and passed a piece of the candy to each of his sisters and brothers with him without being told to do so.
>
> "I looked POVERTY in the face today"...
> They were pastors and CHURCH MEMBERS gathering in a crowded, hot, mud-STRUCTURE church building WITH MEN sitting on homemade benches and WOMEN AND CHILDREN ON mats on the ground, but praising God and dancing and praying as if they were in a cathedral somewhere else.
>
> "I looked POVERTY in the face today"...
> She was bent down from the waist in stagnant dirty water with a hoe in her hand working the rice fields.
>
> "I looked POVERTY in the face today"...
> They were seventy five children and about 87 adults who were sitting and listening to ME tell them about Jesus and His love.
>
> "I looked POVERTY in the face today"...
> They were seventy-five children who have no schooling

---

3. See Flemming, *Contextualization in the New Testament*.

because they are too far from the nearest school and the main roads, but who when I promised that Zinga-Zinga would have a church and a school in the very near future... clapped and sang and shouted on their feet!

"I looked POVERTY in the face today"...
It was three little boys (8–9 years of age) dressed in blue shirts with an HIV/AIDS logo on it and the name of the home from which they had come. They came to me and said: "We are orphans of parents who have died of HIV/AIDS and we would like it if you could give us a donation to support our care." After I gave my gift one looked me in the eyes and said: "Thank you madam, and may God bless you."

"I looked POVERTY in the face today"...
It was a 2 year and 2 months old baby girl, whose eyes just rolled around, never focusing on anyone or anything, as I held her in my arms and prayed for her. Her name is Baby Betinho Albert Olieveira.

"I looked POVERTY in the face today"...
She was a blind lady with her baby on her back and with 2 little girls (I assume her daughters) leading her by the hand begging for whatever was in my hand.

"I looked POVERTY in the face today"...
He was a little black toddler who had flies all over his/her (couldn't tell the gender) face because of an infected open sore on the back of THE ear. The infection caused the ear lobe to be three times the size of the other ear lobe; yet the little toddler had that special smile of "I love you, and I know you love me" which completely swallowed my heart.

"I looked POVERTY in the face today"
They were men and women walking down a long road from Beira to places on the road to Mau (a 2 hour trip by van)... feet in tongs and some barefooted, but walking briskly toward the nearest village or city.[4]

In 2004, the Beira District (18th Episcopal District AMEC), was the fastest growing area in the Mozambique Annual Conference and received the District award for church growth that year with the report

4. Davis, *I Looked Poverty in the Face Today*.

of 247 conversions, 333 accessions, and 267 baptisms. Not only were the people in that region hungry for physical food and sustenance, they were hungry for the Word of God and the message of hope that the good news brings. In every village where we went, hundreds of people would come to hear and see. They would stay as long as we were there sharing the Word of God. However, we encountered many challenges during our two-week visit in Beira and the surrounding provinces of Muda, Chimoio, Caia, Marromeu, and Luabo. Our journey was interrupted with the need to get salve for the sores of a young boy who was suffering with open wounds. On another occasion we gave a ride to a mother and her baby (in an already over loaded van) to the nearest hospital because the baby was very ill. We had to take care of the needs of the people before they could hear our good news!

These situations taught us that we reach the masses by meeting them in their poverty, with their different languages, and through their own cultures and traditions. We join them where they are and stay long enough to see beyond the stereotypical images of our African sisters and brothers portrayed on television or on advertisements. We learned not to let suspicion, doubt, and our own unrealistic expectations divert energy from the more critical work of building relationships of trust.

Scriptural Images

Two passages from scripture paint a compelling portrait that relates directly to mission and evangelism in the Southern African context. The first is Matt 4:18–19 in which Jesus calls the disciples: "As he walked by the Sea of Galilee, he saw two brothers, Simon, who is called Peter, and Andrew his brother, casting a net into the sea—for they were fishermen. And he said to them, 'Follow me, and I will make you fish for people.'" Jesus extended an invitation to the fishermen to join him and to learn a new vocation. This required Jesus' time, patience, teaching, and repeating some lessons more than once. Despite the demands on Jesus of all the people, he made time for teaching the disciples and gave them his full attention. He listened to and heard them. Discipling these fishermen meant that Jesus first had to arrest their minds, convince them to follow a different path, and then teach them how to master that new way. By living with them, he demonstrated how they were to relate to one another. He evangelized their bodies, souls, and minds.

In the same way, during our ministry in Southern Africa, HIV/AIDS orphans had to be given the warmth of a home, the love and caring of the Village Mother, the food needed to fill their bellies, clothes on their backs and the assurance that despite where they had come from, the future looked bright. Once the children's physical needs had been satisfied, their minds began to be transformed from despair to hope through the day by day caring and sharing of the Village Mother. Soon trust and dependence blossomed in their relationships, and the lessons of love, respect, obedience, and responsibility that they saw lived out in their day to day activities took root in their lives. The children were introduced to Sunday School and church and became active participants in the programs and activities. Soon they joined the church and accepted Christ as their Savior.

The second passage which provides a powerful image for the ministry of mission and evangelism is that infamous passage in which Jesus intentionally went out of his way to Samaria so that he might minister to the woman at the well (John 4:1–29). He went to the woman who needed to be made "whole"—a woman who needed to understand she had worth, she could do work for the kingdom, and that she was important to the Master. Jesus in this passage models the holistic ministry which was required as we ministered in Southern Africa. The people in Southern Africa whether in Maseru, Lesotho, or Mbabane, Swaziland, or Maputo, Mozambique, had self righteous attitudes which easily excluded persons who were known to have strayed from the ways of acceptable living and behaving. Those persons in the villages and communities who were intentionally excluded and ostracized were made to feel uncomfortable in the church. The traditions of the different countries in some cases forbade women who were widowed from walking in the village where livestock was kept; these same women were forbidden from coming to the altar for communion for a season. Evangelizing the body, mind, and soul of both those "in the church" and those "out of the church" was critical to the growing and sustaining of the churches. Just as Jesus had to transform the woman's thinking by engaging her in conversation despite her gender, despite her reputation, and despite her ethnicity, so we worked to end the divisiveness among God's people in Southern Africa.

Scripture says that Jesus "had to go through Samaria." Likewise, the very distant places in Mozambique and the hard to get to places in the Mokhotlong mountains were places that had to be visited in order to get to the people who needed to hear the good news. We had to go and sit with people who had been ostracized and cast out so that they too might hear the good news and be transformed to a new way of thinking and living. We are called to minister to people so that they are willing to move out of the places and situations they are in and follow a new path.

Evangelistic Practice

Sharing our Christian faith means spreading the good news of the kingdom of God by word, deed, and sign through the power of the Holy Spirit, and then waiting and watching in respectful humility and working in expectant hope (Mark 1:15, Luke 9:1–2, Rom 15:18–10).[5] Tent revivals and evangelism crusades were held in each of the Conferences of the 18th District. Additionally we moved out to demonstrate the Word of God through meeting the needs of the wider community. Providing schools and orphanages and health care were also part of the mission and evangelism ministry. Paying an outstanding bill to get water pumped again into a community where the water had been off for several weeks brought new vitality to the community. Upon hearing that the outstanding bill had been paid by the church, the people in church that Christmas morning were able to hear the scriptures clearer and sing the hymns of praise with excitement. If we are going to do effective evangelism, we are going to have to minister to the "whole" person and the all the needs of those persons.

Essential principles that guide such holistic witness include:

1. "Loving the other person as we have been loved by God." Our ultimate purpose is to share the gospel, to offer Christ out of love for the person and in obedience to the command of Christ.

2. "Praying in all things at all times." We are to love others deeply and talk to God about them and talk to them about God.

3. "Listening to God so that the door to speak is opened." Listening to God is an essential in prayer, and listening to others is a requirement in witnessing.

---

5. See Wade, "Essentials of Leading a Person to Christ."

4. "Taking people and their environment seriously." Our witness takes both the person and the person's environment seriously. Faith sharing always begins by genuinely caring for the person and as much as possible entering into the persons' situation. Our testimony begins not in our speaking, but in our hearing. When we genuinely love and care for others and hear their story then we are able to tell our faith story.[6]

Christian Vitality

The more our churches reach out and get involved in the communities where they are, the greater will be the vitality and energy of the church. In Botswana, as the youth and young adults got involved in the campaign against HIV/AIDS, holding workshops, Saturday festivals, and church events, the more we could see renewed energy rising in the churches. The sharing of the issue of HIV/AIDS drew audiences to the churches and to the many church activities which gave opportunity for sharing the good news of Jesus and salvation.

New ministries which meet the needs of people in our communities and villages give birth to and increase to Christian vitality. In each of the four countries, Christian vitality most certainly is vested in the youth and young adults who are less loyal to traditions and more open to new ideas, activities, and teachings. The introduction of music competitions as a major event of the annual Christian Education Conference more than doubled the young adult participation. This event brought renewed vitality to the churches and excitement among our young people and it brought young people who had left the church back to the church.

Having ministered in Southern Africa has given us a greater appreciation for the diversity of cultures and traditions of peoples of the world and a greater determination to advocate for more intentional global ministry in our church.

---

6. Wade, "Essentials of Leading a Person to Christ."

25

A Permeable Church of New Disciples

R. F. Leão Neto

I came to the United Kingdom from Brazil in 1996. I was invited by the church to serve as a Mission Partner. Later I candidated for the ordained ministry and was ordained a presbyter in the British Methodist Church. At the time of writing I have been in my present post in central London for eight years.

Critical Challenges

In *World Christianity in the 20th Century*, Martin Conway and Noel David argue that Christianity has only really become a world-wide faith in the last century.[1] They also make the case that, while Christianity grows and expands elsewhere, decline and stagnation continue to characterize the church throughout Europe. The malaise of the church in this part of the world can be understood, in part, against the backdrop of the nineteenth and early twentieth centuries. The serious critiques levelled against institutional Christianity by influential thinkers, scientists, and philosophers such as Charles Darwin, Karl Marx, Sigmund Freud, and Friedrich Nietzsche dealt a critical blow to the hegemony of Christendom. By the end of two world wars, many Europeans increasingly viewed all religion, let alone Christianity, as superstition, the "opiate of the people," illusion, and in most regards irrelevant to the major concerns of life in the Western world. Other historical factors compounded the deterioration of Christian presence and influence throughout the

---

1. See Davies and Conway, *World Christianity in the 20th Century*.

course of the twentieth century.[2] The church in England declines in numbers, loses more and more of its property, and, more significantly, loses influence in society. This challenge to religion has produced an internal reaction within the community of faith—a lack of self-esteem, a depressive condition, and a fatalistic resignation to decline, both among the members and within the leadership of the church.

The church in the United Kingdom faces two particular challenges. Firstly, there is the external challenge to discipleship due to the blatant antagonism of the culture. A general attitude of apathy concerning the open doors the church attempts to offer, however, may be an even more difficult obstacle than direct attack. Furthermore, atheism continues to grow stronger, although, as Karen Armstrong argues in her book *The Case for God*, theologians have engaged atheism for centuries.[3] Arguments concerning the existence of God have been part and parcel of Christian apologetics, and militant atheism seldom represents well the disputes between doubt and faith in God. Although there is resistance and apathy, ironically, people still expect the church to play a role in society, even if it does so vicariously.[4]

Secondly, the lack of keenness on the part of church members presents an internal challenge to discipleship. Church people have tired of the institutional attitudes that have dominated church life. It is not unusual and even common in some quarters to hear sermons against the church, particularly its institutional life. Often pseudo-intellectual analyses, these diatribes fail to recognise that any content requires a structure to hold it. All human organizations operate with some sort of structure, some agreement about purpose and movement, and some arrangement for managing finances. The church will always entail organizations and institutions as a necessary aspect of its life, whether we like it or not. In the current situation, however, those within positions of influence seem to either take the church institution for granted, on one hand, or openly malign it, on the other.

These external and internal challenges/attacks make disciple-making a very difficult task and threaten the health of the church. Internal detractors fail to realize that without the church the story of Jesus would not have been passed down to this generation. Without

2. See Davie, "Understanding Religion in Modern Britain."
3. See Armstrong, *The Case for God*.
4. See Davie, "Understanding Religion in Modern Britain."

the church there would be no Bible, no sacraments, no creeds. Without the church there would be no community of disciples. At a time when Christian leaders were first considering the devastating consequences of secularization, in his *A Rumour of Angels*, Peter Berger predicated a return of a religious spirit. Has his prophecy been realized elsewhere in the world but not in Europe? Is there a remedy for the fact that the church is ignored by the wider society? Is atheism a challenge that will engulf disciples? For how long will the churches be able to continue their religious roles vicariously before disappearing altogether? Could the internal rebellion against the institutional church be replaced by a creative and transformative energy?

From Rebellion to Transformation (Romans 12:1–2)

"I appeal to you therefore, brothers and sisters, by the mercies of God, to present your bodies as a living sacrifice, holy and acceptable to God, which is your spiritual worship," Paul writes to the Roman church. "Do not be conformed to this world, but be transformed by the renewing of your minds, so that you may discern what is the will of God—what is good and acceptable and perfect" (12:1–2).

Whatever the origins of apathy concerning the church on the part of outsiders or rebellion against the institution on the part of insiders, with regard to the missionary task of making and building up a community of disciples, Christians must open themselves up to a culture of transformation. In a society that has "come of age," to use Bonhoeffer's term, transformation relates directly to the posture of the Christian community to the world that surrounds it. Christians find it difficult to deal with medical advances and the ethical concerns that they raise about both life and death, the complexities of living in a multi-religious context and the enormity of ethnic barriers, the plurality of values related to sexuality, the body and family, and the image of what the historical churches represent in terms of class and gender. Without facing these realities, the church will continue struggling to fulfil its task of making disciples. On the other hand, the church must also tackle its internal challenges head on and foster a culture of transformation inside its communities; internal despair and disillusionment must be turned into transformative and creative energy.

Some find hope for the British church among Christian immigrants who have come from other parts of the world. This optimism is due, in part, to the fact that immigrant communities, language specific congregations, and ethnic specific churches represent the growing part of the church in Great Britain. Cross-cultural dynamics, however, may bear even more important fruit. I serve in a multi-lingual circuit. There are congregations worshiping in four languages in addition to English. These communities serve as catalysts for renewal in the present generation. They bring particular theological and liturgical gifts from other parts of the world. The witness of the church of the poor in Latin America, in particular, may offer some of the most important insights related to the making of disciples. These include finding God in the struggle, rediscovering the Bible, and building transformative communities.

Lessons from Latin America

Finding God in the Struggle

The experience of poverty reinforces particular dimensions of spirituality and determines the path of the disciple who seeks to follow Jesus. Oppressed people find God in the middle of the struggle, in the thick of life. This is different from many European cultures that have tended to confine God to Sundays and to specific areas of life. Evangelization from a liberationist perspective emphasizes the message that God is to be found in the context of life as a whole and, in particular, in the struggles with which people grapple. The suffering servant of Isaiah 53 and the crucified Christ reflect an alternative discipleship and a spirituality that challenges and corrects the church's marriage to comfort. The church that is only for Sundays and that is only on the side of respectable society has already lost its relevance in a suffering world. The church of the poor contributes a transformative impulse. It proclaims that God is to be sought in the struggle. Moreover, it bears witness to a God who is involved in the struggle and who is on the side of those who suffer. Such faith scatters seeds of transformation (Matt 13:1–23). Mission and evangelism in the church of the poor necessarily entails participation in political resistance, solidarity with those who suffer, struggle for justice, and is often consummated in persecution, exile, and even martyrdom.

Rediscovering the Bible

The church of the poor has gathered great energy from the rediscovery of the Bible. Rather than approaching the text from a fundamentalist mindset, or reading the Bible mechanically, Latin American Christians view the Bible primarily as a source of inspiration. The questions commonly asked by the Enlightenment reader seldom apply in the context of poverty and oppression. The primary issue is not whether the story is true or false. The poor do not expect the Bible to provide historical, geographical, or scientific answers. They do not even expect the Bible to set the standards of a universal morality that fits all times and all places. The primary question that the disciples and the community of disciples in the church of the poor ask the text is, What does this story mean to us here and now? Suddenly, a dead text of old speaks anew. In the face of despair, miracle stories bring hope. Where injustice reigns, the example of the early church helps people to organise themselves into communities of resistance that imagine a different future. The biblical witness enables them to find courage to cope with persecution and suffering. They find in the eucharistic memory of Jesus a mystical link with many of the martyrs today.

Request a group of theological students to look at a scriptural passage and comment and they will reach for their biblical commentaries. Preachers may feel that at a loss away from their study. But ask a disciple in the church of the poor about the meaning of a text and she or he will tell of their journey in life, their struggles, and the strength they received from the stories of the Bible. They will say that they see the Gospel stories of healing in the campaign for a local clinic, the feeding of the multitude in a new food program at the local school, the well of living water in a prophetic condemnation of the lack of clean water in the neighborhood, the river in the middle of the city and the tree of life in efforts to achieve sanitation and to recover polluted rivers, seas, and forests.

Building Transformative Communities

There is a crisis in the traditional church, a problem of discourse and of imagination. The old language of atonement makes little sense in the culture. Some in the church cling to that old language. Others struggle to find a language that could be affirmative enough to gather the community around a transformative agenda.

Not to deny the personal dimension of the Christian faith, but the community of disciples has to be more than just a collection of individuals who have experienced the divine. The kingdom of God, the God of life, demands a theology that goes beyond an obsession with the atonement. The church must participate in the ideal of the kingdom of God preached by Jesus. That message is more than just a proclamation of the salvation of individual souls. The church of the poor in Latin America has made it clear that the church has a role in building communities of and for transformation. The community of faith is called to promote life in abundance for all (John 10:10).

The liberationist perspective does not offer a tired Marxist ideology; rather, it proclaims the sacredness of life and proposes that a disciple of Jesus is an eternal learner in the school of living, translating old stories into new teleologies. Rooted in the heritage of the past, the church needs to seek new paradigms to interface with society in a way that points to God's future for all people. The community of faithful disciples, in this view, is an eschatological community of those who are re-interpreting experiences of life in the light of faith and pressing on towards a better tomorrow. They are able to draw from the rich wisdom of the past in order to address the complexities of life and to envisage new dreams for the future.

The Ecumenism of Permeability

Cross-cultural experience necessarily entails an ecumenical dimension. Struggle is the common denominator for Christians of different traditions in the church of the poor. Disciples of different denominations engage together in transformative mission. They come together to exercise political pressure. They scatter to be who they are in their local churches. This movement functions somewhat like a hinge. The same hinge effect is true for wider-than-Christianity ecumenical relations. There is an inter-religious ecumenism operating in the church of the poor in Latin America that is hardly recognised by the academic theological community. I call it the ecumenism of permeability. It is porous. It allows people of different religious traditions on occasions to stand side by side to struggle together or to celebrate their faith in ecumenical acts. Again, they come together like a hinge, for particular purposes and occasions, then, they go away from each other, enriched but firm in their own identity.

With that kind of ecumenism in mind, I dream of a church that is more permeable. Perhaps this could inspire the church in the United Kingdom to make its walls more porous in relation to the society, to the youth, and to the different cultures present within the nation today. A more permeable church, I believe, would also be a more secure church, at ease with its own identity, unafraid to mix. This demands disciples that are in tune with the cultures, able to engage with them critically and constructively; new disciples for a new time.

Hopeful Signs

There are signs of good practices that awaken hope for the future of the church in the United Kingdom. The forty-year-old initiative in urban theology and radical discipleship in Sheffield continues to represent the sort of discipleship I have described above in relation to the church of the poor. This initiative has produced extensive literature and an alternative to the Alpha Course called *Journey*.

Considerable progress has been made in inter-religious relations in the United Kingdom. This is well represented by a Network of Inter-faith Practitioners (CIPA). This movement, in part, calls cities and churches to become sanctuaries for undocumented migrants. They have also developed an ecology link network for churches and Christians concerning the environment. Echoing these same concerns, the Methodist Church adopted a statement concerning Christian stewardship as a constitutive part of following Christ: "A commitment to living within sustainable levels of carbon emissions is central to Christian discipleship in our days."[5]

There is hope also in the work of the churches through aid and development agencies such as Christian Aid, Catholic Agency for Overseas Development (CAFOD), and the Methodist Relief and Development Fund (MRDF).

There is much about which to rejoice; there are many challenges that remain. It is urgent that the church move from pilot schemes of

---

5. Methodist Church in Great Britain. *Hope in God's Future*, 55.

discipleship to a disciple-making church, much more intentional in its witness.

In the circuit where I serve we started a volunteering project in our social work services and in other community organisations. It is called Spirituality in Action (SPA). It is a missionary program seeking to streamline opportunities to engage in service and to enter into conversation and relationship with those who are beyond the walls of the church. It is accompanied by theological reflection and pastoral support. Through this program we have seen some homeless people cross the threshold of the church and become followers of Christ and members of the church. We have seen young people discern their vocation and renew their sense of call. We have seen people who might not have been related to the church before, but who have found greater meaning in their lives in serving others.

SPA expects much and demands much of those who are involved in the disciple-making process. Through the encounters and relationships facilitated by this scheme, enhanced by a theological reflection component, opportunities emerge not only for the transformation of those who are served, but also of those who are serving. The practices related to this process demand that the worshiping community go beyond their Sunday commitments. It exposes those who are engaged to the struggles of others in life. This approach to disciple-making, based primarily on the church of the poor in Latin America, while extremely time demanding and work intensive, bears the fruit of renewal in the life of the church.

Recovering the Whole Gospel

The crisis that confronts the church in the United Kingdom calls for a transformation of its message as well. In this regard, the liberationist movement in Latin America offers three important insights. Firstly, it points to the need to recover the mystic element of faith, a message that speaks to the heart and finds God in the struggle. Discipleship should engage people on a deep, emotional level, where the meaning of life is restored and where the joy of being alive is recovered. Discipleship must engage the heart. Secondly, the message of discipleship must have an intellectual component that struggles with the difficult questions of life. The biblical narrative, with its metaphors and symbols, rites and rituals, tragic and triumphant events must be translated into the contemporary context by addressing the question, What does it mean in this situation? Discipleship must engage the mind. Thirdly, the message has got to have some real political impact with regard to the realities of this world. It must expose injustices and bring some relief from poverty. It must combat discrimination and promote peace. Discipleship must engage the moral will. A rediscovery of a whole gospel that engages the heart, the mind, and the will may just lead to a new way of talking about being a disciple of Jesus and a community of disciples in this world.

26

Baptism of Water and Spirit
A Women's Discipleship

Tumani Nyajeka

ON DECEMBER 14, 1998, THE PROGRAM GUIDELINES COMMITTEE OF the World Council of Churches presented "Four Fundamental Questions for Churches" for endorsement by the delegates of the Eighth Assembly held in Harare, Zimbabwe:

1. How do we as churches engage together in missions and evangelism in the midst of a highly pluralistic world?
2. How do we understand baptism as the foundation for life in the community to which we are called to share together?
3. How do we offer our resources, witness and action for the state of the world's very future?
4. How do we walk together on the path towards visible unity?

Sitting within this assembly were Rukwadzano women (Methodist Women United) who would have immediately resonated with these questions related to the nature and meaning of Christian discipleship. Had an opportunity been granted, they would happily have shared a living testimony of what it means to be a Christian disciple in today's world. They would have made it clear to the delegates that, unless one understands the significance of baptism, it is a challenge to engage or respond to the other three fundamental questions. Their own understanding of baptism is expressed through a non-violent spirituality that seeks and finds freedom, justice, and equality in an environment where they suffer every form of gender persecution in both church and society. These women-disciples are a tireless religious community of predominantly poor women who are responding to the HIV/AIDS pandemic by caring for orphaned children, feeding the hungry, and nursing the sick and elderly. They till the soil, build schools, endure torture for their political views, bury the dead, and find themselves in exile. For them, being a baptized Christian means building a joyful community in partnership with God, each other, and all of creation (John 3:16; Acts 2:38; 2 Cor 5:17).

The Birth of a Community of Women-Disciples

In 1928, at Old Mutare, Zimbabwe, a group of nine women of the Methodist Episcopal Church, led by one of their own, Lydia Chimonyo, founded a prayer-group meeting as they were in the forest just outside the mission grounds fetching firewood as wives of the new pastors and evangelists. According to Lydia, this base community was born by inviting colleagues who held similar convictions in the new Christian faith, women who loved prayer and deeply believed in the power of the Holy Spirit to change situations. They had also come to the point of realizing that their backs were against the wall. Both church and society rendered them marginal and powerless. Armed with the courage and conviction of their new faith and a deep respect for their culture and environment, these nine sisters refused to surrender to fear.

They chose two sites outside the mission grounds to rendezvous twice a day for prayer. The site for the early morning prayer was set in the east and named "paDara" (the watchtower), and the time for meeting was set at 4:00 AM, a symbolic time in Shona culture known as "mashambanzou" (the time that elephants bathe). The site for the second daily prayer was set in the west and named "paChingando" (place of deep meditation) and the time was set at sunset.

According to the *Rumano* (Rukwadzano Constitution), as a consequence of these actions, Lydia was brought before a select mission committee to respond to a few questions. First, her interrogators inquired about the purpose or need of such a prayer group. She responded simply, "to pray for the troubles of this world." Secondly, they asked: "by what authority and whose wisdom she assumed leadership of the group?" "By the power," she claimed, "of the Holy Spirit."

Lydia Chimonyo and her sisters were not afraid to stand before the authorities and testify that their baptism into the Christian faith had awakened in them a new spirit that sought to partner with God in Christ and each other to redeem the ignorant, the lost, and all creation. Through reading the scriptures in their own language, Lydia and her sisters understood their role as disciples to be a partnership with God in Christ. As Shona women they belonged to a culture in which everyone and everything had a role in building a beautiful community. In the scriptures they read with clarity and understanding the purpose of God's message and mission in Jesus Christ—announcing the good news of God's reign in every situation, context, and culture (Mark 1:14 ; Luke 4:43). Lydia and her sisters did not doubt the Holy Spirit was guiding their reading, hearing, and understanding of this Word.

These Manyika sisters, by the grace of God, quickly grasped the primary thrust of the gospel as declaring God's love and compassion for all creation. The good news is that God in Christ and the Holy Spirit redeems and guides all creation into the realm of a united yet diverse community for belonging—a unity-in-diversity in which all relationships in community are governed by compassion and love for all. In this realm, love rules supreme and all those who are lost in their ignorance or who are in pain and suffer are sought, invited, and made welcome. Those who accept the call to enter the realm of God's reign become a proclamation-community, partners in proclaiming the good news of God's eternal, active, presence in every situation and context in time and space (Mark 1:14).

These women believed that in God's realm they were called to surrender all self-motivated attitudes and behavior. They identified all structures and attitudes that create and indulge hierarchy or supremacy over others and decried them as a violation of God's principle of compassion for all creation. God called them to destroy boundaries and barriers that stood in the way of genuine community (Gal 3:28). In Jesus Christ, God offered a model of One who surrendered his will to God's will, so that God's mission on earth could be accomplished. Christ set the model of self-emptying in order to become an instrument of God's reign of compassion, mercy, and kindness for all of creation. (2 Cor 5:19; Heb 2:16–18). These founding women of Rukwadzano were convinced that through the work of the Holy Spirit they had attained a glorious unity of faith in a compassionate God that could not be moved. They centered their daily liturgy and prayers on personal testimonies and celebrated the way in which, at baptism, they experienced an awakening to

God's Spirit who quenched all self-seeking appetites, guiding them into God's reign as a united community of Christ's disciples in the church.

The Foundation of Humility and Faithful Obedience (Daniel 1–4)

According to the Rukwadzano, baptism quenches the human struggle for self-aggrandizement, leaving one free to choose a path of a faithful discipleship (Luke 13:22–30). Their interpretation of the stories surrounding King Nebuchadnezzar in the Book of Daniel (1–4) shapes this understanding of baptism and discipleship. Life consists of a struggle to overcome a path of self-seeking indulgence, pride, and power, that threatens the existence of all and to embrace the way of God's covenant—the law of love, equality, diversity and unity (Phil 2:7–8). In this biblical narrative, dreams trouble the spirit of the King. Three Jewish prophet confessors attempt to convince him of his need for a baptism that will quench his self-indulgent cravings. But because of his pride and arrogance the King rejects the free gift and privilege of having been called to participate in the reign of God. The Rukwadzano women viewed this story as a parable concerning the human condition and the struggle to choose the path of righteousness even after God, through God's grace, reveals the truth and the way. Genuine discipleship demands that we humble ourselves and be yoked to God's law of love and compassion for all in creation. Only after a lengthy process of discipline and transformation was the King able to say, in the end: "Now I, Nebuchadnezzar, praise and extol and honor the King of heaven, for all his works are truth, and his ways are justice; and he is able to bring low those who walk in pride" (Dan 4:37).

Abandoning Fear and Anxiety

Rukwadzano women have lived in a fiery furnace for nearly a century in colonial and postcolonial Southern African. In this environment they have known and refused to surrender to fear, terror, lust, and carelessness (Luke 12:32; John 16:33). They are a fearless community of faith that inhabits this fiery furnace unscathed and unafraid, like the prophets of old. Lydia and her sisters taught others and each other that the Holy Spirit forever acts to create a community of disciples who have no fear or anxiety in a violent environment. The women always warn other believers to refuse to surrender to fear because, they argue, fear or anxiety is the greatest enemy to a faithful Christian discipleship. Addressing the reality of fear and anxiety as a challenge to discipleship for Christian communities worldwide, Pope John Paul II wrote in his autobiography:

> At the end of the second millennium, we need, perhaps more than ever, the words of the Risen Christ: "Be not afraid!" . . . Peoples and nations of the entire world need to hear these words. Their conscience needs to grow in the certainty that Someone exists who holds in His hands the destiny of this passing world; Someone who holds the keys to death and the netherworld, (cf. Rev 1:18); Someone who is the Alpha and the Omega of human history (cf. Rev 22:13)—be it the individual or collective history. And this Someone is Love (cf. 1 John 4:8,16)—Love that became man, Love crucified and risen, Love unceasingly present among men. It is Eucharistic Love. It is the infinite source of communion. He alone can give the ultimate assurance when he says, "Be not afraid!"[1]

Christ: Healer in the Village

Rukwadzano women ground their worship and practices in an abiding relationship with Christ and a complete surrender to the Spirit of Christ. In this humble union, they are clear about the mission and mandate of the Holy Spirit—to bring all creation into the compassionate realm of God's power to heal and to reconcile. Drawing from both their culture and scripture, the women conceive God in Christ primarily as a Healer—the face of peace who restores all health and joy in all relationships. Disciples of Christ, therefore, participate with Christ as ambassadors of peace and reconciliation, healing and wholeness. Their Spirit has not been shaken by the HIV/AIDS pandemic, the government's persecution, or the traditional church's late response to the crisis. In this challenging environment, Rukwadzano women share testimonies concerning the power of God to heal the sick and redeem the lost and ignorant.

---

1. John Paul II, *Crossing the Threshold of Hope*, 37.

Jesus is the Healer, the Comforter, the Exorcist, the Companion of the sick and the troubled. He goes to Peter's home and finds his mother-in-law sick with fever, lying down. He lifts her up by the hand, heals her, and transforms her into a ministering person giving hospitality to the crowd that soon gathers in her house. Jesus' fame spreads like lightning: fame about healing and cleansing unclean spirits. Jesus is Healer—that is the word that goes around, that is the word that brings crowds to him in the first case. We only need to transfer this description about Jesus, from Galilee to an African village. Jesus changes lives as he did in Capernaum and Galilee. He heals, he drives out what troubles them, he comforts, he raises the dead, and he eats with them. He brings healing as the epitome of salvation, healing individuals and healing community, giving life in this and the next world.

One Family in Christ

Lydia Chimonyo and her sisters started a prayer-group meeting outside the mission grounds as a protest movement. Rukwadzano women have struggled to liberate the structures and powers in both the church and society that keep them in a second class status in all aspects of their lives. They are the champions of human rights in a social and political context that has decimated millions of people, plundered and pillaged the environment for hundreds of years. As a prophetic movement, the group has been on the forefront of challenging and rejecting all structures of hierarchy along, caste, class, creed, race, gender, sexual orientation, culture, and species. For this proclamation-community of women, discipleship has meant building schools for girls who historically were denied access to education with one hand and reading the Bible with the other (Neh 4).

Two characteristics of discipleship among the Rukwadzano stand out in their struggle against the powers and principalities that deny the full humanity of others. First, Rukwadzano women's ministries and engagements clearly communicate to those who have eyes to see that they have never been victims of these powers and principalities. From the day they accepted God's grace bestowed upon them at baptism and decided to partner with God in God's mission of healing and reconciling, they triumphed over evil. As disciples of Christ, they put their hand to the plough, never to look back.

A second mark of Rukwadzano discipleship is an unwavering compassion for the ignorant, the lost, and those who suffer. Prayer for the liberation of church to awaken and live up to its calling for the salvation of all in creation is ever on the lips of these women as disciples. Women weep over the church in Southern Africa, which often appears lost and confused in this region, where gender, class, and race rule supreme. The church's structural beliefs and practices remain rigid and hierarchic, often mirroring those of the society at large.

Rukwadzano women continue to present a model of discipleship, therefore, that leads from behind. Because they have taken on this posture, they have been able to be a healing presence in every aspect of the community and have never tired of sharing the good news of God incarnated in Jesus Christ and eternally present in the counsel and guidance of the Holy Spirit. They have chosen not to expend their energy in the politics of vying for positions and power in the church, thereby demonstrating that a genuine disciple of Christ can lead from any place when truly seeking to advance God's mission. Women teach the lessons of humility, renunciation of power, greed, and prestige as they exemplify the model of humility, self-emptying, and servanthood set by Jesus Christ (Phil 2:5–11).

Baptism celebrates the way in which God embraces all children and welcomes them into the body of Christ, drawn into the community of faith from all the corners of the globe. Eucharist reminds these disciples about the way in which God in Christ sacrificed himself so that grace may abound to all people—all who are thirsting to be free. In both sacramental practices of the church, we experience the mystery of unity-in-diversity, and both serve as profound symbols of discipleship. Patristic exegesis interpreted the Pentecost experience as the reversal of Babel. The diversity of languages was fatal to the unity and common endeavor of the people in the old Babel. In the new Babel, paradoxically, diversity became a gift of the Spirit and constituted the oneness of the body of Christ. In all of this, the Holy Spirit enables a form of solidarity that transcends all divisions and differences, real or manufactured and establishes the local and universal proclamation-community—the church. Rukwadzano women praise God for this great gift and for the joy and work of redemption that God continues even when they are asleep.

Rukwadzano women believe that through baptism children of God are born of water and Spirit into a living community that is called to be the salt of the earth, partners with Jesus and co-heirs with Christ. They have sought to be faithful disciples in the face of tremendous obstacles and continue to confront the reality of unjust structures, both in the world and in the church. Their discipleship, like that exemplified by the Lutheran martyr, Dietrich Bonhoeffer, involves great cost. They follow Jesus and his way resolutely because their baptism by water and Spirit compels them to do so nonetheless. "Now when Jesus saw great crowds around him, he gave orders to go over to the other side. A scribe then approached and said, 'Teacher, I will follow you wherever you go.' And Jesus said to him, 'Foxes have holes, and birds of the air have nests; but the Son of Man has nowhere to lay his head.' Another of his disciples said to him, 'Lord, first let me go and bury my father.' But Jesus said to him, 'Follow me, and let the dead bury their own dead'"(Matt 8:18–22).

Becoming, Being, and Making Disciples in Cross-Cultural Appointments

Helmut Renders

I AM THANKFUL FOR THE OPPORTUNITY TO ENGAGE WITH COLLEAGUES from the entire world to reflect on and to testify to the importance of cross-cultural experiences. For a decade, this has been my life, living and communicating with people from different countries and continents, in Germany and abroad. Have I made disciples during this time? Yes, but I would prefer to put it somewhat differently. I have tried to become a brother disciple of people whom God has put in my path. Where this has worked well, together we have experienced how God creates spaces to be, to be transformed, to transform one another, and to reform congregations. It may even be that personal and communal transformation extended beyond our communities of faith into the world. Together we have learned that God makes disciples by grace and love and by the tenderness, patience, and sincerity of all the brothers and sisters.

Matthew 28:18–20 orients our thinking about the practice of disciple-making. I would like to suggest a translation of this familiar text that gives proper place to each of the participles related to the primary verb about making disciples: "*Going*, therefore, make disciples of all nations ... *baptizing* ... and *teaching*.[1] I have had to incorporate all three of these dimensions into my ministry of disciple-making over the years. The sacramental dimension was the major accent in my appointment to the first African German charge in Hamburg. The educational dimension was the center of my ministry in São Paulo, Brazil. "Going," I believe, should not be reduced to a kind of geographical dislocation, but

1. See Garcia, "Reflexões sobre," 7–9.

describes disciple-making as an *ongoing* process in daily life. Definitely, this was the challenge in the Amazon region. Going, baptizing, and teaching represent an interwoven tapestry of becoming, being, and making disciples of Christ and relates the various contexts of my own ministry—church, university, and society—with the triune God.

Becoming a Disciple alongside Ghanaian "Adofos" (1994–1998)

Immigration defines nations such as the United States and Brazil. The fact that Germany is a land of immigrants, however, is a little known fact. The complex story of the first African Charge in Hamburg reflects this growing reality.[2] In 1997 I had to substitute for a Ghanaian colleague in an emergency. The worship service was in Twie and one word was frequently repeated: *adofos*. This sounded very much like the Greek word for brother (*adelphos*), and this made me feel very much at home. I later learned that the word for Christian brothers and sisters in Twie, in fact, is based on the Greek. Cross-cultural understanding and becoming, being, and making disciples is all about feeling at home. Words, sounds, smells, food, appearances—all can either facilitate or hinder communication, and meals often become a place in which all of these elements come together. Being disciple, therefore, has something to do with the ability to share one table.[3]

Work alongside Ghanaian brothers and sisters offered me deep insights and experiences, particularly with regard to the Bible. They brought stories of inclusion, rejection, and living side by side to life and afforded new insight with regard to how to treat foreigners (Exod 22:20), how to love enemies (Deut 10:18), and how to live in transformative relationships (Ruth 2:10). In the end, the written Word became the core of our cross-cultural church proposal. In our search for understanding we came across Eph 2:19: "So then you are no longer strangers and aliens, but you are citizens with the saints and also members of the household of God." This phrase became the biblical "icon" upon which we based our ministry—the phrase that described our project. It also helped us to stay on course. In the end we understood that this was

---

2. See Renders, *So seid ihr nun nicht mehr Gäste und Fremdlinge*.
3. See Renders, *Einen anderen Himmel*; cf. Bhogal, *Pluralismo e a missão*.

God's world for us. Knowing this enabled us to embrace the challenges which followed. Looking back I would conclude that this biblical vision was essential. It served well because we understood it both as a sign of God's grace and of God's will—something to which we were called to respond to and to obey.

From 1995 onwards, the Northern Conference of the United Methodist Church in Germany received many new members through its international congregations, but did it make disciples? First, the discipleship of all was enhanced by becoming and being disciple alongside the African-German disciple-makers. The mixed charge did result, secondly, in qualitative church growth among the German membership. Their disposition to serve and to share revived their sense of discipleship and molded their understanding, sending a right and prophetic signal in xenophobic times. It was obviously right and courageous at the time. Two days before the official opening of the church, we announced the service in local newspapers. The Hamburg police department called, offering protection. We declined their assistance, however, knowing that a third of our African participants were illegal. The lively African and monthly German-African Sunday services provided a magnetic attraction in relation to the young, urban professionals in the "yuppie" quarter. It is not too much to say that we became each other's disciples during many encounters, meals, bilingual administrating board, and in all our gatherings. We decided to share as much as possible and to celebrate our differences in every aspect of our common life.

In 2000, the Ghanaian congregation split over underlying internal ethnic or tribal problems and over a question of vision which also involved the policy of appointment. The very first Ghanaian minister had taken particular attention to gather together those who wanted to stay in Germany. The following two ministers, coming from Ghana, favored an approach that would provide cultural and social support for those who were interested in returning to their homeland. On the other hand, in this second phase of the Ghanaian congregation, many reached out, especially to poor members of the Ghanaian community in Hamburg. Obviously, the circumstances called for some kind of double strategy that was sensitive to the needs and desires of the various groups within the Ghanaian community. All of this simply illustrates the fact that becoming and being disciples in these kinds of circumstances necessarily involves a lot of patience on all sides. This whole experiment led to important developments on multiple levels within the life of the church. On the conference level, for example, we introduced the idea of a third commission for foreigners in Germany, something that would stand between the Commission for Evangelization and the Commission for Mission. When the Conference agreed to create this "third pillar of mission," as we called it, we knew that we had implanted a process with a larger, and no longer simply a local, perspective.

Becoming a Disciple in God's Lost Eden (1998–2003)

In 1998 I went to the Amazon region as a "missionary." In my German "mission" board this term was out of use—"collaborator" was preferred—but the Brazilian Methodist Church retained this language with regard to everyone, native or foreigner, who worked in a missionary conference or district. This difference in language, however, reflected some deeper differences in expectation and understanding. Whereas the German perspective emphasized being and becoming a disciple in a foreign context, the Brazilians placed a high level of expectation making disciples. My new home was Porto Velho, the southwest entrance to the endless rainforest. Although the cities are crowed, the Amazon region, in general terms, is not. There are only a small number of people per square kilometer and, in many areas, there are none at all. Nevertheless, the rainforest is not "untouched." Actually it has been continuously transformed by the indigenous population who knew how to live with and in it. It may sound strange, but in the Amazon region, the trees and rivers actually became brothers and sisters to me. I understood that they were suffering and wondered what kind of revelation creation was expecting from the sons and daughters of God. Nature was, at the same time, powerful and formative, fragile and dangerously dysfunctional. As a consequence of my time in the Amazon region, I jettisoned a good part of my exclusively anthropocentric soteriology, and this enlarged my vision of mission, evangelism, and disciple-making as well.[4]

This new friendship was important, but it was not very much appreciated by those in positions of leadership and authority. The Methodist Church had a long but interrupted history in the region. It was only in the middle of the twentieth century that the earlier work of the nineteenth century was resumed, but this new work also entailed the

4. See Renders, "Social Soteriology of John Wesley."

conquest and occupation of the territory under the doctrine of national security. The wild north was not a place for friendship with the environment and the theological discourse of that time favored conquest, expulsion, and victory. To be honest, the conquerors suffered a lot and many families lost their loved ones in the forests in accidents and under seldom-clarified circumstances. The life of the pioneers was rough and the living conditions were bad. Then, around 1991, the church decided to invest in the education of the people and I was one of those invited to contribute as a theological educator and student pastor from 1998 onwards.

All of us knew that the new mission work upon which we were embarking would call for radical change. We were uncertain as to how this change would affect those who were established in the church and whose view of discipleship was shaped by other forces, from the leadership on down. From the early 1990s, charismatic Christians had contributed greatly to the shaping of the church and their vision of evangelism revolved primarily around church growth. Becoming and being a disciple to the people of the Amazon region and becoming and being a disciple to my fellow Methodists presented an immediate double challenge. Our mission involved reforming the church and the nation simultaneously and making disciples included a kind of constructive friendship with the world. In our little seminary we had the opportunity to discuss various missional options. The sheer lack of leadership within Methodism in the region privileged an ecumenical faculty, men and woman, who appreciated the space offered by the Methodist Church. These colleagues turned out to be the "experts" in mission that the church needed. An international congress in Porto Velho called "Amazonia 2002" was the high point of this joint effort and evangelistic proposal.

Unfortunately, the Methodist Church in the region did not embrace the project and continued to perpetuate classical patterns in its relationship with the indigenous people and the environment. On the one side, feeling pressure to grow, the church opted essentially to perpetuate the older patterns of conquest in its vision of mission, although there were always some exceptions. In general they did not realize how near their position came to the old myth that declared the indigenous population a sub-human species. Others, instead of this, sought to transform the Amazon into a kind of anthropological zoo, basing their approach on the myth of untouched "nature" and the "noble savage."

Over against these attitudes, many have embraced the idea that we have to learn together to become disciples and have resisted the temptation to transform others into disciples who simply mimic their own concepts and guiding ideas. The development of a course that interfaced mission/evangelism and context moved the thinking of many in a positive direction, but this did not result directly in an advance in making disciples among local indigenous communities. Some of the younger local pastors have looked for alternative methods and models of evangelism, and perspectives continue to change in a direction that is more sensitive to the context and the environment. A more holistic paradigm of being, becoming, and making disciples can be seen in a number of their projects.

At the heart of these new efforts is the conviction that we need to invest in fraternal encounters and true and faithful relations. Those who commit themselves to an appreciation of difference within the church are better prepared to understand difference beyond the church. Also central to these efforts is the need for a sustainable form of discipleship. Often, programs in the church depend upon financial resources, but the church's mission in this region is founded upon understanding, respect and love and the desire to serve the people as part of a complex and fragile environment. This means that all, together, have to learn from the environment. Where the unexpected is the normal, our own mission history does not provide sufficient "know-how." To become and to be disciples in the Amazon region necessitates learning from and being shaped by the local people in faithfulness to the gospel in a context that is neither urban nor rural, but forestall.

Cross-Cultural Teaching Ministries in a Wesleyan Perspective (2003–2009)

In 2003 I was invited to participate in founding the Wesleyan Study Center of the Theological Faculty of the Methodist University in São Paulo. I left the Amazon region and went to the industrial heart of Brazil the "great ABCD," four cities between São Paulo and Santos. Here I actually started to discuss and to write specifically about a unique aspect of disciple making, namely, discipleship groups. I engaged with the basic ideas of David Lowes Watson´s "accountable discipleship" and Brazilian proposals and tried to help develop a program where Sunday school and discipleship groups, in particular, could work together.[5]

During this time, I became aware of an underlying and very influential Brazilian cultural expression, the "religion of the heart." The confluence of a number of influences shaped this idea: a characteristic colonial and post-Tridentine reading of Teresa of Avila, the devotion of the sacred heart of Jesus as part of an ultra-monastic project, the wide distribution of the Book of the Heart of Johann Evangelist Gossner by Presbyterian, Methodist, Pentecostal, and Baptist publishers, a new interpretation of the "warmed heart of Wesley" (Aldersgate) by the pentecostal Wesleyan Methodist Church as the baptism of the Holy Spirit, and a new revival movement within the Methodist Church. All of these movements grabbed my attention. All were, basically, promoting forms of a mythic union with God and, in some cases, ecstasy, as the highest expression of Christian existence—and not the imitation of Christ in daily life.[6]

I observed that this had a direct influence on the understanding of how to "make" disciples. For those who sought mystical union, the practice of discipleship was oriented primarily around experiences of God; those who understood discipleship as faithfulness in daily life, however, emphasized spiritual guidance related to the imitation of Christ. Becoming and being a disciple in this context involved the attempt to help people understand better what was at stake on either end of this polarization. Whereas revivalist, charismatic, and Pentecostal Methodists where mainly promoting a part of the Catholic substance of Brazilian spirituality—although a good number of them would declare themselves, in a militant way, anti-ecumenical—the other group concentrated on aspects of what Paul Tillich described as the "Protestant principle."[7]

In order to more fully understand this division within the church I knew that it was important for me to explore more fully the background of these different perspectives. I learned that early twentieth century Brazilian historians and sociologists labeled the kind of Brazilian citizen who cannot distinguish between the public and the private—so that, in the end, the private always invades the public—as "homem cordial,"

5. Renders, "Pequenos Grupos," 68–95.
6. See Renders, "Deus, o ser humano e um mundo," 373–413.
7. See Tillich, *Protestant Era*, chapter 11.

the "cordial man."[8] No doubt, there is a link between the Brazilian concept of the religion of the heart and the typology of the "cordial man." Both views are based upon the concept of the family and extend their understanding of the family to the church. The "cordial man" does not trust any person from the outer circle of his clan. He or she is guided by emotional impulses and sympathy, not by empathy and the quest for justice. Enemies cannot be tolerated and have to be destroyed. The "cordial man" is the "colonial man," characterized by "coronelismo"—an extremely hierarchical and androcentric organization of relations. Some discipleship programs in Brazil, as one would imagine, are based on these principles. They fit the culture but, in my view, stand at odds with important aspects of the gospel. We need the "courage" to address them with mercy—*misercordia*—in search of concord—*concordia*.

In the end, I am asking myself: Have I become a Ghanaian to the Ghanaians? Have I become an Amazonian to the Amazonians? Have I become a Brazilian to the Brazilians? Have I cried with those who were crying and laughed with those who were laughing? Have I been able to understand their preoccupations, intentions, and logic? Am I able to articulate the reasons, understandings, and hopes that led me to offer Christ the way I did and to engage my brothers and sisters in the way in which I did? I believe that we became disciples of Christ in our relationships with one another in the mix of it all, but I have to leave the final conclusion to others. And although I hope so and I believe so, I can certainly testify with great joy that many of my Ghanaian, Amazonian, and Brazilian friends made the effort to become a German to this German, and taught me much as a consequence of their courage. I am profoundly thankful for this.

---

8. See Araújo and Schwarcz, *Raízes do Brasil*.

28

Christian Vitality in Cuba

An Apparent Contradiction in a Land of Paradoxes

Philip Wingeier-Rayo

CUBA IS A LAND OF MANY CONTRADICTIONS. IT IS A VERY FERTILE tropical island, yet there is not an abundance of produce for its population. It is the country with the highest per capita number of doctors, yet medicine for treating illnesses is scarce. It is ninety miles away from the United States, yet Americans are not allowed to travel there without a license. It was legally atheist until 1991, yet it has one of the fastest growing churches in the Western hemisphere. The Communist government of Cuba is both the greatest obstacle to church growth, and at the same time the greatest contributor. In the midst of these apparent paradoxes, the church in Cuba is experiencing unprecedented growth. This chapter will discuss the phenomenal growth of Protestantism in Cuba with particular emphasis on the Christian vitality within the Wesleyan tradition. Specifically it will begin with the critical challenges that the Protestant church in Cuba has faced, then reflect on the passage of the walk to Emmaus that has been helpful for Cuban evangelistic growth. In the later part of the chapter I will turn to a specific evangelistic practice, namely, the leadership of the laity in small group ministries, which brings Christian vitality and offers a general contribution to the global church.

When the Cuban revolution ousted General Batista on January 1, 1959 the overwhelming majority of Cubans were supportive of the change, including Christians, and many were excited about the platform of the incoming government against gambling and prostitution. These optimistic feelings turned to concern when Fidel Castro announced on the eve of the Bay of Pigs invasion in April of 1961 that the young revolution was to be "socialist in character." Protestantism in Cuba had enjoyed very good relations with the United States and up to that point had received and depended on U.S. missionaries for its growth and support. The Methodist Church in Cuba, for example, had fifty-four U.S. missionaries in 1959 as opposed to only fifty-one Cuban pastors.[1] Moreover, the majority of financial support came from the United States. This suddenly changed when in the summer of 1960 the U.S. embassy in Havana started urging missionaries to return home.[2] Many resisted and stayed as long as they could until they finally realized in the 1960s that their very presence endangered their Cuban friends and had adverse effects on the mission itself. The Protestant churches had developed a pro-U.S. mindset and the presence of "Yankees" made the church appear unpatriotic in the midst of a nationalistic revolution. The financial support also was cut back dramatically after the U.S. government broke off diplomatic ties with Cuba in January 1961 and started an economic embargo. While some U.S. mission boards were able to get around the embargo by sending some funds to their sister denominations through the World Council of Churches, the cut-backs were dramatic and Cuban Protestants were forced to take steps toward autonomy.

Another major challenge that the Cuban church has faced under socialism has been the shortage of trained pastors. The Methodist Church in Cuba, for example, was still a mission under the episcopal area of the Florida Annual Conference, however, it quickly moved toward financial and ecclesial independence out of necessity. As the missionaries left, so too did many Cuban pastors. Out of the fifty-one pastors, only eight would remain after the 1960s. Faced with a shortage of pastors, the Methodist superintendent of eastern Cuba, Rev. Armando Rodriguez, organized a weekend youth rally and had an altar call seeking lay missioners willing to replace those departed pastors. Remarkably the young men and women responded and became lay missioners serving in remote parishes. Making up with faith what they lacked in training and experience, those young people were able to shepherd several wayward congregations and save several vacant church properties in the process. Finally, in 1967 the Methodist Church in Cuba voted to become auton-

---

1. Perez, *Un Resumen*, 46.
2. Course, *Protestants, Revolution, and the Cuba-U.S. Bond*, 52.

omous of North American Methodism, and Rev. Armando Rodriguez became the church's first bishop in 1968.

The 1960s were very difficult years for Cuban Protestantism. The Cuban government nationalized church schools, camps, and hospitals, relegating the church to exclusively "spiritual" guidance. In 1965 the Cuban government started re-education camps for delinquents, homosexuals, and clergy. Several pastors were forced to cut sugar cane from dawn to dusk for close to two years until international human rights groups complained and the program was disbanded.[3] The government began to hope that the church would soon disappear, and the church felt the same way about the government. The churches continued to function, but membership decreased dramatically as Christians faced discrimination at every level of secular society. "Individual clergy were persecuted, religious services were obstructed or disrupted, church property was vandalized, education and occupational access for believers was restricted, and, for a brief period in the 1960s, 'reeducation camps' grouped priests with prostitutes, criminals, and other 'anti-social elements.'"[4] School children were told that God did not exist and only those students faithful to the revolution received access to higher education. Lay persons were passed over for promotions in their jobs and considered untrustworthy in the neighborhood block committees. Basically the Protestant church went into survival mode in the 1960s and bunkered down.

By the 1970s and 1980s, both the government and the church realized that their adversaries were here to stay. The governmental Office of Religious Affairs took a more conciliatory tone and identified those denominations that were willing to work with the government. The Ecumenical Council emerged as the church entity that could represent and negotiate with the government on behalf of all Protestants. Christians were definitely a minority in Cuba, but they were a significant minority with important ties abroad. The church continued to function in Cuba, although with reduced numbers, and individual Christians were treated as second class citizens.

In the late 1980s and early 1990s the balance of church-state power began to change, starting with the fall of the Berlin Wall in 1989, the election loss of the Sandinistas in 1990, and the fall of communism in

3. Interview with Bishop Armando Rodriguez, Des Plaines, IL, January 20, 1998.
4. Malone, "Conflict, Coexistence, and Cooperation," 3.

Eastern Europe in 1991. Simultaneous to these ground-shaking events was the changing attitude of the Cuban government to the Protestants in Cuba. In April 1990, Fidel Castro met openly with Protestant leaders for the first time—and the meeting was broadcast on Cuban television. In this meeting Methodist pastor and future bishop Joel Ajo courageously addressed Fidel:

> We have to speak on behalf of our congregations where there are brothers and sisters who have wanted to study to become psychologists, but they have not been able to because it has been pointed out that they are Christians. They have wanted to do something, wanted to occupy an important position, for example in the Popular Power [parliament], but they haven't been able to because it has been pointed out, "This person is Christian." And we believe that the principal leader of our Revolution should be aware of all of this, just as Dr. Carneado is, to whom we have expressed the problems that we are confronting on several occasions. In this hour of definition where the evangelical church says that we will stay in Cuba working for the well-being of our people and to back the Revolution in all that is just, we believe the correct thing to do is to tell the Revolution where we do not agree.[5]

This meeting exemplified the changing mood in church-state relations. The following year, the Cuban Communist Party held its IV Congress and voted to change the constitutional status of the Cuban state from atheist to lay, thus allowing people of religious affiliation to hold government posts and be elected to parliament. Although this constitutional amendment was intended by the communist party to allow believers to participate in the political system, it actually had the opposite effect. Namely, it lifted the ban of government officials to have faith, which gave the opposite latent message to the Cuban people that it was acceptable to believe in God.

While these changes were occurring at governmental levels, a revival had started at the grassroots. The Holy Spirit had started to move among a small group of pastors. Within the Methodist Church a number of lay pastors had never had the opportunity to attend seminary—which was a luxury, given the shortage of clergy. This group also included pastors from other denominations that the Methodist Church had hired to fill vacant pastoral charges. All these pastors were being trained to-

---

5. Video: "Con Dios y Con La Patria."

gether in the 1970s and 1980s through extension courses or modules organized two or three times a year. They became very close to one another as they shared their mutual challenges together. During their training modules the pastors organized their own late-night devotions and prayer vigils. Here they began to experiment with non-traditional prayers and music. While the majority of Methodist Churches still used traditional-style worship and hymns, this group of pastors introduced extemporary spontaneous prayers and contemporary music that was popular among Pentecostals in Latin America. Initially the pastors only prayed and sang with this style among themselves at these extension courses. They gradually introduced this contemporary worship style, however, to the youth, and eventually to the congregation in general.

This more contemporary and more spontaneous style became very popular in a short period of time. The lyrics of the praise songs were short and easier to memorize then hymns, making the music easily mobile—no hymnals needed. Also, Cuban popular culture is comprised of Spanish and African influence. The guitar was imported from Spain and the drums from Africa. The melodies of contemporary music were played with guitars and drums, which had a more familiar sound than the traditional piano and organ. Also, the songs were upbeat and congregants clapped their hands and danced—much more in line with their Caribbean idiosyncrasy. In the words of current Methodist Cuban Bishop Ricardo Pereira: "Cubans are very enthusiastic and now the worship style allows people to express their Cuban culture. One doesn't have to stop being Cuban just to enter a church."[6] The extemporaneous nature of charismatic worship seemed to fit better with the Cuban personality which is very free and spontaneous.

Simultaneous to this revival within the church, the 1990s also brought tremendous economic hardship to Cuba. Already under a U.S. embargo, the collapse of the Soviet Union meant the end of economic subsidies. In 1989, seventy percent of Cuba's foreign trade was with the Soviet Union, and eighty percent of all foreign trade was with Eastern Bloc countries.[7] With very little warning, the Soviet Union reneged on its commitments in 1990 which started a devastating chain reaction of economic and social crisis in Cuba. The shortage of oil, in particular, led to power outages, factory closings, transportation shortages, and thus

6. Interview with Bishop Ricardo Pereira, Havana, Cuba, March 7, 2005.
7. Background Notes, U.S. State Department, 1993, 4.

crops rotting in the fields with no transportation to carry the produce to markets.

Anticipating that the end of Castro's regime might be near, the U.S. government acted to tighten the screws of the U.S. embargo. Representative Robert Torricelli sponsored a bill that was signed into law by President George H. Bush in October of 1992 that prohibited foreign ships that traded with Cuba from entering U.S. ports. The law also denied foreign aid to any country that traded with Cuba. Cuba had become overly dependent on the Soviet Union, and the purpose of the Torricelli bill was to isolate Cuba even further from the Western world and new trade partners.

Certainly the economic crisis was real, but the worst crisis was spiritual. The Cuban government had taught its populace that the Soviet Union—with its socialist style government—was the model after which they should design their country. It was their great benefactor. All of sudden this sugar daddy was no more, and Cuba was in dire straits. The Cuban people started to despair. There was both the literal concern of day-to-day survival and the existential concern of identity. Cubans began to ask: Who am I? Why am I alive? What is the purpose of life? In 1993 the Council of Catholic Bishops of Cuba issued a pastoral letter stating: "The fathers, mothers, priests, educators, agents of the public order and authorities feel uneasy about the growth of delinquency: robberies, assaults, growth of prostitution and violence for generally disproportionate causes. This behavior is many times the manifestation of a repressed aggression that generates personal insecurity in the street and even at home. The scarcity of the most elemental materials: food, medicine, transportation, electricity, etc. favor a tense environment which, on occasions, makes the usual peaceful and cordial Cuban behavior disappear."[8]

This anxiety reached its climax in the summer of 1994 when Fidel lifted the ban on immigrating to the United States. Tens of thousands of Cubans lanced themselves across the Florida Straits in unseaworthy vessels: inner tubes, small boats, and styrofoam rafts. This was the epitome of despair.

The revival within the Cuban church began to fill this spiritual void. Pastors and church members went down to the beaches to dissuade would-be rafters from taking the risk. They preached that the

---

8. Conference of Catholic Bishops of Cuba, "El Amor todo lo Espera," 408.

God who created them had a purpose for their life. Cuban Christians witnessed that they could do more good for their family alive in Cuba, than lost at sea.

The Emmaus Paradigm (Luke 24:13–35)

There was a time when Jesus' disciples also were in despair and they wanted to run away. After Jesus had been crucified the disciples were afraid that the same could happen to them. Peter denied Jesus three times, and the other disciples locked themselves out of fear (John 20:19). Feeling discouraged and defeated, Cleopas and an unnamed disciple walked seven miles to Emmaus to escape from the danger and turmoil of Jerusalem. Along the way they were accompanied by Jesus who listened to their disillusionment. When Jesus revealed himself to them their eyes were opened and they discovered that Jesus had been with them the whole journey. Immediately they jumped up to go back to Jerusalem and share of the good news of Jesus' resurrection (Luke 24:13–35). Similarly Cubans have been so discouraged by their circumstances that many have not realized that Jesus is accompanying them along their journey. As their eyes are opened Christians are filled with joy and want to go back to their communities and families to witness to what God has done.

As a missionary serving in Cuba during the 1990s, I remember the story of José Luis, a new convert to Christianity. He was a card-carrying member of the Communist Youth organization, but in 1992 a friend witnessed to him about the love of Jesus Christ and he came to church. Still suspicious of the governmental opening toward religion, he traveled twenty miles on a bicycle away from his home in Old Havana to our church in the town of Punta Brava. He accepted Christ in our church, but kept his newfound faith a secret and continued in his government job at a dollar store for tourists. One Sunday after church he asked about the spiritual disciplines of prayer and fasting. I explained the biblical and Wesleyan understanding of the means of grace. He asked if he could come to pray and fast in the church for forty-eight hours. For two days and two nights we carried water to the sanctuary and periodically checked on José Luis. At the conclusion of his fast he felt that God was calling him into the ministry. He shared this calling with his wife, Mercedes, and we introduced him into the candidacy process. During the discipleship of José Luis and Mercedes we opened a small group ministry in his home. When the doors opened for him to do full-time ministry he resigned from his governmental job and was assigned to a mission outside of Havana and began leading other people to Christ.

Discipleship in Small Groups

The small group ministry is an important part of the revival of the Cuban church. This is a very popular style of evangelism in Cuba since the government does not allow churches to build new buildings. The church is restricted to the same properties that they owned at the time of the revolution, but towns and cities have continued to grow throughout the island. So in order to reach communities where there are no churches, house-churches (*casas-culto* in Spanish) are an effective way of ministering to the community.

As the revival began in the late 1980s and early 1990s *casas-culto* began to proliferate throughout the island without permission from the government. In an international meeting hosted by the Cuban Ecumenical Council with representatives from the National Council of Churches USA, the Canadian Council of Churches, the Latin American Council of Churches, the European Council of Churches and even a representative from the China Christian Council, then bishop Joel Ajo had the opportunity to point out the contradiction between the rules of assembly in the Cuban constitution and the church's *casas-culto* directly to Fidel Castro. Bishop Ajo recalled that Fidel stood up, stroked his beard and responded: "You are not disobeying the Constitution, you are only showing us where it needs to be amended."[9] And so within a few months the government issued a series of requirements and a procedure to register the house-churches throughout the island. At the time, the Methodist Church alone already had about two hundred operating across the country. By the year 2005, this number had grown to seven hundred fifty house-churches.[10]

In another house-church that we helped to start in the area of *Alturas de La Lisa* outside of Havana we reached out to an aging population that was having a difficult time coming to church due to the shortage of public transportation. This group had been faithful members of the church, but could rarely come to worship on a Sunday un-

9. Interview with Bishop Joel Ajo, Racine, Wisconsin, April 8, 1998.
10. Interview with Bishop Ricardo Pereira, Havana, Cuba, March 7, 2005.

less the church provided transportation. Therefore my wife and I went to sister Juanita's home every Saturday morning and offered a worship service. The members faithfully gathered and invited their children and grandchildren, as well as neighbors and friends. We read the Bible, sang, gave testimonies, took up an offering, and preached a sermon. We even provided children's education while the adults were worshipping. The service was also designated a fasting service, as the members carried out a partial fast until noon, and then we broke fast as a community with refreshments after the service. The members would sometimes joke that it was a good thing they were fasting because they did not have anything to eat for breakfast anyway. It was a joyous occasion for the members and their families and gradually began to grow as friends and neighbors were invited. We also invited the small group members to the mother church on Sunday mornings and occasionally provided transportation.

These house-churches were led by lay people. When individuals experienced personal transformation they had the passion and desire to share this new-found love of Jesus Christ with others. Many lay people have felt the call to go into the ministry, like José Luis, but others have assumed greater responsibilities in the local church. The Protestant principle of the priesthood of all believers has become a real part of the Cuban church as believers take serious their vows of baptism to witness to Jesus Christ.

A Legacy of Vital Christian Witness

Oftentimes when people hear about the growth of Christianity in Cuba, they are skeptical of how the church can grow under a communist government. In a country of many contradictions, this is one more paradox. When we take a closer look, however, and see how the church is growing, we should not be surprised. Their methods of Christian vitality are not new. They are simply implementing the classic spiritual disciplines of prayer, fasting, and the centrality of the Word of God. The laity participate in the Protestant belief in the priesthood of all believers and lead others to Christ by witnessing to the love of God. New believers are discipled in small groups where they sing, pray, and hear the proclamation of the Word. In the face of many contradictions, Cuban Christians are connected with Christians around the world through a firm foundation in the classic spiritual disciplines.

Further Reading on Global Witness

Adeney, Frances, and Terry Muck. *Christianity Encountering World Religions: The Practice of Mission in the Twenty-first Century*. Grand Rapids: Baker, 2009.

Carpenter, Joel A., and Lamin Sanneh. *The Changing Face of Christianity: Africa, the West and the World*. Oxford: Oxford University Press, 2005.

Castro, Emilio. *Freedom in Mission: The Perspective of the Kingdom of God: An Ecumenical Inquiry*. Geneva: WCC, 1985.

Elmer, Duane. *Cross-cultural Servanthood: Serving the World in Christlike Humility*. Downers Grove, IL: InterVarsity, 2006.

Escobar, Samuel. *The New Global Mission: The Gospel from Everywhere to Everyone*. Downers Grove, IL: InterVarsity, 2003.

Fung, Raymond, editor. *Not a Solitary Way: Evangelism Stories from around the World*. Geneva: WCC, 1992.

Gallagher, Robert L., and Paul Hertig. *Landmark Essays in Mission and World Christianity*. Maryknoll, NY: Orbis, 2009.

Jenkins, Philip. *The New Faces of Christianity: Believing the Bible in the Global South*. New York: Oxford University Press, 2008.

Kalu, Ogbu U., and Alaine M. Low. *Interpreting Contemporary Christianity: Global Processes and Local Identities*. Grand Rapids: Eerdmans, 2008.

Kew, Richard, and Cyril C. Okorocha. *Vision Bearers: Dynamic Evangelism in the 21st Century*. Harrisburg, PA: Morehouse, 1996.

Kim, Sebastian, and Kirsteen Kim. *Christianity as a World Religion*. New York: Continuum, 2008.

Mayers, Marvin K. *Christianity Confronts Culture: A Strategy for Crosscultural Evangelism*. Rev. ed. Grand Rapids: Zondervan, 1987.

Mignolo, Walter. *Local Histories, Global Designs: Coloniality, Subaltern Knowledges and Border Thinking*. Princeton: Princeton University Press, 2000.

Moore, Rebecca. *Voices of Christianity: A Global Introduction*. Columbus, OH: McGraw-Hill, 2005.

Noll, Mark A. *The New Shape of World Christianity: How American Experience Reflects Global Faith*. Downers Grove, IL: InterVarsity, 2009.

Premnath, D. N., editor. *Border Crossings: Cross-Cultural Hermeneutics*. Maryknoll, NY: Orbis, 2007.

Rhodes, Stephen. *Where the Nations Meet: The Church in a Multicultural World*. Downers Grove, IL: InterVarsity, 1998.

Robert, Dana L. *Christian Mission: How Christianity Became a World Religion*. Hoboken, NJ: Wiley-Blackwell, 2009.

———. *Joy to the World: Mission in the Age of Global Christianity*. New York: GBGM, 2010.

Sanneh, Lamin. *Translating the Message: The Missionary Impact on Culture.* Maryknoll, NY: Orbis, 1991.
Tennent, Timothy. *Theology in the Context of World Christianity: How the Global Church Is Influencing the Way We Think about and Discuss Theology.* Grand Rapids: Zondervan, 2007.
Walls, Andrew F. *The Missionary Movement in Christian History: Studies in the Transmission of the Faith.* Maryknoll, NY: Orbis, 1996.
Walls, Andrew F., and Cathy Ross. *Mission in the Twenty-First Century: Exploring the Five Marks of Global Mission.* Maryknoll, NY: Orbis, 2008.
World Council of Churches. *Mission and Evangelism: An Ecumenical Affirmation.* Geneva: WCC, 1982.
Yrigoyen, Charles, Jr., editor. *The Global Impact of the Wesleyan Traditions and Their Related Movements.* Lanham, MD: Scarecrow, 2002.

Conclusion: Lessons from the World Parish
Some Concluding Observations

FIVE PRIMARY QUESTIONS PROVIDED A BASIC FRAMEWORK FOR THE preceding reflections on making disciples, mission, and evangelism from various perspectives around the globe. While not all of the contributors adhered slavishly to these questions, all of the essays together give us a clear sense of the diversity that exists just in one part of the Christian family around these concerns. They also reflect a striking consensus across the boundaries of culture and context. All of this is anecdotal, nothing approaching a scientific study of these questions from all possible angles, but these reflections inspire, challenge, and offer some lessons for the community of faith.

1. What are the most critical challenges related to disciple-making in your context?

With regard to the various African contexts, two recurrent themes stand out: poverty and the legacy of colonialism/racism. Mission among the poor immediately reveals the necessity of a holistic vision of disciple-making that refuses to separate the spiritual and the physical realities of life. Poverty breeds bitterness, violence, and ethnic animosity. So faithfulness to the way of Jesus mandates a vision of mission intimately connected with the Christian calling to be ambassadors of reconciliation in the world. In a post-colonial situation in Africa today, the primary question is, What does it mean to be fully African and fully Christian? This challenge calls for cultural sensitivity, openness to the other, and attentiveness to the multifarious ways in which the gospel may be proclaimed and lived.

Almost all of the Asian contributors identified the multi-cultural, multi-religious dynamic of their contexts as the most critical challenge. How does one do evangelism as a minority group within a sea of other religions and often in the face of repressive government controls? This situation raises a whole host of additional questions, oriented around practical concerns. What language do we use? How do we create a sense of identity? What methods and practices are culturally appropriate and communicate the gospel most effectively? While some of the Asian contexts, South Korea, for example, demonstrate a remarkable expansion of the Christian faith—"from a trail of tears to a highway for the gospel"— most struggle to find a "space" in which "to be."

Europe presents a completely different contextual situation. Here, two concerns surface quickly: a post-Christendom, Western culture that is increasingly secular and emergence from the legacy of Soviet oppression. The former concern resonates with a North American cultural scene, in which Christians struggle with the same demise of Western religious hegemony and where massive cultural shifts have led so many to proclaim the irrelevance of Christianity. The concern of those from the "Eastern Bloc" strikes a chord, perhaps, with those in Asia who find themselves in oppressive circumstances or emerging from them without any clear sense yet as to how they "hold together" these disparate aspects of their history. The thread that runs through both scenarios has to do with the experience of being "alien" to the environment or context.

Similar to the African experience, that in Latin America revolves around forms of colonial Christianity in which converts to the faith were forced to reject their indigenous cultures and practices. It seems as though the church has had to learn the lesson of the Jerusalem Council (Acts 15) over and over again. Rather than embracing the universal reach of God's love for all, the inertia of human self-centeredness seems to draw the community in the direction of shaping all others in its own image. This leads to a dominant centripetal force within the community of faith and a failure to embrace mission as the church's reason for being. Also, as in Africa, poverty plagues the life of the Latin American world, as systems of injustice exploit and dehumanize people, who are the children of God.

2. What images/stories from scripture are most pertinent to your context in this regard?

References to various biblical images and stories in these essays range widely across the canon of both Testaments, literally, from Genesis to

Revelation. It would be dangerous to make any generalizations from region to region based upon these allusions and specific identifications. There was as much variation within the regions as among them. But frequency of use does draw attention to several images and texts. One should not be surprised by the fact that several mention the Great Commission (Matt 28:18-20), although none of the authors used this text in a typical, Western, triumphalist manner. The multi-cultural Pentecost event (particularly Acts 1:8), the call of the disciples (Mark 1:15-20), the image of the vine and the branches (John 15), and the whole armor of God (Eph 6:12-18) all figured prominently as well in more than one presentation. Several narratives, however, call for particular attention.

The Walk to Emmaus (Luke 24:13-35). Discussion of the walk to Emmaus event revolved around several important aspects of the disciple-making process. The primary image of journey or pilgrimage dominates the narrative. Like the "walk" to Emmaus, disciple-making is a journey that is shared with others in community. Jesus comes alongside those who walk in his way. He explains the scriptures—translates it into their lives in ways that connect and make sense—and helps the disciples rediscover the central place of the Word. The journey itself concludes in a sacramental act that propels the followers of Jesus into the world—back to Jerusalem—to share all that they have heard and seen.

The Jerusalem Council (Acts 15). Perhaps no text of the New Testament addresses the issue of gospel and culture more directly than Luke's account of the Jerusalem Council. Given the fact that so many around the world have experienced the imposition of cultural forms and practices that, truth to be told, are incidental to the gospel, this event in the early life of the church bears perennial witness to the translatability of the gospel and the need for the gospel to penetrate the lives of all who seek to follow Jesus.

Several other expositions of scripture stand out, although they receive singular treatment in this volume: One of the most important rediscoveries today relates to the centrality of the reign of God to the practice of evangelism, an insight articulated in these ancient words: "If there is among you anyone in need, a member of your community in any of your towns within the land that the Lord your God is giving you, do not be hard-hearted or tight-fisted toward your needy neighbor.

... I therefore command you, 'Open your hand to the poor and needy neighbor in your land'" (Deut 15:7, 11). The Priest Hilkiah's rediscovery of the sacred scriptures (2 Kgs 22–23) provides a reminder to each generation concerning the indispensable, character-shaping nature of the Word. Nehemiah 8:10 puts "the joy of the Lord" at the very center of God's life-shaping process. The Parable of the Five Friends (Mark 2:1–12) provides a paradigm of emancipation for mission and evangelism, including the call to "open holes in the roof of the church." Of the many texts alluded to and images explicated, however, one stands out, referred to by someone from almost every continent.

The Samaritan Woman at the Well (John 4:1–42). At least five of the contributors to this volume find a significant paradigm for mission and evangelism in this story. Providence figures prominently in this narrative. The Gospel-writer makes it clear that Jesus "had" to make his journey through this particular place. Prevenient grace, the Wesleyan might say, prepared the way for all that followed, in the same way that God's grace precedes all else in mission, evangelism, and the process of forming disciples. In his encounter with this woman, Jesus crosses boundaries. He engages a *woman* who is a *Samaritan* at the wrong time and the wrong place. He extends the offer of relationship across the chasm created by culture and religion. But first, rather than engaging this woman from a position of power or strength, he approaches her in his need and weakness, permitting her to be the provider, the giver. He listens before he speaks, receives before he gives, and then offers life. The encounter proves to be transformative for the woman who then hurries home to share the good news that she has heard and seen in the Christ.

3. How do you envisage and practice evangelism/disciple-making, therefore, in your context?

As might be expected, the African vision of evangelism articulated here reflects a holistic approach to making disciples. Gitonga talks about this in terms of a connection between conversion and nurture, all of which must be done in a manner that values genuine inculturation. Forster emphasizes the importance of holding personal piety and social transformation together. Kurewa discusses the way in which evangelism and education can be held together under the paradigm of *dzvikiti*—

journey through struggle. Kwaramba observes that the practice of evangelism extends beyond conversion and regeneration into initiation and maturation. W'Ehusha identifies the early Methodist classes and African small groups as the places where the personal and the communal meet.

The same theme pervades the Asian perspectives. Lung-kwong defines the heart of evangelistic practice as "living out the life of Jesus by word and deed." Tiong calls for an "integrated evangelism" that combines evangelism, social work, and education. In the Philippines, according to Arichea, quite a number of exemplary institutions model a "holistic approach" to evangelism. In his discussion of the scope of Jesus' evangelistic commission, Solomon describes an authentic partnership with God in the *missio Dei* as a deeper relationship with Jesus and a more profound response to the poor and marginalized. Park describes the vertical pole of evangelism and the horizontal pole of liberation; *tongsung* prayer—a central Korean practice which he explicates—demonstrates the unity of the individual and the community.

Reflecting European concerns, Rüütel advocates "engagement in holistic mission." For Kim, social ministry and educational programs must be combined with life transforming engagement with Christ. "Fresh expressions" of church in Britain, according to Horsley, reflect a concern for "whole-life, world-changing" discipleship. Employing the metaphor of "spaces," Härtner's strategy unites spaces of "immersion in the story" with spaces of "growth in grace": disciple-making entails both personal transformation through faith and movement toward deeper levels of love. Mulrain's Carribean perspective conjoins personal evangelism—the core of missional practice—with humanitarian activities that seek to address the "whole person." Fonseca develops a "holistic model of disciple formation" for a Costa Rican context that combines biological, psychological, social, and spiritual concerns. To say the least, the theme of "holistic practice" pervades these essays and represents, incidentally, a central Wesleyan image.

While not averse to these various holistic practices in any way, the contributors from North America and cross-cultural contexts reflect a range of different concerns related to practice. The primary images that come from Canada and the United States reflect the importance of authenticity and integrity in building relationships with those who are befriended on a Spirit-led journey. Each of these terms is critical—

authenticity, integrity, relationships, befriending, journey—and reflects the requisite response to cultures that have become cynical and skeptical with regard to the Christian faith. This vision calls for a "grace-full" understanding of disciple-making that stands in stark contrast to the out-moded, close-minded, judgmental stereotype of the Christian that tends to dominate in the West. Those speaking from cross-cultural perspectives reflect a heightened sense of mutuality in their description of evangelistic practice. Not only do they appreciate the gifts of their own heritage that they have to offer, but they celebrate the ways in which they have learned from the agonies and ecstasies of their hosts. In particular, they bear witness to the way in which they have been evangelized by the poor.

4. Where do you see signs of new life and vitality in the life of the church as a result of this vision and practice?

Almost all of the contributors point to the youth of their various constituencies as the vital center of new life, growth, and hope. African colleagues identify group life as the locus of energy (particularly some of the established groups like United Methodist Women) and the experience of worship as the core of formational activity. The African church sings and dances its faith; worshipping in an authentic African mode, with spirited singing and testimony, bears witness to this new life that abounds. The unbridled enthusiasm of new converts to the faith animates the Asian contributors. But authenticity can also be found among those Christians "who are willing to die for their faith." One of the most interesting signs of new life in the European context is the immigrant church. Intentional multi-national congregations are also breathing new life into stagnant urban centers. "Base Christian communities," as well as intentional communities for poor women and children, reflect the vibrant ambiance of the Latin American church. Various forms of "emergent Christianity," parallel to the "Fresh Expressions" movement in Britain, show hopeful signs for a renewal of vibrant Christianity in North America.

5. What do the lessons you are learning about disciple-making in your context contribute to the rest of the world parish?

There is a certain sense in which the contributors to this volume were more interested in listening to the celebrations and victories of others than in imposing their own vision of success. This was actually quite refreshing; while this spirit was never overt, it was extremely transparent. Perhaps it reflects their understanding that every context is characterized by its own set of challenges, pathways, and goals. Nevertheless, there are some important gifts that need to be shared with the global church. Without identifying the source, here are twelve lessons the contributors have learned about disciple-making in their own contexts:

> Disciple-making must begin where people are.
>
> Living the gospel means affirming diversity.
>
> Evangelistic practice, whatever its form, must revolve around Jesus Christ.
>
> All people will face evil in life, but good will always triumph in the end.
>
> A pluralistic world demands a cross-cultural evangelism.
>
> Those who seek to follow Jesus must know that authentic discipleship is costly.
>
> Disciple-making involves participation in the *missio Dei*.
>
> Mission/evangelism begins with listening.
>
> The evangelist invites others to rediscover a biblical vision of life.
>
> Christians must learn how to connect the gospel to the culture.
>
> Disciples of Jesus cannot be made apart from the intimacy of small groups.
>
> The gospel can be translated into any culture.

In the words of one contributor: "A rediscovery of a whole gospel that engages the heart, the mind, and the will may just lead to a new way of talking about being a disciple of Jesus and a community of disciples in this world." May it be so, to the glory of God.

Bibliography

2006 Yearbook of the Methodist Church of Southern Africa. Cape Town: Methodist Publishing House, 2006.
Abraham, William J. *The Logic of Evangelism.* Grand Rapids: Eerdmanns, 1989.
Achtemeier, Paul J. *Harper's Bible Dictionary.* San Francisco: Harper & Row, 1985.
Adeyemo, Tokunboh. *Is Africa Cursed?* Nairobi: Christian Learning Materials Centre, 1983.
Altnurme, Lea. *Kristlusest oma usuni. Uurimus muutustest eestlaste religioossuses 20. sajandi II poolel.* Tartu: Tartu Ülikooli Kirjastus, 2006.
Altnurme, Riho. *Estonian Culture.* No pages. Online: http://www.einst.ee/culture/index3.html.
Araújo, Ricardo Benzaquen, and Lilia Moritz Schwarcz, editors. *Raízes do Brasil.* São Paulo: Companhia das Letras, 2006.
Araya, Victorio. *El Dios de los pobres.* San José: Sebila, 1983.
Armstrong, Karen. *The Case for God.* New York: Knopf, 2009.
Attwell, Arthur. *What Wesley Believed and Taught: The Essentials of Wesley's Theology.* Cape Town: Methodist Publishing House, 1994.
Baker, Frank. *Practical Divinity: John Wesley's Doctrinal Agenda for Methodism.* No pages. Online: http://wesley.nnu.edu/wesleyan_theology/theojrnl/21-25/22-01.htm.
Balia, Daryl M. *Black Methodists and White Supremacy in South Africa.* Durban: Midiba, 1991.
Bamouin, Barbara, and Changgen Yu. *Ten Years of Turbulence: The Chinese Cultural Revolution.* New York: Kegan Paul, 1993.
Barrett, David B., editor. *World Christian Encyclopedia: A Comparative Survey of Churches and Religions in the Modern World, A. D. 1900 to 2000.* New York: Oxford University Press, 1982.
Barrett, David B., and Todd M. Johnson, editors. *World Christian Trends, AD 30—AD 2200: Interpreting the Annual Christian Megacensus.* Pasadena, CA: William Carey Library, 2001.
Barrett, David B., et al. *World Christian Encyclopedia: A Comparative Survey of Churches and Religions in the Modern World.* 2nd ed. New York: Oxford University Press, 2001.
Barrett, David B., et al. *Kenya Churches Handbook: The Development of Kenyan Christianity, 1498–1973.* Kisumu: Evangel, 1973.
Barth, Karl. *Church Dogmatics*, IV.2. Edinburgh: T. & T. Clark, 1978.
Beckford, Martin. "Atheist bus: three Christian groups launch counter-adverts." No pages. Online: http://www.telegraph.co.uk/news/newstopics/howaboutthat/4523445/Atheist-bus-three-Christian-groups-launch-counter-adverts.html.

Bhogal, Inderjit S. *Pluralismo e a missão da igreja na atualidade*. São Bernardo do Campo: Editeo, 2007.
Bisnauth, Dale. *History of Religions in the Caribbean*. Nassau: Kingston, 1989.
Blair, William Newton, and Bruce F. Hunt. *The Korean Pentecost and the Suffering which Followed*. Carlisle, PA: Banner of Truth, 1977.
Blakely, Thomas D., et al. *Religion in Africa*. London: James Currey, 1994.
Boff, Leonardo. *Ecclesiogenesis: The Base Communities Reinvent the Church*. Trans. Robert R. Barr. Maryknoll, NY: Orbis, 1986.
Bonhoeffer, Dietrich. *The Cost of Discipleship*. Trans. R. H. Fuller. London: SCM, 1959.
Bonino, José Míguez. *Ama y haz lo que quieras: la ética para el hombre Nuevo*. Buenos Aires: Aurora, 1976.
Book of Discipline of The United Methodist Church. Nashville: Methodist Publishing House, 2004.
Bosch, David J. "The Structure of Mission: An Exposition of Matthew 28:16-20." In *The Study of Evangelism: Exploring a Missional Practice of the Church*. Edited by Paul W. Chilcote and Laceye C. Warner, 73-92. Grand Rapids: Eerdmans, 2008.
———. *Transforming Mission: Paradigm Shifts in Theology of Mission*. Maryknoll, NY: Orbis, 1991.
Browning, W. R. F. *A Dictionary of the Bible*. Oxford: Oxford University Press, 1996.
Brueggemann, Walter. *Interpretation and Obedience: From Faithful Reading to Faithful Living*. Minneapolis: Fortress, 1991.
Camargo, Gonzalo Báez, and Kenneth G. Grubb. *Religion in the Republic of Mexico*. New York: World Dominion, 1935.
Cavanaugh, William. *Torture and Eucharist: Theology, Politics, and the Body of Christ*. Oxford: Blackwell, 1998.
Chilcote, Paul W. "Evangelistic Practices of the Wesleyan Revival." In *Methodist Evangelism: Wesleyan Mission, Equipping Global Ministry: Wesleyan Studies Project*. Edited by Laceye C. Warner. Washington: Wesley Theological Seminary, forthcoming.
———. "The Mission-Church Paradigm of the Wesleyan Revival." In *World Mission in the Wesleyan Spirit*, edited by Darrell Whiteman and Gerald H. Anderson, 151-64. Franklin, TN: Providence House, 2009.
———. *The Wesleyan Tradition: A Paradigm for Renewal*. Nashville: Abingdon, 2002.
Chilcote, Paul W., and Laceye C. Warner, editors. *The Study of Evangelism: Exploring a Missional Practice of the Church*. Grand Rapids: Eerdmans, 2008.
Choon, Lee Min. *Freedom of Religion in Malaysia*. Kuala Lumpur: Selangor: Kairos Research Center, 1999.
Chui, Tina, et al. "Canada's Ethnocultural Mosaic: 2006 Census." *Statistics Canada*, April 2008.
Clark, Warren, and Grant Schellenberg. "Who's Religious?" *Canadian Social Trends* (Summer 2006) 2-8.
Coggins, Jim. "The State of the Canadian Church—Part VI: Those pesky moral, social issues." No pages. Online: http://www.canadianchristianity.com/national updates/080117state.html.
Conference of Catholic Bishops of Cuba. "El Amor todo lo Espera." In *La Voz de La Iglesia en Cuba*. Havanna: Obra Nacional de la Buena Prensa, 1995.

Coomes, Anne. *Africa Harvest: The Captivating Story of Michael Cassidy and Africa Enterprise*. London: Monarch, 2003.
"Couple found guilty of sending seditious tracts." *The Straits Times*. May 29, 2009.
Course, Theron. *Protestants, Revolution, and the Cuba-U.S. Bond*. Gainesville: University of Florida Press, 2007.
Cox, L. G. *John Wesley's Concept of Perfection*. Kansas City: Beacon Hill, 1968.
Cray, Graham, et al. *Mission Shaped Church*. London: Church House, 2004.
Croft, Steven, et al. *Mission Shaped Questions*. London: Church House, 2008.
Davie, Grace. *Europe: The Exceptional Case*. London: Dartman Longman & Todd, 2002.
———. "Understanding Religion in Modern Britain: The Factors to Take into Account." Hugh Price Hughes Lectures 2008. No pages. Online: http://www.hindestreet.org.uk/Groups/99353/Hugh_Price_Hughes.aspx.
Davies, Noel, and Martin Conway. *World Christianity in the 20th Century*. London: SCM, 2008.
Davies, Rupert E. *Methodism*. New York: Penguin, 1963.
Davis, Sarah F. *I Looked Poverty in the Face Today*. Self-published poetry, 2005.
De Gruchy, John W. *The Church Struggle in South Africa*. Minneapolis: Fortress, 2004.
De Santa Ana, Julio. *El Desafío de los Pobres a la iglesia*. San José: Educa, 1977.
Dickerson, Dennis. "The Worldwide Mission of the African Methodist Episcopal Church." *The Doctrine and Discipline of the African Methodist Episcopal Church*. Nashville: African Methodist Episcopal Church, 2008.
Dubach, Alfred, and Roland Campiche, editors. *Jede/r ein Sonderfall. Religion in der Schweiz.Ergebnisse einer Repräsentativbefragung*. Basel, 1993.
Dunn, James D. G. *Jesus' Call to Discipleship*. Cambridge: Cambridge University Press, 1992.
Duque Z., José. *Módulo Misión de la Iglesia*. Unpublished manuscript, 2009.
Eitel, K. E. *Transforming Culture: Developing a Biblical Ethic in an African Context*. Nairobi: Evangel, 1986.
Erb-Kanzleiter, Christine. "Peace Church News." Special 25th Anniversary Edition. No pages. Online: http://www.peacechurch.de.
Escott, Phillip, and Alison Gelder. *Church Life Profile 2001: Denominational Results for The Methodist Church*. London: CIM, 2002.
"Eurasia UMC Roundtable." *Russia Initiative Newsletter*, November 2009. No pages. Online: http://new.gbgm-umc.org/work/initiatives/russia/newsletter/index.cfm?i=31049.
Eurobarometer Survey, 2005. No pages. Online: http://www.gallup.com/poll/13117/Religion-Europe-Trust-Filling-Pews.aspx.
European Council of Methodist Churches. "Minutes." Velletri, Italy, Sept. 15–16, 2008.
Federal Constitution of Malaysia. No pages. Online: http://confinder.richmond.edu/admin/docs/malaysia.pdf.
Finney, John. *Recovering the Past: Celtic and Roman Mission*. London: Darton, Longman and Todd, 1996.
Flemming, Dean. *Contextualization in the New Testament: A Biblical Model*. Downers Grove, IL: InterVarsity, 2005.

Forster, Dion Angus. *Wesleyan Spirituality: An Introduction.* Cape Town: Methodist Publishing House, 2001.
Forster, Dion, and Wessel Bentley, editors. *Methodism in Southern Africa: A Celebration of Wesleyan Mission.* Kempton Park: AcadSA, 2008.
The Freeway, "Church?" No pages. Online: http://www.frwy.ca.
Freire, Paolo. *Pedagogy of the Oppressed.* New York: Penguin, 1972.
Garcia, Paulo Roberto. "Reflexões sobre os desafios para o discipulado: uma abordagem a partir de Mateus 28.16-20." *Mosaico: apoio pastoral* 13:34 (July-Sept.) 3-23.
Gibbs, Eddie, and Ian Coffey. *Church Next: Quantum Change in Christian Ministry.* Downers Grove, IL: InterVarsity, 2000.
Gill, David W. *The Opening of the Christian Mind: Taking Every Thought Captive to Christ.* Downers Grove, IL: InterVarsity, 1989.
Gitonga, Nahashon. *Evangelization and Inculturation in an African Context.* Kijabe: Today in Africa, 2008.
Gnadenteich, J. *Kodumaa kirikulugu.* Tallinn: Logos, 1995.
Green, Laurie. *Let's Do Theology: A Pastoral Cycle Resource Book.* London: Mowbray, 1990.
Green, Michael. *Evangelism through the Local Church: A Comprehensive Guide to All Aspects of Evangelism.* Nashville: Nelson, 1990.
Grözinger, Albrecht. "Geschichtenlos inmitten von Geschichten." *Wege zum Menschen* 48 (1996) 480-96.
Grözinger, Albrecht, editor. *Predigen aus Leidenschaft,.* Karlsruhe, 1996.
Guichard, Jean. *Iglesia, lucha de clases y estrategias políticas.* Salamanca: Ediciones Sígueme, 1973.
Härle, Wilfried. *Dogmatik.* Berlin: de Gruyter, 1995.
Härtner, Achim, and Holger Eschmann. *Predigen Lernen: Ein Lehrbuch für die Praxis.* Darmstadt: Wissenschaftliche Buchgesellschaft, 2008.
Hanes, A. "Theology of Evangelization." In *Dynamizing Evangelical Witness,* edited by Pavel Procházka, 99-121. Praha: ECM, 2008.
Hanesová, Dana. *Nabozenska vychova v Europskej Unii.* Banska Bystrica: Univerzita Mateja Bela, 2006.
Heath, Elaine A. *The Mystic Way of Evangelism: A Contemplative Vision for Christian Outreach.* Grand Rapids: Baker, 2008.
Heitzenrater, Richard P. *Wesley and the People Called Methodists.* Nashville: Abingdon, 1995.
Hengel, Martin. *The Charismatic Leader and His Followers.* Translated by James C. G. Creig. Edinburgh: T. & T. Clark, 1981.
Horsley, Graham, et al. *May I Call You Friend.* Peterborough: Methodist Publishing House, 2006.
Hunsberger, George, "Sizing Up the Shape of the Church." In *Church Between Gospel and Culture,* edited by George Hunsberger and Van Gelder. Grand Rapids: Eerdmans, 1996.
Hunsberger, George, and Craig Van Gelder, editors. *The Church Between Gospel and Culture.* Grand Rapids: Eerdmans, 1996.
Hunt, Robert, et al. *Christianity in Malaysia.* Petaling Jaya: Pelanduk, 1992.
Hunter, George G., III. *The Contagious Congregation: Frontiers of Evangelism and Church Growth.* Nashville: Abingdon, 1979.

Huntley, M. *Caring, Growing, Changing: A History of the Protestant Mission in Korea*. New York: Friendship, 1984.
Il'in, Ivan Aleksandrovich. *Crisis of Atheism*. Moscow: Dar, 2005.
Janvier, George E. *Discipleship: A West African Perspective*. Lagos: Baraka, 1995.
John Paul II. *Crossing the Threshold of Hope*. New York: Knopf, 1995.
Johnson, Todd M., and Brian J. Grim, editors. *World Religion Database: International Religious Demographic Statistics and Sources*. No pages. Online: http://www.worldreligiondatabase.org.
Johnson, Todd M., and Kenneth R. Ross, editors. *Atlas of Global Christianity*. Edinburgh: Edinburgh University Press, 2009.
Jenkins, Philip. *The Next Christendom: The Coming of Global Christianity*. New York: Oxford University Press, 2002.
Jüngel, Eberhard. "To Tell the World about God: The Task for the Mission of the Church on the Threshold of the Third Millennium." *International Review of Mission* 89, 353 (2000) 203–16.
Kimbrough, S T, Jr., editor. *Songs for the Poor*. New York: GBGM, 1997.
Kinnaman, David, and Gabe Lyons. *Unchristian: What a New Generation Really Thinks about Christianity . . . and Why It Matters*. Grand Rapids: Baker, 2007.
Klaiber, Walter. *Call and Response: Biblical Foundations of a Theology of Evangelism*. Translated by Howard Perry-Trauthig and James A. Dwyer. Nashville: Abingdon, 1997.
La Voz de La Iglesia en Cuba. Mexico: Buena Prensa, S.A., 1995.
Lee, Duk Joo. *The Life and Thought of Rev. Jung-do Sohn*. Seoul: Methodist Theological University Press, 2004.
Liiman, Raigo. *Usklikkus muutuvas Eesti ühiskonnas*. Tartu: Tartu Ülikooli Kirjastus, 2001.
Lumen Gentium: Dogmatic Constitution on the Church. Promulgated by Pope Paul VI, Nov. 21, 1964. No pages. Online: http://www.ewtn.com/library/COUNCILS/v2church.htm.
Lung-kwong, Lo. "Ecclesiology from the Perspective of Scripture in Wesleyan and Asian Contexts." In *Our Calling to Fulfill: Wesleyan Views of the Church in Mission*, edited by M. Douglas Meeks. Nashville: Kingswood, 2009.
Magesa, L. *Anatomy of Inculturation: Transforming the Church in Africa*. Nairobi: Paulines, 2004.
Malone, Shawn T. "Conflict, Coexistence, and Cooperation: Church-State Relations in Cuba." Georgetown University, Center for Latin American Studies, August 1996.
Mana, Kä. *Christians and Churches of Africa Envisioning the Future*. Yaoundé: Edition Cle, 2002.
Masarik, A., editor. *Homileticka cinnost cirkvi a kvalita sucasneho zivota*. Banska Bystrica: Univerzita Mateja Bela, 2009.
Mbiti, John. *African Religion and Philosophy*. 2nd ed. Oxford: Heinemann, 1989.
McCune, G. S. "The Holy Spirit in Pyengyang." *The Korean Mission Field*. January 1907.
Mears, William James Gordon. *Methodism in the Cape: An Outline*. Cape Town: Methodist Publishing House, 1973.
Meeks, M. Douglas, editor. *Our Calling to Fulfill: Wesleyan Views of the Church in Mission*. Nashville: Kingswood, 2009.

Mehta, Hemant. *I Sold My Soul on eBay: Viewing Faith through an Atheist's Eyes.* Colorado Springs: WaterBrook, 2007.

Methodist Church in Great Britain. *Hope in God's Future: Christian Discipleship in the Context of Climate Change.* No pages. Online: http://www.methodist.org.uk/downloads/10-hope-in-gods-future-210509.pdf.

Migliore, Daniel. *Faith Seeking Understanding: An Introduction to Christian Theology.* Grand Rapids: Eerdmans, 1991.

Millard-Jackson, J. "Who Called the Tune? Methodist Missionary Policy in South Africa during the 19th Century." In *Methodism in Southern Africa: A Celebration of Wesleyan Mission,* edited by Dion Forster and Wessel Bentley, 31–39. Kempton Park: AcadSA, 2008.

Moore, J. Z. "The Great Revival Year." *The Korea Mission Field.* August 1907.

Mugambi, J. N. K., editor. *Christian Mission and Social Transformation: A Kenyan Perspective.* Nairobi: NCCK, 1989.

Murray, Stuart. *Post-Christendom.* Carlisle: Paternoster, 2004.

Nichols, Christopher McKnight. "The 'New' No Religionists." *Culture* 3:2 (2009) 1–23.

Nthamburi, Zablon. *The Pilgrimage of the African Church: Towards the Twenty-First Century.* Nairobi: Uzima, 2000.

Nthamburi, Zablon, editor. *From Mission to Church.* Nairobi: Uzima, 1991.

Outler, Albert C. *Evangelism in the Wesleyan Spirit.* Nashville: Tidings, 1971.

Pajusoo, Toomas. *The United Methodist Church in Estonia, 1907–2007.* Tallinn: Eesti Metodisti Kirik, 2007.

Parra, Alberto. *De la iglesia ministerio a la iglesia de los pobres.* Bogotá: Pontifica Universidad Javeriana, 1984.

Perez, Carlos. *Un Resumen de los Setenta Años de Labor de La Iglesia Metodista en Cuba, 1898–1968.* Miami: Self-published, 1983.

The Pew Forum on Religion & Public Life. "U.S. Religious Landscape Survey." No pages. Online: http://religions.pewforum.org/reports.

Pine, B. Joseph, and James H. Gilmore. *The Experience Economy.* Boston: Harvard Business School Press, 1999.

Procházka, Pavel. "Slovak Small Membership Churches and Social Cohesion." In *Europe,* edited by Hans-Georg Ziebertz and Ulrich Riegel, 143–53. Berlin: Lit Verlag, 2008.

Procházka, Pavel, editor. *Dynamizing Evangelical Witness in Post-Communist Era.* Praha: ECM, 2008.

Rack, Henry D. *Reasonable Enthusiast: John Wesley and the Rise of Methodism.* London: Epworth, 1992.

Recinos, Harold, J. *Good News from the Barrio: Prophetic Witness for the Church.* Louisville: Westminster John Knox, 2006.

Religion in Europe. No pages. Online: http://www.gallup.com/poll/13117/Religion-Europe-Trust-Filling-Pews.aspx.

Renders, Helmut. "Deus, o ser humano e um mundo nas linguagens imagéticas da religião do coração: códigos e projetos." *Pistis & Práxis* 1:2 (2009) 373–413.

———. *Einen anderen Himmel erbitten wir nicht: Urchristliche Agapen und methodistische Liebesfeste.* Stuttgart: Medienwerk der EmK, 2001.

———. "Pequenos Grupos na tradição metodista. Observações, análises e teses." *Caminhando* 6:8 (2002) 68–95.

———. "So seid ihr nun nicht mehr Gäste und Fremdlinge, sondern Mitbürger der Heiligen und Gottes Hausgenossen." DMin diss., Wesley Theological Seminary, 1998.

———. "The Social Soteriology of John Wesley and its Communitarian, Arminian and Public Elements: Comments on its Development, Purpose, Inspirations, and Spirituality." No pages. Online: http://www.oxford-institute.org/docs/2007 papers/2007-2Renders.pdf.

Republic of Estonia. *2000 Census.* No pages. Online: http://pub.stat.ee/px-web.2001/Dialog/statfile2.asp.

Reuter, Ingo. *Predigt verstehen. Grundlagen einer homiletischen Hermeneutik.* Leipzig: EVA, 2000.

Richardson, Neville, et al. *God, Truth, and Witness: Engaging Stanley Hauerwas.* Grand Rapids: Brazos, 2005.

Richardson, Neville R., and Purity Malinga, editors. *Rediscovering Wesley for Africa.* Pretoria: Education for Ministry and Mission Unit, 2005.

Rieger, Joerg. *Christ and Empire: From Paul to Postcolonial Times.* Minneapolis: Fortress, 2007.

Ritsbek, Heigo. "The Mission of Methodism in Estonia." DMin diss., Boston University School of Theology, 1996.

Robert, Dana L. *Evangelism as the Heart of Mission.* Mission Evangelism Series, Number 1. New York: GBGM, 1997.

Rollins, Peter. *How (not) to Speak of God.* Brewster, MA: Paraclete, 2006.

Russell, Letty. *La iglesia como comunidad inclusiva.* Trans. Carlos Bonilla. San José: Sebila, 2004.

Samuel, Ang, et al. *Religious Liberty after 50 Years of Independence.* Petaling Jaya: Malaysia Research Commission, 2008.

Schmemann, Alexander. *For the Life of the World: Sacraments and Orthodoxy.* Rev. ed. Crestwood, NY: St. Vladimir's Seminary Press, 1997.

Shah, Timothy Samuel. "Born Again in the U.S.A.: The Enduring Power of American Evangelicalism." *Foreign Affairs.* No pages. Online: http://www.foreignaffairs.com/print/65231.

Sheffield, Dan. "Encountering the Other: Mission and Transformation." *Common Ground Journal* 5:2 (2008).

Siuhengalu, Tevita M. "In Search of a New Identity: The Tonga Parish in Sydney." MTh thesis, Sydney College of Divinity, 1991.

———. "Renewal of All Things and Personal Salvation: A Pacific Island Perspective." Paper presented to the Evangelism and Ecumenism Working Group of the 11th Oxford Institute of Methodist Theological Studies, Christ Church College, Oxford University, 2002.

Slovak Academy of Science. "Národná identita a hodnoty spoločnosti. Z Prognózy rozvoja Slovenska do roku 2010, ktorú pripravili pracovníci SAV. No pages. Online: http://www.civil.gov.sk/archiv/casopis/2002/1120ho.htm.

Snyder, Howard. *La Comunidad del Rey.* Miami: Caribe, 1983.

Sobrino, Jon. *The True Church and the Poor.* Eugene, OR: Wipf & Stock, 2004.

Sparks, A. *The Mind of South Africa.* New York: Ballantine, 1990.

Special Eurobarometer Survey: Social values, Science and Technology. June 2005. No pages. Online: http://ec.europa.eu/public_opinion/archives/ebs/ebs_225_report_en.pdf.

Spencer, Nick. *Beyond the Fringe*. Calver: Cliff College, 2005.
Stackhouse, John, Jr. "Whose Dominion? Christianity and Canadian Culture Historically Considered." *Channels* 12:2 (1996).
Stafford, William Stafford. *A Glass Face in the Rain*. New York: Harper & Row, 1982.
Stone, Bryan P. *Evangelism after Christendom: The Theology and Practice of Christian Witness*. Grand Rapids: Brazos, 2007.
The Story, "Handles." No pages. Online: http://www.thestory.ca.
Tamayo-Acosta, Juan José. *Para comprender la Teología de la liberación*. Estella: Verbo divino, 2000.
Tennent, Timothy. *Invitation to World Missions: A Trinitarian Missiology for the Twenty-first Century*. Grand Rapids: Kregel, 2010.
Thompson, Marjorie. *Soul Feast: An Invitation to the Christian Spiritual Life*. Louisville: Westminster, 1995.
Tillich, Paul. *The Protestant Era*. Chicago: University of Chicago Press, 1951.
Ting, K. H. "A Rationale for Three-Self." In *A Chinese Contribution to Ecumenical Theology: Selected Writings of Bishop K. H. Ting*, edited by Janice and Philip Wickeri, 60–72. Geneva: WCC, 2002.
Tippett, Alan R. *People Movements in Southern Polynesia: A Study in Church Growth*. Chicago: Moody, 1971.
Trueblood, Elton. *The Company of the Committed*. New York: Harper, 1961.
Wade, James C. "The Essentials of Leading a Person to Christ." Department of Church Growth and Development, African Methodist Episcopal Church of Mozambique, March 2007.
Ward, K. "'Tuku tendereza Yesu': The Balokole Revival in Uganda." In *From Mission to Church*, edited by Zablon Nthamburi, 97–115. Nairobi: Uzima, 1991.
Warner, Laceye C., editor. *Methodist Evangelism: Wesleyan Mission. Equipping Global Ministry: Wesleyan Studies Project*. Washington: Wesley Theological Seminary, forthcoming.
Waruta, D. W. "The Church as a Teaching Community: Special Reference to the Church in Africa." In *Christian Mission and Social Transformation: A Kenyan Perspective*, edited by J. N. K. Mugambi, 76–92. Nairobi: NCCK, 1989.
Wei-Ming, Tu. *Confucian Thought*. New York: State University of New York Press, 1991.
Wesley, John. *The Works of John Wesley. Volume 1. Sermons I*. Edited by Albert C. Outler. Nashville: Abingdon, 1984.
———. *The Works of John Wesley. Volume 2. Sermons II*. Edited by Albert C. Outler. Nashville: Abingdon, 1985.
———. *The Works of John* Wesley. 14 vols. Edited by Thomas Jackson. Grand Rapids: Baker, 1978.
———. *The Works of John Wesley. Volume 19. Journal and Diaries II (1738–1743)*. Edited by W. Reginald Ward and Richard P. Heitzenrater. Nashville: Abingdon, 1990.
Whiteman, Darrell, and Gerald H. Anderson, editors. *World Mission in the Wesleyan Spirit*. Franklin, TN: Providence House, 2009.
Wickeri, Janice, and Philip Wickeri, editors. *A Chinese Contribution to Ecumenical Theology: Selected Writings of Bishop K. H. Ting*. Geneva: WCC, 2002.
Williams, Colin W. *John Wesley's Theology Today*. Nashville: Abingdon, 1960.

World Christian Database. No pages. Online: http://www.worldchristiandatabase.org.
World Methodist Council Handbook of Information, 1997–2001. Lake Junaluska, NC: The World Methodist Council, 1997.
World Methodist Council Handbook of Information, 2007–2011. Lake Junaluska, NC: The World Methodist Council, 2007.
Wright, Christopher J. H. *The Mission of God: Unlocking the Bible Grand Narrative*. Downers Grove, IL: InterVarsity, 2006.
Ying, Crystal Kuek Chee. "Religious Liberty: Trends of Legislation and Court Judgments." In *Religious Liberty after 50 Years of Independence*, edited by Ang Samuel, et al., 70–85. Petaling Jaya: Malaysia Research Commission, 2008.
Yung, Hwa, and Robert Hunt. "The Methodist Church." In *Christianity in Malaysia*, edited by Robert Hunt et al. Petaling Jaya: Pelanduk, 1992.
Ziebertz, Hans-Georg, and Ulrich Riegel, editors. *Europe: Secular or Post-secular*. Berlin: Lit Verlag, 2008.
Zimbabwe East Annual Conference Report. Harare: Methodist Conference Office, 2007.
Zulehner, Paul M. *Helft den Menschen leben. Für ein neues Klima in der Pastoral*. Freiburg/Basel: Herder, 1978.

www.ingramcontent.com/pod-product-compliance
Lightning Source LLC
Chambersburg PA
CBHW061425300426
44114CB00014B/1541